PRAISE FOR
MYTHS OF PR

'At a time when "fake news" is a common term it's no wonder there's a lack of trust in PR. Rich Leigh is restoring the faith at a crucial time with his book *Myths in PR*. It's an essential guide for practitioners, an inspiring read for PR hopefuls and an open door for anyone interested in 21st-century PR. Let's bury the myths and enjoy the most exciting time in history for communications.' **Stella Bayles, director, CoverageBook**

'Rich Leigh does a great job debunking much of the nonsense attributed to the art of public relations, from making things go viral, to the death of the news release. As a young practitioner of the profession, he belies his tender age with words of wisdom and common sense beyond his years. *Myths of PR* is written in plain English with helpful anecdotes, case studies and links to further reading. If your reputation is what people say about you when you leave the room, Rich can walk out head held high safe in the knowledge we'll all be waxing lyrical about this book.' **Dom Burch, Managing Director, Why Social, and former Head of PR, Head of Social and Senior Director of Marketing Innovation at Asda**

'*Myths of PR* is one of the first books to realistically capture what public relations is today and educate the business community about its value and role in achieving commercial success. Not only does it quote many of the great and the good in PR today and showcase the worst, it's basically an ethics manual every practitioner in PR should be forced to read. Massive thumbs up from me.' **Sarah Hall, Director, Sarah Hall Consulting, Founder and Editor of #FuturePRoof, and CIPR President-Elect 2017**

'Rich busts many myths both within and about the PR business in spectacular style. Essential reading!' **James Herring, Owner, Taylor Herring**

'At a time when telling the truth is a revolutionary act, Rich Leigh tackles misconceptions and strategy head on with facts, tact and wit. This book is required reading for current and aspiring communications professionals and, frankly, anybody affected by or contributing to the daily onslaught of misinformation; a practice exercised at present, most damagingly and disconcertingly, by even the highest offices in the world.' **Nick Hewer, PR impresario, *Countdown* host and Lord Sugar's aide on *The Apprentice*, having spent decades as his PR adviser**

'Rich Leigh is one of the good guys of PR, and his book proves that our industry is a realm not as easily understood as it is underestimated. He cuts through the mirage of *Ab Fab* lunches and spin doctors to cast new light on what makes the contemporary world of communications tick.' **Alex Myers, Founder and CEO, Manifest London**

'Rich Leigh has put together an invaluable overview of PR in the 21st century, and all the facets which sit under it, and how to become a talented, strategic operator in the industry (and thus stand out from all the tactical, archaic practitioners still spray and praying for coverage). This is a must-read for anyone starting out in the industry and essential for those who need reminding of the core values they must hold dear. It's a refreshing mix of counsel, insight, and real-life examples, pulling from a rich vein of material to showcase the theories being discussed.' **Chris Owen, Director, M&C Saatchi**

'This is a candid, punchy and practical book. Buy one for your mum or your children when they ask what you do. Buy one for your employer to underline the value of public relations. And buy one for yourself if you want to advance your practice. Rich also quotes me throughout – what's not to love?' **Stephen Waddington, Partner and Chief Engagement Officer, Ketchum, and Visiting Professor at Newcastle University**

'Rich Leigh has written an interesting book with many lessons for PRs. He is right to draw attention to the importance of the gender pay gap. Gender is the third reason to affect pay in the PR Industry, after seniority and length of service. I completely agree with Rich that every percentage point counts. I will not cease to draw attention to the facts of the embarrassing, illegal situation in my profession until gender drops off any list of reasons affecting pay and the gap is closed for my own sake, for my daughter and for Rich's.' **Sarah Pinch ChartPR FCIPR MIoD, Managing Director, Pinch Point Communications, and CIPR President 2015**

'Rich Leigh's passion, experience and creativity sets him aside as one of the top PR professionals in the country with a breadth of knowledge that belies his years. In *Myths of PR* he blows the b*****ksology that surrounds the industry out of the water and backs up each of his assertions with cold, hard facts and solid evidence. The book is an easy read with its entertaining anecdotes and nuggets from industry leaders and is a must-read for any aspiring PR guru.' **Paddy Power, Head of Communications, Paddy Power Betfair**

'Rich Leigh's punchy approach to dispelling PR myths makes for an entertaining and informative read. Is PR really glamorous? Do you have to be an extrovert to succeed in the industry? Can you make something go viral? Rich gives his experienced insights into all these questions and more.' **Sarah Stimson, Chief Executive, Taylor Bennett Foundation**

'If I could marry a book, this would be the one! There is almost nothing worse than someone saying that all publicity is good publicity and Rich Leigh hits that myth head on. What's more, I have dedicated the better part of the past 10 years working towards changing the perception that people have of the PR industry (through *Spin Sucks*) and everything Rich writes in this book speaks to that vision. I love it so much, I wish I'd written it. If you think PR is just getting your name in the paper so the phone will ring, this book is for you. Buy it, read it, highlight it, read it again and share it. Your business depends on it.' **Gini Dietrich, CEO, Arment Dietrich, and author of *Spin Sucks***

Myths of PR

All publicity is good publicity and other popular misconceptions

Rich Leigh

To an exceptional PR & communications creative. Good luck with your Masters

Best
DoC
_Aug 2018

KoganPage

First published in Great Britain and the United States in 2017 by Kogan Page Limited

2nd Floor, 45 Gee Street	c/o Martin P Hill Consulting	4737/23 Ansari Road
London	122 W 27th St, 10th Floor	Daryaganj
EC1V 3RS	New York, NY 10001	New Delhi 110002
United Kingdom	USA	India

www.koganpage.com

© Rich Leigh, 2017

The right of Rich Leigh to be identified as the author of this work has been asserted by him in accordance with the Copyright, Designs and Patents Act 1988.

ISBN   978 0 7494 7959 6
E-ISBN 978 0 7494 7960 2

British Library Cataloguing-in-Publication Data

A CIP record for this book is available from the British Library.

Library of Congress Control Number

2017001790

Typeset by Integra Software Services, Pondicherry
Print production managed by Jellyfish
Printed and bound by Ashford Colour Press Ltd.

CONTENTS

ABOUT THE AUTHOR

Rich Leigh is a UK-based public relations professional. He founded his agency, Radioactive PR, weeks after his 27th birthday, and has led the accounts of leading brands and organizations including IKEA, Just-Eat, Premier Inn, the National Gallery, Paddy Power and many others. At first, the agency was (imaginatively) called 'Rich Leigh & Company'.

Rich's passions lie in helping individuals build personal brands, as well as creative stunts and campaigns. He founded leading PR blog PRexamples.com in 2012.

ACKNOWLEDGEMENTS

There are many, many people to thank for helping me with this book.

Firstly, to my wife Emma. I massively underestimated the amount of time and effort that goes into writing a book, and, coinciding as it did with the running of a young agency, I was often stressed. You were the perfect balance of supportive and scolding, always helping me to see the bigger picture. I extend these thanks to my two children, Maia and Noah – but none to our dog, Jackson, whose confused but always enthusiastic 5 am barking as I, bleary-eyed, sat to write endeared me none to neither my family nor neighbours.

Thank you to my awesome team at Radioactive PR for your support, ideas and proofreading, and helping to give me the headspace to do what it took to get this book done. I'm very proud to be building the company we're building.

Thank you to Andy and Jill Barr for taking a chance on me. I know I'm a pain, but I wouldn't be anywhere without you, and am just grateful you saw past my flaws. I can't thank you enough.

Thanks to Graham Goodkind, Andrew Bloch, Alex Grier and David Fraser for your kind welcome, flexibility and ongoing support. I learnt a great deal in what was a relatively short space of time from each of you.

To my friend Jamie McDonald, thank you. I'll never forget your reaction, chicken in hand, to the email containing the publishing contract coming in – the point at which it became 'real'. Your support in everything I do and have done means the world to me. It was made even more special by you getting your own publishing deal a month or so later, you copycat.

Thank you to Andrew Peart at Kogan Page for first getting in touch at the start of 2016 – this wouldn't have happened without you – and thereafter, my thanks for putting up with my faffing go to Jenny Volich and Charlotte Owen. Even if you did, though no doubt for my own professional good, take out things that made me laugh. Charlotte, in particular, you were incredibly calm, collected and reassuring in the face of many a deadline panic. Thank you, all.

I am enormously grateful to Dom Burch, Anthony Tuite, Marc Cowlin and Susan HayesCulleton for your contributions to the book. Special thanks go to Leanne Ross for putting me on to Susan – she's as amazing as you said she'd be.

Finally, I made hideous use of one hell of a group of professionals, but thank you to Victoria Leyton, Mark Perkins, Chris Owen, Joe Sinclair and Alex Wilson for initially offering to support the development of this book. I struggled to balance everything to bring you all in effectively, but owe you all a drink or two, definitely.

Special thanks to 'uncle' Matt Muir, who, as well as being part of that group, pushed to read an early stage of the manuscript and regularly checked in. You lose points for your Johnny Five-like ability to read it as quickly as you did though, highlighting a stark contrast between the amount of time I put into this and how long people will likely take to finish it.

INTRODUCTION

The question 'What is public relations?' is something countless people in PR have debated. It's something that has been defined and redefined over the course of decades by the great and the good of the industry, but an awkward point remains: the general public are near clueless as to what PR is and actually does.

This lack of awareness is all the more interesting given that PR is silently present in near enough everything we read, watch, listen to and consume in the media. Every time you scroll down the Mail Online's sidebar of shame; every time you turn the news or a talk show on; whenever you listen to interviews or the news on the radio; when you make a note to download an app Mashable has mentioned or read your favourite singer's social media feeds – the fingerprints of PR can be found.

Where there isn't a complete lack of understanding amongst the public and even practitioners, many damaging misconceptions exist. Before we jump straight into myths, I wanted to highlight my PR ethos – and bear with me, as I realize it might be somewhat controversial.

I want my work to make somebody (the audience my client wants to reach) think – but in a way that makes them think that they thought it. That way, they're malleable and their reactions all the more predictable.

Allow me to explain. You might like a certain celebrity, or want to watch a certain film, or want to buy a certain product, or want to donate to a specific charity. Somewhere along the line, the chances are I or somebody like me had a hand in the process of making that happen.

Our aim is to affect the media, social media feeds and other content our target audience consumes to achieve whatever our clients want to achieve, and, like Keyser Söze, it's without said audience ever having known we were there, convinced that celebrity is the person they imagine them to be, or that they need that product as much as they think they do. There's no malice to it, but while they're busy doing what we want them to do, we're straightening up our respective limps and riding on to the next town getting ready to do it all over again.

This sounds deeply cynical, but it's important to mention because, of course, myths and misconceptions are more likely to endure in a profession where the practitioners and the individuals and businesses that pay them don't really want their existence to be noticed or scrutinized, anyway.

All that said, PR activity is, more often than not, quite inoffensive and often genuinely quite mundane, but whether you're reading *Garage and MOT Professional* or watching *Good Morning America*, we're there, hidden in plain sight, hoping to pull opinion in a certain direction and very often succeeding.

Throughout this book, I'll be dispelling myths that exist in and around the public relations industry, as well as looking at commonly held misconceptions about the impact of our work – the most obvious and prevalent being that 'all publicity is good publicity'. But first...

A bit about me

So, Rich Leigh is kind of my stage name; Leigh being my middle name. I usually just discard my actual surname, Smith. When I first started out in PR aged 20, I was convinced Richard Smith was the most common name in the world and that I'd be more memorable without it to journalists. I'm sure a psychiatrist would have another explanation but that's the best I have.

In the near decade I've worked in PR, I've been fortunate enough to work on and lead campaigns for the likes of Confused.com, Paddy Power, Premier Inn, IKEA, Gocompare.com, Just-Eat.com and hundreds of other clients.

I've directed award-winning campaigns while working at 10 Yetis PR agency in Gloucester and Frank PR in London; been named in industry magazine PRWeek's '29 under 29', a list of 'promising young professionals'; been shortlisted for the Mark Hanson Award celebrating 'the brightest young social media communicators' in the UK Social Media Communications Awards; and founded popular independent PR blog PRexamples.com. I also co-founded blogger database bloggabase.com.

I now manage my own PR agency, Radioactive PR (RadioactivePR.com), having founded it in 2014. We have two offices in the UK – one in the north in Manchester and one in the south in Gloucester – and we work with clients of all shapes and sizes.

Why this book?

Myths are damaging. They hold us back and prevent us from looking at and assessing things clearly and intelligently.

The range of PR books and materials currently available is excellent, but many are particularly theory-laden, and sometimes none too accessible.

Among the people championing public relations progress in the UK are: Laura Sutherland, one of Scotland's most prominent public relations practitioners and the founder of the PR Festival; former CIPR president Stephen Waddington, prolific blogger, author, partner and chief engagement officer at renowned agency Ketchum; Stella Bayles, author of *Public Relations'*

Digital Resolution and director at tool Coverage Book (who, with Gary Preston and their team, are also creating some other great progressive tools); and #FutureProof author and PR consultant Sarah Hall. I therefore feel in good company to, in what is a slightly different style, attempt to do the same.

My aim in writing this is to create something that reads more like an insider's guide to an industry. Something that could be understood, and, importantly, enjoyed by students, business owners, individuals that could (or perhaps currently do) benefit from PR and, of course, PR professionals. It's hoped that each camp will take something different from this book.

The media landscape is less certain than ever. The ability to interact with, and proactively find, an audience is, conversely, easier than ever, unhindered by those same journalistic gatekeepers. PR is in a unique position, where, as an industry for and of influence, we must either understand this shifting world of influence or get left behind.

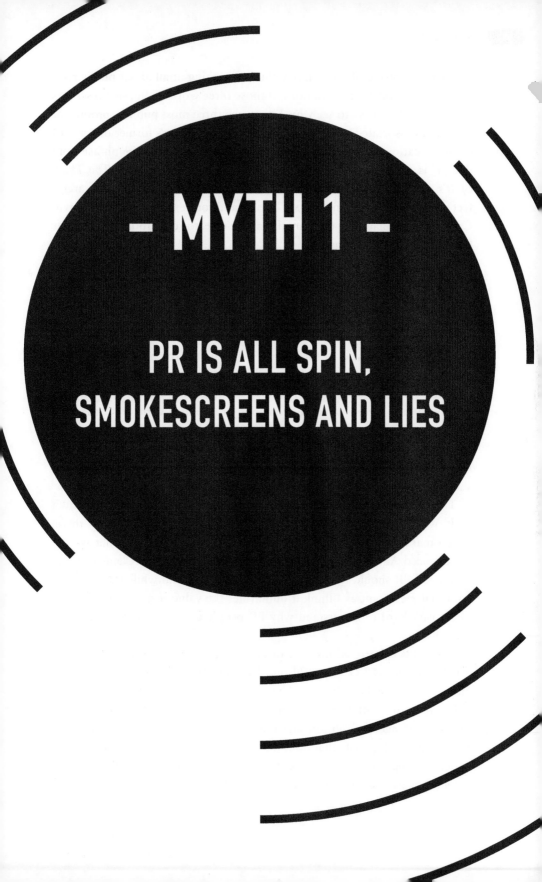

– MYTH 1 –

PR IS ALL SPIN, SMOKESCREENS AND LIES

If anybody outside of the industry thinks anything at all about public relations, it likely relates to variations of those three words. Spin, smokescreens and lies. And it's easy to see why. I'd say the three most publicly prominent characters associated with PR in the UK are Tony Blair's former director of communications Alastair Campbell – somebody to whom the phrase 'spin doctor' is often attributed (and supposedly the inspiration for *The Thick of It*'s wonderfully sweary Scot, Malcolm Tucker); tabloid scandal architect and convicted criminal Max Clifford; and former Prime Minister David Cameron, who had a seven-year stint as the director of corporate affairs for Carlton Communications.

Now, look again at those three words. It's no wonder PR has a PR problem, as journalist Brian Groom said (Groom, 2013), though not the only voice either inside or outside the industry to have said so.

When I discuss my career with anybody outside of PR, I'm usually met with one of two responses – the first: 'I don't really know what that is' and the second: 'Ah, so you lie for a living?' The first is the most common and has taken years of practice to respond in a concise way that doesn't leave the other person bored rigid. I've lost count of the number of times I'd previously just agreed whenever somebody responded with 'oh, is that like a <insert profession that is nothing like PR, like a personal assistant>'. I'm aware that it's a fairly common occurrence in PR, but my mum has only recently stopped feeling aggrieved on my behalf when a journalist's name stands above a story I told her I had a hand in.

That second and less common response is, for the most part, our own fault. We hide behind our clients just as much as they want us to stay there, which makes it very hard for an outsider to understand just what we do. Experienced Atlanta, Georgia-based PR professional Tracy Clement wrote that 'good PR should be invisible' (Clement, 2011) and while I do disagree with that viewpoint as I think it diminishes the value society puts on good PR, it isn't hard to understand why PR people and our clients want us to stay unseen.

The CIPR (Chartered Institute of Public Relations) is an industry organization. Its then-CEO, Jane Wilson, discussed the topic of PR 'spin' with industry website PR Moment. She said, 'For years people have equated public relations with "spin", taking the truth and representing it in a way that suits an agenda.' Wilson says that 'although PROs craft messages, the aim is not to tell people that up is down or that black is white, but to build understanding and trust, which can only be achieved if the activity is transparent, honest and engaging' (Wilson, 2012).

Agreeing with Wilson is Alex Honeysett, a Marketing and Brand Strategist who spent nearly a decade working in communications for brands like NASDAQ and Thomson Reuters. Alex says that while 'there may have been a time and a place when companies put out messaging that misrepresented what was actually happening within the company – whether about their executives, products, or overall company health – that's definitely not the chosen approach anymore' (Honeysett, 2016).

Alex continues, citing the move from the shadows as one of necessity in an era of digital footprints and mistrust: 'With the backlash around the financial collapse, the rise of social media, and a significant decrease in the patience investors and clients have for company BS, most PR people are actually focused on the opposite: helping companies be as transparent as possible.'

Having given it a great deal of thought, there are three main reasons for the misconception that public relations is synonymous with spin and lies.

1 The people who most publicly represent our industry

Kiss and tell PR is a tiny and fatuous corner of our world – and something the majority of practitioners will never have experience of. However, throughout the 1990s and 2000s, Max Clifford, who specialized in this style of publicity, became the self-appointed face of PR. Clifford's face and the word 'PR guru' appeared together on-screen and in print regularly, each time creating a negative public association with the industry despite the fact that he barely represented it at all.

Once people have the idea that we trade in salaciousness, perpetuated by Clifford's every TV appearance, each one serving to act as adverts for his services, it's difficult to alter that perception of PR. Practitioners are quick to correctly highlight that there's a difference between them and Clifford as a 'publicist', but to the public there isn't – yet. I believe, though I couldn't find any data to back this up, that if you were to ask a stranger on the street for the name of a PR person – and if they're able to recall one at all – Clifford's would be the one they'd come up with. Add all of the above to the fact that Clifford repeatedly and publicly said that lying was a key part of his job, declaring during a 2007 PRWeek debate that he'd 'been telling lies on behalf of people, businessmen, politicians and countries for 40 years' (BBC, 2014), and the dots connecting public opinion of PRs and the most vocal spokesperson the industry has had are easy to see.

In the US (and I'm sure there are other publicly well-known ones, but being a Brit, my exposure is limited) there's Ryan Holiday, former director of marketing for American Apparel and author of the controversial book *Trust Me, I'm Lying: Confessions of a Media Manipulator*, which debuted on the *Wall Street Journal*'s best-seller list. It's a great read about the flaws in online publishing's focus on low-quality, high-traffic tactics, all with a focus on monetization, and how Holiday and others exploit them for client gain by, essentially, lying.

I couldn't tell you how prominent Holiday is beyond media, marketing and PR circles, but his best-seller status gives us an indication that a good number of people have read what he has to say. One tactic Holiday hones in on is something he calls 'trading up the chain'. To explain what he readily defined as a 'scam', Holiday says he used a strategy that 'manipulates the media through recursion', turning 'nothing into something by placing a story with a small blog that has very low standards, which then becomes the source for a story by a larger blog, and that, in turn, for a story by larger media outlets', claiming that 'people like me do this every day'.

2 Silence

As mentioned, I barely knew what the job entailed until I started doing it – and I place the blame firmly at the feet of the industry itself and the behind-closed-doors operation of it. Transparency is something we talk about a lot within communications on behalf of our clients, but there's a reluctance to be transparent about our own tactics and work.

There's a certain pressure when working with clients to ensure that good PR appears organic. This is understandable, because people don't much like being told what to think, feel or do and clients should really be the ones we shine the light on, but this invariably means skulking around somewhere in the shadows. Given they're the ones holding the purse strings, clients don't often want to admit that they didn't come up with an idea or message and with that, our function is diminished to nothing more than somebody that presses the 'send' button to share a pitch with journalists, if we're acknowledged at all.

One of the earliest clients I got to work on was a project called Tribewanted, a 'social experiment' in which a couple of 20-somethings leased a paradisiacal Fijian island called Vorovoro, formed a partnership with its indigenous tribe and, by appealing to socially responsible tourists, aimed to build an environmentally friendly and sustainable model of what the National Geographic dubbed 'low-impact development'. *The Beach*, the

2000 movie starring Leonardo DiCaprio, provided imagery that both the media and our target audience understood, so we ensured journalists associated the project with that idea of isolated beauty... with fewer deaths than in the film, all being well.

Tribewanted became an international success, achieving media coverage in dozens of countries around the world. After what Founder Ben Keene defined as a slow start, my first agency boss, Andy Barr, helped Keene and – in particular, the brilliant and unique concept – achieve global notoriety by securing interview after interview by communicating the project in just the right way to the right audience, something that led to a TV and book publishing deal. By the time I was up and running as a PR executive within 10 Yetis, I was already promoting Ben to the media as an author with an upcoming BBC documentary, something that stands out amongst the noise, whether I realized it at the time or not.

I only use this example out of plenty of others I could choose because, as a fledgling PR in a job, I felt lucky to have scored. I marvelled at the behind-the-scenes and around-the-clock work Andy put in to make this happen for Tribewanted and others. It actually transpired that Andy settled on the agency's name, 10 Yetis, by incorporating an old nickname of his from his days in financial PR – where he tells me he was known by others in his company as 'the Yeti' on account of his ability to remain hidden.

Of course, there's merit to this given that clients do pay agency professionals for their expertise and confidence, and it does tally with the views of Tracy Clement that good PR is invisible. However, it means:

a) There is little in the way of appreciation when you're the person or group making other brands and individuals look good, or enabling them the platform to do so. This lack of praise and recognition is actually something I attribute the high quantity of industry awards to – we're happy, maybe even desperate, to pay for the potential to be recognized.

Yet far more importantly:

b) The fact that the wider public are barely aware of your existence serves to enshroud the role of a PR person in secrecy, leaving our actual role open to guesswork. This allows for myths and misconceptions – like the notion that all PR people lie – to propagate, unchecked.

3 Education

Like every person with an agenda – I'm turning into Jamie Oliver – I think the state education system should, at the very least, acknowledge a profession that plays a significant role in the success of businesses, charities and other organizations.

Advertising, a separate discipline that sits alongside public relations under the banner of 'marketing', is otherwise widely understood on at least a very basic level, because it's there – it's in your face. In 2015, I judged in a 'Dragons' Den' (Shark Tank for American readers)-style school competition for kids aged 13–16. During a talk I gave about PR, just one hand of more than twenty went up when I asked at the outset if anybody knew what public relations was. I spoke to that person afterwards and they said, 'It's basically advertising, isn't it?'

Many of the people I know and/or have worked with were educated in private, paid-for, schools (I... well, I was the first in my family for generations to sit exams you could actually put on your CV). Of the questions asked related to diversity in the State of the Profession 2016 paper (CIPR, 2016) – taking in responses about ethnicity, disability, sexuality and religion, I would have liked to see something in relation to secondary education.

According to the Independent Schools Council, around 6.5 per cent of the total number of schoolchildren in the UK are educated privately. However, in the PR Census (PRCA, 2016), educational backgrounds were looked at and, according to the results, there is a disproportionate number of privately-educated people working in the industry compared to the general profile of the UK population. The study found that 27 per cent were educated privately, a figure that rose to 33 per cent for practitioners in London. To put this into context, 32 per cent of Members of Parliament went to a private school (Burns, 2015).

Sixty-six per cent of census respondents attended a state school.

Privately educated people are more likely to have jobs in agencies than in-house teams, with around one in three privately educated professionals in agencies compared to one in five in in-house roles.

It's not that I think private school kids shuffle from double English Literature to the PR classroom where they take turns trying to beat the lie detector (I joke), but perhaps there's more exposure to the realities of business amongst the children whose parents earn well enough to pay for their education, alongside which a basic idea of PR's role in marketing is picked up.

Beyond secondary education, the CIPR State of the Profession 2015 report found that 'four per cent of public relations practitioners who were university graduates attended either Cambridge or Oxford University to study an undergraduate or master's degree'. This was based on interviews with more than two thousand practitioners across the UK and was interpreted by previous CIPR president and Ketchum's Chief Engagement Officer Stephen Waddington.

With an above-average number of people within the industry educated to at least degree standard – 84 per cent – I believe there's merit in an introduction to public relations and its role within business being added to syllabi in state secondary education. Not only would it expose a wider population of pupils to the industry, but I believe it would positively impact on the world's economy and charitable organizations, too, as future employees and employers are taught the basics and merits of effectively communicating to internal stakeholders and an external audience.

Wrapping Up

I'm conscious that something I haven't yet done in this chapter is explain the role of PR in defence of it, nor have I gone into detail with regards to what we actually do. I was keen to demonstrate that the misconception (where there's a perception at all) that we are all somehow looking for a way to hoodwink the public is something that we've allowed to happen. People outside the industry have filled in the gaps where we are otherwise silent.

If we are keen to improve not only the public perception of PR but also the diversity of the people who make it up, and we seemingly are, then the above has to change. We can't let people who don't speak for the industry speak for us. We have to resist the urge to be silent, simply because that's what we've always done, and we have to consider ways to further the reach of PR into mainstream education. As I'll get to in future chapters, I believe PR can do incredible things, for businesses, causes and individuals, and the perception of the industry that runs contrary to that should bother us.

In this next chapter, I'll explain what PR does, the impact it can have and how it can be measured.

Further reading

Burns, J, 2015. Almost a third of MPs went to private school. *BBC News*, 11 May. Available at: <http://www.bbc.co.uk/news/education-32692789> [Accessed 11 April 2016]

CIPR, 2016. *CIPR State of the Profession*. Available at: <http://www.cipr.co.uk/content/policy-resources/research/cipr-state-profession-2016> [Accessed 11 April 2016]

Clement, T, 2011. Good PR should be invisible. *Robin Tracy PR*. Available at: <www.robintracy.com/good-pr-should-be-invisible/> [Accessed 11 April 2016]

Groom, B, 2013. PR, an industry with a PR problem. *Financial Times*, 29 July. Available at: <http://www.ft.com/cms/s/0/516618ea-f83b-11e2-b4c4-00144feabdc0.html#axzz45WMidW6I> [Accessed 11 April 2016]

Honeysett, A, 2016. The 3 biggest myths about working in PR. *The Muse*. Available at: <https://www.themuse.com/advice/the-3-biggest-myths-about-working-in-pr> [Accessed 11 April 2016]

Unnamed journalist, 2014. Max Clifford: the fallen king of spin, *BBC News*, 28 April. Available at: <http://www.bbc.co.uk/news/entertainment-arts-26465728> [Accessed 11 April 2016]

Waddington, S, 2015. 10 areas of pain in public relations. *Influence*, 24 February. Available at: <http://influence.cipr.co.uk/2015/02/24/10-areas-pain-public-relations/> [Accessed 11 April 2016]

Wilson, J, 2012. Eight misconceptions about PR. *PRmoment.com*, 8 November. Available at: <http://www.prmoment.com/1198/eight-misconceptions-about-pr.aspx> [Accessed 11 April 2016]

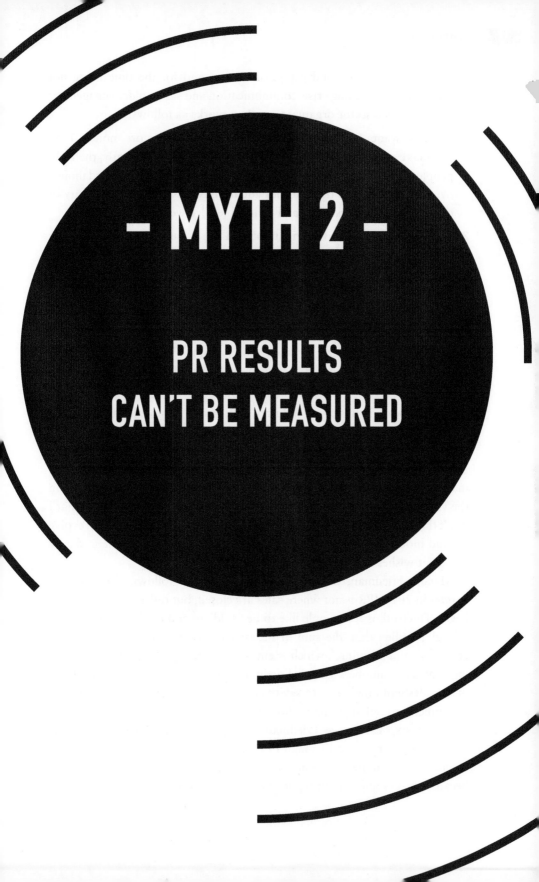

PR – in its most basic and capitalistic form, and for the time being not including areas including crisis communication and stakeholder engagement work that public-sector organizations do – works as follows:

1 Client A wants (and in many cases needs) to make more money. They can make more money if more people – but, most importantly, the right people – know who they are and actually like them enough to hand money over to them. This is true for individuals, businesses and the majority of organizations (professional and charitable) I've worked with.

2 Once we know who the 'right' people are – our target audience (or 'market') – we get onto thinking about how to best reach and communicate to or with them. In short, we think – what do these people watch, read, listen to and consume?

3 As soon as we have an idea of where our efforts might have the best chance to be consumed by our target audience, we think of ways to best represent our client or paymaster there, aiming to pique audience interest enough to achieve our client's aims. Essentially – what do we want them to think?

Public relations is a service industry. We, as professionals, are there to provide a service to fee-paying clients or, if in-house, whoever's paying our wages. And when somebody is paying for a service, that somebody – assuming they subscribe to the standard and time-honoured business approach of making more money than they are spending – will soon start to question the value they are getting in return. It's important at this point to say that I don't think PR is a direct sales channel. Of course it isn't, but it does revolve around money, just as all marketing does; again, focusing on the audience the client wishes to reach.

Marsha Friedman, CEO of EMSI PR, said the following to *Business Insider* in 2010: 'PR is not where sales are closed, but rather, it's where sales begin. The truth is few people like to be "sold" to and that's why PR works so well', adding that 'the soul of PR isn't promotion or sales, but rather, education and branding', which is entirely different to advertising, describing that as 'a numbers game'. Friedman's response to the question 'How many sales will I make?' is to say that PR isn't a direct sales venue but that 'it's difficult to sell anything without it'.

In the six years since Friedman's analysis of PR, though, much has changed. It's rarely good enough in my personal experience to rely on the promise of 'awareness', or the assertion that PR will educate consumers, because those things are unreportable. In recent years, and having worked with hundreds of clients, I've found that, if there's anything post-recession business owners like less than vague talk of branding, it's money they spend that can't be tracked.

PR is about attempting to create an action or reaction that usually, at *some* point, revolves around making money. It's where the buck stops. I've never had a client for whom this wasn't the case – even charity PR work is about money raised through donations, and personal PR clients almost always have earning power at the forefront of their goals.

The myth that PR activity can't be measured in any meaningful way is a damaging one. I have no hard facts to prove it, but one can assume business owners of a certain mindset that see our industry as 'fluffy' would sooner put their money into PPC (pay-per-click) advertising, where the cost per user or customer is much easier to arrive at. My agency works with a number of clients with investors to report to and I've been told this is one of the first figures the investor will want to look at.

Throughout the recession and in the immediate years thereafter, PR held on well, but as reported by Cameron Clarke, 'PR agencies [had] to stomach shorter contracts and a continuing pressure on costs because their clients' confidence [had] been dented by the economic gloom' (Clarke, 2011).

I was actually quoted in that same article and (although nowhere in the manuscript preparation document does it say how to deal with quoting yourself) I said that retained clients were keeping a very close eye on costs, leading to us working with their wider marketing teams and service suppliers more closely than ever. I said and still believe that one good result of the downturn was that both prospective project and retained clients came with tighter and better defined briefs and objectives, leading to more accountability. I noted that this was indicative of market nervousness and a sign that the industry's practices would have to adapt to this, meaning the way we reported results to clients.

An ugly fact of the agency world, and something rarely touched upon, is that client retention is a problem. At the outset for near enough every client I've worked with, from start-ups to global brands, they've said a variation of 'if this is successful during our trial period' – small to medium-sized clients tend to want to try before they buy and ask for X month contracts – 'there's no reason we wouldn't carry on'. Sometimes that's in the form of a break clause or a three-month notice period if you're going for a longer retained contract, but there's always that Damoclean pressure from the off – after all, a client can't pay you with the 'awareness' you've achieved for them alone.

I'm going to have to talk about AVE, aren't I?

Sometime decades ago, AVE was born as an answer to that one pesky client question: 'Why should we keep paying you money?'

AVE is a marketing industry term that stands for 'Advertising Value Equivalent' and is a measure that has been used in the public relations industry to 'measure' the benefit to a client of media coverage. PRs would measure the actual size of the coverage gained, account for its placement and calculate what the equivalent amount of space, if paid for as advertising, would cost.

Often a multiplier would also be used – commonly in the range of three to ten – to allow for the credibility of editorial coverage over advertising. Alongside AVE, I've also encountered PRV – as in, PR Value. I never really knew the difference, but I'm not sure it much matters.

I worked with a handful of agencies as a consultant prior to setting my agency up and once, whilst sitting in a meeting – and this was in 2014 – the account director proudly declared that the PR 'value' of the activity for that month-long reporting period was something like £3,000:£1. What was meant by that was, for every pound spent on PR, the activity had, according to this team's analysis and factoring up of the results (on account of being better trusted, remember), been responsible for £3,000 worth of exposure.

To give a basis for comparison, the rate card price for a full-page colour advert in the *Daily Mail* was £45,612 (Jackson, 2012). Let's say that client was spending £1,000 per month with that agency (it wasn't) – the agency was saying that it'd achieved £3 million worth of exposure for this client. Divide that by even the highest 'credibility' factoring most articles online say agencies would plump for – ten times – and you get to £300,000, or the equivalent of six and a half full pages in the *Daily Mail*, an achievable coverage goal in a month. But as I say – that's not taking into account a) the client was paying much more than £1,000 per month, b) the factoring might not have been ten times, and c) this is all utterly, utterly imaginary. The client did not make a minimum of £3 million that month as a direct result of PR…!

It doesn't take a genius to work out that, while it's one way to assign a figure to our activity, AVE is a broken metric. Then-CEO of PR mega-shop Edelman Robert Phillips was on the money when he said that AVE 'is a lazy way of persuading marketers schooled in old ad ways that PR counts, rather than working to find new and better systems of measurement' (Wallace, 2009).

Despite widespread industry ridicule, though, in a bid to determine ROI (return on investment) from public relations outcomes, I've heard regularly from clients I've worked with that finance directors, investors and other senior executives accept AVE as a barometer of PR success. In line with this and hoping to shift that expectation, Jon Sellors, head of communications at insurance company LV, recently stated that 'public relations agencies and measurement suppliers need to help in-house teams educate boards/exec teams about the role of communications and therefore what should be measured and reported back to them' (Starbutts, 2016).

As with many aspects of public relations, marketing and even business as a whole, the internet has changed things – but practitioners have often been too heads-down, or too stuck in their ways to adapt. I'll run through one fictional scenario, which many PR people will recognize, dealing with it on a daily basis.

If PR can be measured – how?

If AVE is so terrible (and it is), this leaves us with a problem. How do we provide clients or employers with the metrics they need to see to decide upon the benefit of PR?

It's important to say that industry bodies have realized the importance of better measurement and, with guidelines including the Barcelona Principles, the topic has been considered by people far brighter than me. Personally, I prefer a more explicit approach and am weary of tokenistic adherence to guidelines – something I'll move onto as I re-evaluate the above fictional scenario from a different, much more direct and digital perspective – but in principle, the methodology is sound.

The Barcelona Principles were agreed upon by PR practitioners from 33 countries at a summit in Barcelona, Spain in 2010, convened by the International Association for Measurement and Evaluation of Communication (AMEC). The Barcelona Principles identify 'the need for outcome-, instead of output-based measurement of PR campaigns, call for the exclusion of ad value equivalency metrics, and recognize the communications value of social media'.

A document is available courtesy of AMEC called the 'Paid, Owned and Earned Social Media Measurement Framework menu of potential metrics' (AMEC, 2014). It isn't perfect and as former CIPR president Stephen Waddington says in the same article as Sellors, 'in trying to get buyers of public relations services to adopt the Barcelona Principles – my hunch (backed up by judging a big public relations awards scheme for two years and the briefs I see) is that they simply don't appear on the radar of clients and are not really observed in practice'.

There is a measurement framework put forward by the AMEC and agreed upon by the coalition of PR practitioners for 'earned' media – in other words, outcomes often attributable to PR. Take a look here to see the table: http://amecorg.com/wp-content/uploads/2014/06/Social-media-measurement-frameworks-menu-of-potential-metrics.pdf.

I've only ever cast my eyes over the Barcelona Principles a few times. It's not that they aren't a helpful guideline – they are – but that in practice, we should be asking clients from the outset what their hopes are results-wise, and then advising on or suggesting other KPIs (key performance indicators) alongside those. Then, once we understand our client's aims, we should know how we're going to lift that outcome we're hoping for from the above table and actually measure it.

If agencies are failing to report using these suggested metrics as suggested, what are we reporting as an industry? And although, again, PR isn't a direct sales service, is there a way to more clearly attribute a value to our activity in a way that will satisfy those client-side that still insist on AVE and the like because it's a £value figure – focusing on outcomes, not outputs, as identified by AMEC?

The answer is yes – and it lies, in my opinion, outside of the conventional public relations toolset. In the above table, six metrics down under the heading 'Impact' is the fact that the majority of clients I've ever worked with most care about 'Sales & % increase over time'. Yet, there's still little in the way of measurement that goes on to demonstrate our usefulness because, after all, it's hard to prove PR activity, which led to some favourable and well-read print coverage, was responsible for somebody walking into a shop and buying from that client. There's just no way to know that without perhaps asking them – and then, who's to say they'll remember where they read about the client or product? But, much like the ways we can reach clients have evolved, the internet has changed the way we can prove our worth too.

Let's look at an example. X client has been written about on a popular news website, with a follow link (more on this shortly). The story is in the print version the following day.

What gets reported back to the client?

- A link to the coverage?
- The combined number of unique visitors per month the site gets/tells us it gets (in no way hiking it for ad-selling purposes, ononono) and the

readership figures as quoted by the monitoring service used, likely pulled from ABC statistics?

- The page's domain and/or page authority?
- The number of times that link was shared on social media?
- An estimate of the reach/impressions of said shares?

There is a way to then tell that client how much money, if any, that link on the website made for them – and, over time, there's a way to prove how beneficial that follow link and authoritative links from other sites are to the client's search engine performance, too. I'll run through both, below.

The fact is – and I'm aware PR purists will say our value is more than the total sum of money attributable to our activity come the end of the month (I entirely agree and accept that) – we're big and ugly enough as practitioners to accept that we are an extended function of a business and that very few businesses will sink money endlessly into PR.

Digital measurement is possible but it seems that some a) don't understand it, b) don't care or, worse, c) know about it, but are petrified because, after years of AVE or little-to-no measurement at all, it mightn't make PR look like a good investment.

As laid out in the Barcelona Principles, there are many other benefits to what we do, though it's light on the 'how'. If we're talking about straightforward digital measurement, however, Google Analytics – and specifically Google Goals – is the PR industry's saviour.

Here's where, when I've tried to discuss digital measurement of the value of our activity in the past, a certain type of person attracted to the PR industry might switch off. One individual that handles the accounts of global brands – the type of person who'd die happy if a reality TV star retweeted her – actually said, and it's stuck with me: 'I'll never be geeky enough to care.'

If your client has a website (even if a traditionally 'offline' business, they should have), you can already go one step better than the fictional report I mentioned above. Does your client's site:

- Ask visitors to sign up to a newsletter?
- Give visitors the ability to download information?
- Ask visitors to fill out contact forms?
- Or, perhaps most importantly, give visitors the chance to buy direct from the site?

If you've answered yes to any of the above (most will), you can prove your worth in a way that's much simpler than you think and way, way more realistic than AVE.

Your client very likely already uses some form of website analytics. Google Analytics is the most popular and gives site owners (and those allowed access) the ability to see:

- how much traffic they get;
- where that traffic comes from (geographically and in terms of what links people clicked to reach their site);
- how long visitors stay onsite for, and much more.

What Google Analytics also allows you to do is set up Goals. Put simply, Goals will allow you and/or your client to measure your marketing activity. It goes beyond the traffic measurement mentioned above and gets into what those visitors you've sent them actually *do* when onsite.

You can show your clients how many newsletter subscribers, downloads or sales came as a direct result of PR activity. You can highlight how PR activity sent X,000 unique visitors. Of these, Y% converted into sales, spending £Z. That's £ZZZ we can prove you made as a direct result of our work.

Better than a meaningless ratio of [how much the client pays per month]: [the AVE of that month's coverage], no?

How to set up Google Goals

It all begins at the end. The 'thank you' page which a completed online form or purchase sends you to, acts as the 'goal' from which we, if allowed access, can work back. You can check drop-off rates using 'funnels'.

Using the pages leading up to the 'goal' page, you can see the visitor path, including the stages visitors drop off. Going back from there, you start to see where that traffic came from, how much money they spend, which traffic converted and even what links they clicked on.

You might be surprised by the social network, media outlet, blog or ads that send the most profitable traffic and, as such, you can alter your efforts accordingly. This can save you time and your client's money – but, most importantly, begins to prove value beyond the 'we got you coverage and/or people tweeting about you, what more do you want!?' PR approach.

This is all entirely possible right now – and has been for a few years.

I'm conscious of recommending tools and services to use, for one main reason I've been bitten by before – tools come and go, aging guides and recommendations quickly. For instance, I used to regularly recommend

Topsy.com as a free social media measurement tool, until Apple bought it and, in early 2016, decided it wasn't worth keeping live.

Despite being an industry as prone to adaptation and the shifting media and social media landscape as PR is, which means services suppliers rise, adapt and fall regularly, it's my hope that as well as demonstrating that outcomes can be measured, it's made as simple as possible for professionals.

That's why, built to help the process of evaluating Google Goals, I wanted to highlight 'Answer the Client', which I was first introduced to via a tweet that started with the hashtag #f***AVE (asterisks mine) with a link and a brief description: 'It's Google Analytics for your PR coverage' (Preston, 2016).

Answertheclient.com is a free, better-looking and less complicated way for PRs to access client (or their own, if in-house) Analytics, if going into actual Google Analytics is too confusing and/or time-consuming. If the wider industry is to embrace measurement, and I firmly believe it would benefit us all to do so, the fewer barriers to doing so there are, the better. Answer the Client struck me as something everybody from interns to CEOs could use and understand.

I called the team behind the tool with a few questions and found out that it had started life as an add-on for another industry service they'd developed, but the team had decided it was worth spinning out – for free – to simplify measurement for those in the industry and to hopefully move us beyond a point of repeatedly having the same arguments and debates.

Google Goals need to already be in place, but if you have an email address with access to your employer's or client's Google Analytics – ask the person or team that deals with development to add you – you can then paste in coverage URLs to see a simplified set of results, showing a) any traffic that came about as a result of it, and b) if anybody that visited actually *did* anything, whether that's spending any money or ticking off any other Goals (be it newsletter sign-ups or requests for information).

Measuring the SEO benefit of PR

Another aspect I'd like to touch on is the measurement of the search engine optimization benefits of PR. I've worked with a number of search marketers and agencies, and wanted to leave it to one of these to touch on the search benefits of PR, and how to measure them.

Anthony Tuite is the head of digital at Barracuda Digital, and somebody I've worked with many times in recent years. Here's his take on the subject:

CASE STUDY

One particular foible experienced by SEO professionals, vis-à-vis their role, is a fairly persistent misconception over what they should be employed to do and what value their role can deliver. True enough, most people in marketing now have at least a vague idea what it is all about, 'They do keywords and Google rankings, right?!' But confusion is pervasive and the cause is rooted in the pace of change in the digital landscape and the subsequent increasing overlaps with other areas of marketing.

The fast-evolving digital landscape can be something of a poisoned chalice for SEO folk: on the one hand the role of the SEO is always changing, and that is interesting and stimulating; on the other hand, if you are caught napping, you may end up with a skill set that is insufficient and no longer profitable.

This is exactly and precisely how PR and SEO have come across one another, and in many ways (although it may not be too freely admitted) the PR folk are in a better position than those in SEO, with regard to the specific SEO discipline of link building. SEOs often have the edge when it comes to digital knowledge, but PR folks have the skills for getting links built in the right way, and these days that is all-important. If only you knew how to convey that value to your clients/employer – there lies the PR's opportunity.

It all goes back to Google and a little thing called PageRank. PageRank is Google's representation of democracy on the web, and it leverages that principle in algorithm form to rank web pages in its search results. When a website or webpage is of high value to users, other websites will naturally 'link' to those websites – because that is useful to their audiences. More links is more power to rank for keywords in Google's search. That means more money for websites selling things. So, build good, useful and engaging content and you will naturally attain links from other websites that like what you are saying and doing, and hence you will rank better... right? Wrong. This is the real world.

That is the foundation on which Google is built. But how does this relate back to PR? Focus on the links, the fairy dust of the web, those 'democratic' votes of confidence that make websites fly. Put simply, without links you cannot rank in Google. SEOs used to be able to use any number of tactics to build links, and it worked. Not so any more. In the perpetual grudge match that is 'Google vs The Spammers,' Google has been able to implement technology to police the acquisition of links across the web. Get it wrong and irreversible damage can be done to a website's ability to rank in Google's search result pages. So although we do need to build good, useful and engaging content, we also need to promote what we are doing to receive the credit we deserve for that hard work. And we need to do it in a way that is not 'spammy'. How do you do that in the most effective way? PR.

It turns out that the best links are from websites that have large readerships and are in some way thematically similar to a given website that we are trying to promote. These websites have large readerships because they are genuinely interesting and/or offer real value to users. Because of that, they have generated lots of links from external websites and hence have a lot of power to rank. It also means they have a lot of power to pass on to other websites they link to.

That is all well and good but, as PRs know, those websites with big readerships can be very picky about who and what they feature on their precious web pages. What you need is a hook and a story. That is something PR folk already know and breathe on a daily basis. What I am saying is, that is a seriously relevant and important SEO skill set – and not one that 'traditional' SEOs naturally have or find easy to acquire.

Public relations professionals have a massive leg-up when it comes to digital marketing. The trinity for earned media success online, in terms of ranking in Google's search results is:

1 Website technical health (speed, architecture, markup, internal linking).

2 Keyword targeting and on-site content quality.

3 Links.

As a PR, you're already nailing a third of it, and, from an agency point of view, building good links is the lynchpin that secures longer-term contracts and client retainers. Why? Because links mean Google rankings, which turn into money. Over simplified, but that is the reality. Fine-tuning a car engine is all well and good, but without fuel it is not going to go anywhere. And while we are talking car engines and fuel, you probably want to use the high-grade fuel over the dirty stuff to stop your engine breaking. Links are website fuel and PR delivers the highest grade website fuel.

That just leaves measurement. How do you, as a PR, show increased value in what you are now doing in terms of link acquisition? The answer is relatively simple: keyword rankings increases and overall website visibility increases (a value that is an amalgamation of the majority of keywords a website ranks for and the associated value that delivers, based on monthly search volumes and ranking positions).

There are many keyword rank trackers out there, but for tracking overall website visibility in Google search, our favourites are Search Metrics, BrightEdge, Linkdex and SEM Rush (all four platforms also do rank tracking as well).

It is not just coverage and its equivalent value anymore. As a PR, your work leads to a website ranking better, so long as the other two parts of the earned media trinity are being taken care of; it is definitely a case of 'you are only as strong as your weakest part'.

And finally we get to it: Search Engine Marketers (note the change in vernacular from SEO to SEM) need PR to max out the value of what they are doing with a website's search engine marketing strategy. PRs need SEMs to max out the value they are delivering in terms of links, making us ideal bedfellows.

Further reading

AMEC, 2014. *Paid, Owned and Earned Social Media Measurement Framework menu of potential metrics*. [pdf] Available at: <http://amecorg.com/wp-content/uploads/2014/06/Social-media-measurement-frameworks-menu-of-potential-metrics.pdf> [Accessed 11 April 2016]

Clarke, C, 2011. Marketing budget cuts: a view from the PR industry. *The Drum*, 27 December. Available at: <http://www.thedrum.com/news/2011/12/27/marketing-budget-cuts-view-pr-industry> [Accessed 11 April 2016]

Friedman, M, 2010. So, I'm launching a PR campaign – how many sales will I make? *Business Insider*, 17 September. Available at: <http://www.businessinsider.com/so-im-launching-a-pr-campaign-how-many-sales-will-i-make-2010-9?IR=T> [Accessed 11 April 2016]

Jackson, J, 2012. How much do newspapers think their audiences are worth? *The Media Briefing*, 10 October. Available at: <https://www.themediabriefing.com/article/how-much-do-newspapers-think-their-audiences-are-worth> [Accessed 11 April 2016]

Preston, G, 2016. #f**AVE Our new free tool answertheclient.com – It's Google Analytics data for your PR coverage. #prmeasurement [Twitter]. 5 February. Available at: https://twitter.com/garydpreston/status/695585180904456192 [Accessed 11 April 2016]

Sarbutts, N, 2016. Measurement: time to look up, not down. *CIPR Influence*, 1 March. Available at: <http://influence.cipr.co.uk/2016/03/01/measurement-time-look-not/> [Accessed 11 April 2016]

Wallace, C, 2009. The AVE debate: measuring the value of PR. *PRWeek*, 6 May. Available at: <http://www.prweek.com/article/903837/ave-debate-measuring-value-pr> [Accessed 11 April 2016]

Wikipedia. *Barcelona Principles*. Available at: <https://en.wikipedia.org/wiki/Barcelona_Principles> [Accessed 11 April 2016]

- MYTH 3 -

ALL PUBLICITY IS GOOD PUBLICITY

Public relations is a little-understood discipline. In the chapter 'PR is all spin, smokescreens and lies', I look at why I think this is. Where psychology is no more present in society than PR, it's certainly more visible, with experts invited to opine on everything from celebrity culture to the latest lifestyle trends. Partly, this visibility and the keenness for the Next Big Thing in psychology has led to myths such as the notion that we only use a certain percentage of our brain.

I reference the brain potentiality myth because it was one of the inspirations behind this book. It caused me to consider which myths and misconceptions exist in and around PR, being as publicly misunderstood and even unknown as the profession is. After talking to friends both in and out of the industry, it was clear that certain misconceptions existed to varying degrees of popularity where a minimal understanding of the industry existed – that all PRs lie and that all PRs go to glamorous parties and hang out with celebrities, for instance. One kept coming up that was bigger than PR though, and will have embedded itself within the minds of people entirely unaware even of the existence of public relations – and that's the idea that all publicity is good publicity.

The phrase in its various guises – 'there's no such thing as bad press', 'all news is good news', 'any PR is good PR' – has been so often repeated that it's difficult to say with certainty exactly where it came from.

In my research, I found an incredibly in-depth look at the saying by etymology expert Barry Popik, a contributor to the *Oxford English Dictionary, Dictionary of American Regional English, Historical Dictionary of American Slang, Yale Book of Quotations* and *Dictionary of Modern Proverbs.*

The origin of this line of thinking is most commonly linked to P T Barnum, the nineteenth-century circus owner and oft-cited grandfather of modern day public relations. He has been credited with having said 'I don't care what people say about me as long as they say something', though Popik was keen to clarify that it is 'not known if Barnum ever said the quote for which he has long been attributed'.

Oscar Wilde is another the sentiment is aligned with, having written in his only novel, *The Picture of Dorian Gray* (1910), '... there is only one thing in the world worse than being talked about, and that is not being talked about'. Variations of the expression began to be used in the early twentieth century, and have been written in print since at least 1916, when the November edition of *The Retail Coalman* reported a coalman as saying 'Good publicity? What does he think he means by good publicity? There isn't any such thing as bad publicity.'

PR professionals with a few scars on their face will happily dispel this myth. Brand and marketing strategist Alex Honeysett wrote on career website The Muse about this myth. Honeysett said that having been on the inside of some major companies going through some major crises, 'those execs would have happily traded in their front-page status for a whole lot of nothing if it was possible'.

Shawn Paul Wood, a 20-year veteran of traditional and digital public relations and now digital strategist at Ketchum, backs up Honeysett's statement, going as far as to say 'anyone who has handled a major crisis will gladly arm-wrestle you for saying [that all press is good press]' (Wood, 2014).

Like the others, I have my own tales to tell, and will go into just why I think this enduring misconception is far from being accurate.

Personal PR

Firstly, I'll focus on personal PR, most commonly associated as being 'publicity'. Ours is a celebrity-obsessed and somewhat attention-seeking culture here in the West. We celebrate those in the public eye, often with little regard for the reasons for their fame. In fact, as multiple surveys in the last decade have found, when asking young children what they wanted to be when they grew up, the majority simply said 'famous'.

Other studies back this up. In 2007, Dr Yalda T Uhls, an award-winning child psychology researcher, did a study with Dr Patricia Greenfield at the UCLA campus of the Children's Digital Media Center@LA. The study, published in *Cyberpsychology* (Uhls and Greenfield, 2011), found that fame was 'the number one value communicated to pre-teens on popular TV'.

In response to this longing for fame that can be found not only among children but among the adults you'll see with every other thumb flick on Instagram, I'd say that anybody can be famous. You could be famous within the week. But, besides the fact that you might not like the reasons for your fame in the long run, there's a catch. Instant fame ends almost as quickly as it begins.

I once worked with somebody who achieved a level of insta-fame through a prime-time TV show. How? Well, this person did something very stupid in front of millions of people and, unsurprisingly, the public talked about it, for about as long as could be expected, before the person disappeared from public thought. It was a textbook Warhol '15 minutes of fame' situation.

But… that wasn't enough for this person (whom I'll take care to avoid identifying). They'd had a taste and they wanted more, so they got in touch with the agency I was working at, asking how we could improve upon this with further media and public attention. The truth was – after racking our collective brain – there was little we could do, and here's why.

To achieve fame of any meaningful kind (and this applies to brands, too), the secret is never allow fame to be the goal. In my opinion, fame should always be a by-product of success and/or talent. If you sat down with Sir David Attenborough, Adele or Muhammad Ali, every single one would say the same thing (or one would hope) – that their craft or work comes first. Celebrity is an aside.

Interesting, inspirational and talented people are all around us and, in turn, need the right people around them, guiding, promoting and supporting them. Even with all that, fame can be fleeting. There's no formula, but perseverance in terms of developing in your chosen field, continued success and the ability to say yes to the right things and no to the wrong things all contribute to longevity.

One of my current personal PR clients has had the chance to be in front of millions and millions of people through numerous reality TV 'opportunities'. It's a large carrot to dangle in front of people, especially those without guidance, who might feel like it's an opportunity too big to miss. That if they turn this down, there won't be another chance. As Ricky Gervais said of his creation David Brent, Brent 'made the mistake of confusing attention for respect', and in circumstances where there's a choice to be made, the questions 'How does this achieve the goals we're working towards?' and 'Really, who does this opportunity serve?' have to be asked. My litmus test is usually, if truly A-list celebrities such as David Beckham, J K Rowling or Stevie Wonder wouldn't agree to it, neither should your client. Any publicity should be, as much as possible, because it benefits your client. The opportunities you say no to are every bit as important as the ones you say yes to.

The person I mentioned earlier – the one who'd done something daft on a primetime TV show – I last saw them doing 'challenges', asking their social media audience to suggest demeaning things they could film themselves doing then upload them. It was sad to see, but all reasonable advice ignored, any publicity and attention was seen to be good publicity and attention at this stage, clearly.

Sometimes, contrary to the scenarios I've highlighted above, where there's an element of choice with regards to publicity, a PR person or team is faced with a client crisis and must react to defuse or improve a situation.

In March of 2016, 29-year-old tennis star Maria Sharapova failed a drug test. Sharapova and the team around her reacted quickly, conscious of the damage the inevitable media attention could do to her and the personal brand she'd cultivated over many years both on and off the court. Until 2016, she was *Forbes*' highest paid athlete for eleven consecutive years, when Serena Williams overtook her and her reputation was, as this relatively tennis-avoiding writer is aware, unblemished. The five-time Grand Slam winner was banned for two years by the International Tennis Federation.

While still at a point where the player was provisionally banned, and before the story could run away from them, Sharapova admitted to taking heart disease drug meldonium since 2006 due to health issues, drawing attention to the fact that the drug had only recently been banned by officials.

Tag Heuer and Porsche suspended their sponsorships, but other sponsors stood by more steadfastly. Johan Eliasch, the chairman of racquet sponsor Head, said he 'looks forward to many more years of working with Maria', calling her 'honest and courageous' in her handling of the issue. Head's statement of support followed similar lines to those of Nike and bottled water company Evian, which each pointed to Sharapova's insistence that she had not intentionally violated doping rules. Serena Williams was also quick to say Sharapova displayed 'a lot of courage' in admitting her offence.

The next major Sharapova will be able to enter is the 2018 tournament in Paris, when she will be 31. Had her camp acted more slowly, or not at all, I have no doubt things would have looked very different for the player. In PR terms, she got 'out' in front of the story, and far from allowing the media to speculate as to the infraction or let public condemnation grow, a clear and concise statement delivered on her Facebook page means the damage to her playing career, earning power and legacy has been reduced significantly. The fact that the player chose to use social media versus, say, a turn on Oprah or an exclusive with a media outlet shows the power of this direct and unfiltered connection to the public. In a tactic I've unfortunately had to use as I'll discuss, it's impossible to be misquoted when supporters could quite quickly highlight media omissions.

I'd go as far as to say Sharapova's handling of the ban was as good as it could have been, from a PR perspective. Compare this to the cases of cyclist Lance Armstrong, or former US president Bill Clinton, where both parties decided a 'deny, deny, deny' strategy was the best decision to make in the face of cheating claims despite the fact that the truth would eventually surface, and it's not difficult to see how being more honest might have helped. Although these were cases from admittedly far less direct and digital times, where news was more often than not filtered through the media's audience-grabbing perspectives and the subjects had less in the way of control, and taking into account the fact that the duo's actions were decidedly worse and more damaging, I wonder just how different their legacies might be had they followed a more concise and transparent path.

A personal example

I'll give you an insight into one such personal PR crisis I had to manage and can detail. It stands out as proof to me that all publicity is not good publicity, as I genuinely believe that this person's reputation and life would have been significantly impacted without quick, decisive management.

CASE STUDY

It was New Year's Day, 2014. I was with my family at a friend's house, having arrived early for lunch, when a journalist called, asking me to confirm allegations a client of mine had made on social media. The journalist, working for a leading international news service, demanded that I give them my client's number so that they could speak to them personally, too.

That client was – and still is – Jamie McDonald, a Pride of Britain award–winning, Guinness World Record–holding fundraising adventurer. At this point, he's nearing the end of an historic 5,000-mile, 200-marathon run across Canada in a bid to raise money and give back to the children's hospitals that helped him as a very unwell child; he was aiming to be the first person to complete the east-to-west trip without a support crew. Oh – and he's dressed as superhero 'The Flash', as the result of a social media poll we conducted. Averaging a marathon most days despite having injured his foot, Jamie was sleeping rough, self-filming, and editing footage we were updating followers with and spending the dwindling amount of money he'd saved himself, having raised a huge amount of money already (to be split between two hospital charities). Separately, he was raising money, province by province, for Canadian children's hospitals. As you can no doubt imagine from this description – of all the clients I've ever worked with, he is the last person I imagined I'd have to mount a crisis plan on behalf of.

'Is it true Jamie was mugged?' the journalist asked, their tone nothing short of accusatory. I was taken aback. This was around 11 am, making it around 4 am where Jamie was. It was easy to know where he was. We'd had a tracking website made up that updated regularly so you can follow his journey. I explained that I'd need to call them back. As soon as I'd hung up, I received another call. A national journalist, a similar conversation.

Afterwards, I pulled up Jamie's Facebook page, logged into his Twitter and did a full-tweet search for his Twitter handle in three separate tabs, trying to make sense of what had happened.

Jamie had, that morning, posted a status explaining that he'd been beaten up and that his bag had been stolen at a New Year's Eve party. His bag contained near enough everything he didn't want to leave on the buggy he ran with to carry his belongings. In the bag was his laptop, his camera (with hours and hours of footage) and an external hard drive he used, ironically, to back up this footage. His wallet had also been taken. He'd already contacted the police and had also had journalists call him after his social media updates were seen.

Initial shock and concern displayed by followers slowly began to be interrupted by questions as to whether or not this was some kind of publicity play. Others began to unpick aspects of what Jamie had initially said, with some highlighting the fact that he'd been drinking (on New Year's Eve, remember). It read like victim-blaming and I had the feeling that, if left unchecked and unclear, the story would take a turn for the worse, bypassing the fact that a crime had taken place and instead focusing on discrediting both Jamie and the story.

Fortunately, Jamie was still up and we spoke many times that morning. My first and most important role was to draft a clear and concise statement based on his experience that the media, who'd also been emailing me for confirmation, could quote. The statement is still up on Jamie's website and, given he was shaken by the incident (though more dismayed at the loss of his footage than having been attacked), it was important for me that he didn't have to speak to the media. I asked that any contact made with him was diverted to me and, once the statement was posted to his social media profiles, it would be his final say on the matter and the source from which the media and social media onlookers would be able to both use in reporting and digest.

As soon as the statement was live, the tone shifted. Not for everybody – there were some unhappy that their town, a travel destination, had been associated with a negative story and, understandably, they wanted to defend it. Jamie was clear, though, via the statement, that his experiences leading up to that point both in Canada and in that town had been incredible, that the people of Canada had been nothing short of welcoming and supportive, and that a minority wouldn't affect that opinion.

The majority of international coverage and opinion changed to what I feel it should have been – that a man running solo across the second biggest country in the world to raise money for the hospitals that helped him, and also children's hospitals in that country, was the victim of a reported crime. Jamie – who was understandably upset and unsure of how to deal with the onslaught of questions and doubt in the direct aftermath of the attack – was able to rest easy knowing all that needed to be said had been. Careful management of the incident, through minimal and to-the-point messaging, and by restricting media access beyond it, encouraged a groundswell of support, both in Canada and the UK. Every cloud has a silver lining, but in this case there were two. Firstly, donations increased, and secondly, Jamie's bag was soon discovered, with only the wallet still missing.

Less than two months later, on 4 February 2014, Jamie completed the final day's 15-mile run accompanied through the streets of Vancouver flanked by a police motorcade and hundreds of cheering runners and supporters. The plan was that he would, as he had in Newfoundland on the Atlantic coast 11 months prior, place his hand into the Pacific Ocean. Instead, he naïvely dived headfirst into hypothermic conditions and the history books.

£250,000 was raised as a result of the run for hospitals in the UK and Canada.

Brands and organizations

It doesn't just go for individuals, especially those longing to be celebrities and willing to do anything to be famous. There's a feeling among business owners that the same applies; that all press is good press. As an unnamed writer on Luminous PR's blog (2015) agrees, though, 'the belief that any press and media coverage, including negative coverage, is a good thing is very naïve, and many established companies who should know better have fallen foul of this misconception'.

Alex Honeysett stated that 'brands live and die by their reputations, and a really bad crisis can impact the company for years', highlighting the Lehman Brothers. 'Sure, there are absolutely ways to show great leadership, customer service, and transparency during a crisis – but since a company can make headlines for those things without the crisis, I'd suggest opting for the less dramatic option.'

Shawn Paul Wood added to his earlier statement that those who've handled crises would 'arm-wrestle' those that believe all publicity is good publicity, by saying about negative press: 'Sure, the brand you represent gets a little exposure but that's why content is so important. Prior to contrary opinion, people actually read the article (for which, our friends in the media thank you). And that's where we discover not all headlines create smiles or profit.'

There are times when poorly managed publicity can do more than impact a company's reputation and, to illustrate this point, there is no better-known nor apt story than that of Gerald Ratner.

CASE STUDY

'Doing a Ratner' is a term that has entered business lexicon, describing somebody who is or has personally crafted their own downfall.

Gerald Ratner was the owner of the Ratners chain of jewellery stores. Gerald Ratner wiped £500 million from the value of the company, all wrapped up in the stock market, with one speech at the Institute of Directors in 1991.

He had said to a crowd of 5,000, 'We also do cut-glass sherry decanters complete with six glasses on a silver-plated tray that your butler can serve you drinks on, all for £4.95. People say, "How can you sell this for such a low price?" I say, "Because it's total crap".' He added that his earrings were 'cheaper than an M&S prawn sandwich but probably wouldn't last as long'.

The comments were said jokingly, Ratner said, but combined with the impact of a recession, the chain was irrevocably damaged by the adverse publicity. Before the comments and Ratner's exit aged 43, his company was making profits of £125 million a year. At its height in the 1980s, with 1,500 stores in the UK and 1,000 in the United States, The Ratners Group consisted of H Samuel, Ernest Jones and Watches of Switzerland.

Ratner told the *Financial Times* in a 2013 interview that he lost everything he had 'because all [his] money was tied up in shares', stating that stocks went from £4.50 to 'tuppence' within six months, not helped by allowing a national newspaper to photograph him with a gun to his head. In November 1992, after an underperforming Christmas in 1991, Ratner was forced out, and resigned. The company changed its name to Signet Group plc in September 1993.

He claims that he was penniless for seven years, saying that he 'got further into debt', did not earn any money and was in a state of depression. Personal turmoil ensued, including the divorce from his first wife and the death of his mother in 1991. 'It doesn't seem to matter that in the eighties I was Britain's largest high-street jeweller, with over 50 per cent of the UK market. My obituary will be all about being a disaster', he told This is Money in 2013.

Now called Signet Jewelers, the company's fortunes have changed dramatically. Signet operates approximately 5,000 stores according to its 2016 annual report, employs 29,000 people and made $6.55 billion in that year. The group owns Kay Jewelers, Zales Jewelers and Jared in the United States, H Samuel and Ernest Jones in the UK, Peoples in Canada, and Piercing Pagoda in the United States and Puerto Rico.

Having changed its name and distanced itself from the Ratner family name, the company has bounced back and I'd say the general public is barely aware of the relationship between both companies. For Gerald Ratner, though, despite having since remortgaged his house to set up a health club company he eventually sold for £3.9 million, his name will forever be synonymous with this gaffe. Any inference that all publicity is good publicity might be met with vehement disagreement from Ratner.

Why does this myth exist?

I believe it has to do with people mistaking controversial campaigns leading to critical publicity or public response for controversial campaigns that in any way affect or bother that brand's target audience.

Betting company Paddy Power, airline Ryanair and clothing brand American Apparel are masters of this style of marketing and their continued success and popularity belies the critical reaction many of these brands' campaigns have received from vocal opponents. Eminem, Donald Trump and Lady Gaga are examples of celebrities who've benefited from courting controversy, yet were unaffected by it.

In 2014, Paddy Power tweeted an image. The image appeared to be a view from above a rainforest. It seemed that, relying on its notoriety for controversial campaigns, the brand had deforested a large portion of the 'Brazilian' landscape with a message of support for England's football team. 'Come on England', it read.

And almost immediately, in response to the purposely minimal details Paddy Power had provided alongside the purported photo, the public and media responded with messages of shock and anger. Paddy Power trended worldwide and even stoked the fire by tweeting an irate Twitter user back to say 'We haven't cut down that much!'

Only of course, Paddy Power had not deforested a rainforest in the name of showing its support for England (and our frankly meagre chances) at the 2014 FIFA World Cup in Brazil. The team failed even to get out of the group stages. The entire story was a ruse, as explained by the brand. The image was a doctored photograph of a rainforest, and, having judged the probable backlash, released as little more than promotional bait.

I don't think I'm giving the game away too much to reveal that, in a brief I received from Paddy Power, the brand states that 'one of the ways [they] differentiate [themselves] from the competition is by making mischief.

It entertains customers and that's what [Paddy Power] love doing'. Essentially, it's all about marketing fun that the core customer base will enjoy, at the expense of people that aren't customers.

Richard Bailey, a course leader at the University of the West of England, once said that 'judgement is the most valuable and most underrated skill in PR' and the Brazilian stunt from Paddy Power was an example of judgement being used to stoke controversy, for little-to-no budget, in a way that provokes a reaction from the general public but sits well with its customers, whom the brand understand incredibly well.

Irish budget airline Ryanair play a similar PR game, inciting furious responses with inexpensive campaigns, such as its claim it would charge people to use the toilet on flights, or that it would be introducing standing 'seats' for only £4. In an interview with *Campaign* in 2013, quote-machine CEO Michael O'Leary said that 'short of committing murder, negative publicity sells more seats than positive publicity'. He referenced the charging-for-toilets story, calling it 'the number one story that resurfaces in the press' and 'the gift that keeps on giving'. 'We've never done it, but it keeps coming up on social networks every three or four months, the media picks up on it and then someone writes a story on it.'

He also said in the same interview that 'as long as you run around generating noise, which is now easier because you've got all these halfwits on social media ranting and raving, inventing stories, it drives people on to our website'.

Every time the brand talks about cutting costs for its customers, in stories such as reportedly asking its pilots to slow down in order to save fuel, it further highlights itself as a budget airline and, as with Paddy Power but with a less humorous dint, it aligns itself with the spending intentions of people looking for a cheaper flight.

With brands, organizations and celebrities seemingly immune to the results of negative press on the face of things, it's unsurprising that the general public might consider there to be no ramifications of bad publicity. What isn't seen, though, throughout these campaigns, incidents and scandals is that they often require a great deal of management and engineering behind the scenes. I do believe, though, that, as with all good proactive PR, the intended audience's reaction is the most important consideration and something lost in the noise of a headline-grabbing and seemingly negative story.

There is a legal side to negative publicity that warrants discussion, too. Paddy Power has its own legal team in-house and all proactive ideas are run through them first in order to assess and mitigate possible legal repercussions.

I once worked on a company that was subject to an OFT (Office of Fair Trading) investigation at the same time as ASA (Advertising Standards Authority) action, as a direct result of company marketing. The company was raked over hot coals and no longer exists, unable to recover from the loss of confidence of users and key stakeholders after legal action was both very publicly levied and upheld.

I can't say much more than this on the issue, other than to say it was one of the most stressful work weeks of my life. It was perhaps the first time I realized that the myth that all publicity is good publicity was far from true and should finally be put to bed.

Further reading

Eleftheriou-Smith, L-M, 2013. Ryanair's Michael O'Leary: 'Short of committing murder, bad publicity sells more seats'. *Campaign*, 1 August. Available at: <http://www.campaignlive.co.uk/article/1193681/ryanairs-michael-oleary-short-committing-murder-bad-publicity-sells-seats#vseJwfgWdyBWHGwM.99> [Accessed 2 September 2016]

Graham, N, 2013. Gerald Ratner – the rise and fall of a rough diamond. *Financial Times*, 1 November. Available at: <http://www.ft.com/cms/s/0/b138e81a-29cd-11e3-9bc6-00144feab7de.html#axzz4HkjJKETA> [Accessed 2 September 2016]

Levin, A, 2013. Gerald Ratner interview: 'How I cut the cr*p' – the return of UK's biggest online jeweller. *This is Money*, 20 July. Available at: <http://www.thisismoney.co.uk/money/markets/article-2371730/GERALD-RATNER-INTERVIEW-How-I-cut-cr-p--The-return-UKs-biggest-online-jeweller.html> [Accessed 2 September 2016]

Luminous PR team, 2015. Debunking the top 5 PR myths and some PR tips to make your brand shine. *Luminous PR blog*, [blog] 24 March. Available at: <http://www.luminouspr.com/debunking-the-top-5-pr-myths/> [Accessed 2 September 2016]

Uhls, Y T, and Greenfield, PM, 2011. The rise of fame: an historical content analysis. *Cyberpsychology: Journal of Psychosocial Research on Cyberspace*, 5 (1) [e-journal]. Available at: <http://www.cyberpsychology.eu/view.php?cisloclanku=2011061601> [Accessed 2 September 2016]

Wood, S P, 2014. Top 7 myths in public relations. *Ketchum blog*, [blog] 11 May. Available at: <https://www.ketchum.com/de/top-7-myths-public-relations> [Accessed 2 September 2016]

– MYTH 4 –

THE PRESS RELEASE
IS DEAD

A press release is, traditionally, the most common way PR practitioners communicate a story to journalists and producers. Agencies and in-house teams around the world have used press releases for more than a century to piece stories together in a media-friendly way: packaging facts, figures and, ideally, a newsworthy story up into a useful bundle and thus, making a journalist's or producer's job of sharing that story easier.

CASE STUDY

Before we get into the myth itself, a chapter about press releases would be incomplete if I omitted the origin of something so fundamentally intertwined with the industry – something that started with a horrific and tragic train wreck on 28 October 1906 in Atlantic City, New Jersey. The accident left more than 50 people dead.

Ivy Lee was a newspaper reporter at the *World* newspaper in New York City, before he left for the world of politics, handling the publicity for Seth Low's 1903 campaign for mayor of New York and Judge Alton B Parker's unsuccessful presidential race against Theodore Roosevelt in 1904.

Partnering with a fellow ex-journalist, George F Parker, Lee co-founded the third public relations firm in the United States, Parker and Lee. Pennsylvania Railroad owner George F Baer was a client of Lee's at this time (quite why all these men are referred to with their middle name initials, I've no idea).

The train crash was big news. In response to the disaster, Lee convinced the railroad to issue a statement. *The New York Times* printed it exactly as it was written and, just like that, Lee created the early template with which public relations professionals would disseminate news and, ahem, 'news'. Lee took the release another step, further differentiating between press releases and advertisements with what he called his 'Declaration of Principles'.

During a coal strike, a coal company hired Lee to represent them. Lee sent newspapers daily updates containing what he deemed to be the pertinent facts of the strike – a move that was met with hostility, as journalists took issue with what they dubbed little more than ads. Lee then wrote the following and sent it to newspapers, in what was seen as a significant move from 'press agentry' to public relations.

This is not a secret press bureau. All our work is done in the open. We aim to supply news. This is not an advertising agency. If you think any of our matter ought properly to go to your business office, do not use it. Our matter is accurate. Further details on any subject treated will be supplied promptly, and any editor will be assisted most carefully in verifying directly any statement of fact. ... In brief, our plan is frankly, and openly, on behalf of business concerns and public institutions, to supply the press and public of the United States prompt and accurate information concerning subjects which it is of value and interest to the public to know about.

In 1948, business writer Eric Goldman said in his book *Two-Way Street: The Emergence of the Public Relations Counsel* that the statement 'marked the emergence of a second stage of public relations. The public was no longer to be ignored, in the traditional manner of business, nor fooled, in the continuing manner of the press agent. It was to be informed.'

Edward Bernays, referred to in his 1995 *New York Times* obituary as the 'father of public relations', is said to have refined Lee's press release as a PR tool.

Writing a release, set against the somewhat-flexible template passed on down the line since Lee, was one of the first things I learnt to do in PR. I often use mistake-laden releases in interviews, as a way to test a candidate's attention to detail (with a few purposefully misplaced 'there's and 'their's thrown in, that kind of thing) and, if particularly undecided between people, have introduced press release writing into the mix, too.

With media relations still an important function of PR practitioners, the majority of PR people will write, approve, send or at least be involved in the development of, press releases. Yet an exact match for the phrase 'press release is dead' returns 'about' 28,000 search results in Google.

Before debunking the myth, let's look at why it might exist.

Because influential people keep saying the press release is dead

1 Governments have spoken about the death of press releases...

In an official blog post on a Canadian Government's website, the URL of which no longer works, Kim McKinnon of the Communications Community Office wrote, as reported by PR Daily in January 2014, that Government communicators would be encouraged to 'repurpose the quick facts and quotes for Facebook and Twitter posts'.

It's difficult to say whether McKinnon was so explicit in her wording as to say that the press release was 'dead', but the now defunct official blog URL includes the ending */press-release-dead-government-canada*, so it's highly probable that's how the post was supposed to be received and reported on.

PR Daily introduced the change by saying 'the Canadian government is ditching the traditional press release for an entirely different format designed for the Internet age'. Sherrilynne Starkie, an executive vice president at Thornley Fallis Communications, an agency with branches in Ottawa, Toronto and Chicago, also wrote about the announcement, saying 'if ever there was a sign that the press release is truly and finally dead, surely it must be that the Government of Canada's announced that it's retiring the traditional format'.

PR Daily said of an example of the government's new release format that 'after some brief introductory paragraphs, the release goes into "quick facts" bullet points, followed by a quote, and some links'. I'm not going to poke too much fun at this but, I recommend Googling the phrase 'Archived – January 1 Marks 20th Anniversary of North American Free Trade Agreement' to see an example of the apparently new and improved format.

If that's anything other than a press release then I'm Michael Jackson.

My personal opinion is that an attention-seeking and arresting title was deemed necessary, to show that the Canadian government was digitally progressive. Being an 'official' announcement on a governmental website adds weight to what, as I read it, is essentially a release with subtitles.

A similarly aggressive stance was taken in the UK, a few short months earlier. In September 2013, the executive director of government communications Alex Aiken told an audience that 'the press release is dead' during a speech at the PRCA's National Conference (Magee, 2013). He called the process of writing a press release and sending it out to journalists 'just telesales' and argued that press officers should be content producers, saying 'you should not start with three pages of A4, but a tweet, an infographic or a video. If you are writing more than 200 words on any subject, you're probably in the wrong place.'

There we have two governmental rejections of press releases between late 2013 and early 2014. It continued as...

2 ... one of the world's biggest companies spoke about 'killing' press releases...

'I'm on a mission. What I want to do is kill the press release.'

That's what Ashley Brown said in December 2013, when still group director of digital communications and social media at Coca-Cola. His comments were made in a Ragan Training session called 'Brand journalism at Coca-Cola: Content, data, and cutting through noise' (Working, 2013) in which Brown discussed the creation of brand journalism project, 'Coca-Cola Journey', a digital magazine staffed by a newsroom of people with backgrounds in journalism.

The magazine was reported to have been 'so successful' that the company planned to ditch news releases altogether. Ragan reports that 'Coke has a goal of reducing press releases by half this year' (2014) and eventually 'getting rid of them entirely', stating that 'by 2015, the press release will be a thing of the past at Coke'.

At the time of writing, Coca-Cola Journey is still being written for but, contrary to the above statement, press releases are still being added to the company's press centre, with a new release added most weeks.

As with the example of the second-largest country's government declaring that press releases were dead, we're talking about one of the world's biggest, best-known and iconic brands publicly stating it wanted to kill the press release in favour of content marketing – but failing to. This will inevitably affect the opinion of public relations professionals, journalists and business owners, amongst others, the world over.

3 ... and a highly influential journalist has, too

Mike Butcher is editor-at-large of TechCrunch, a big fish in the big pond of technology publishing. Mike has been listed amongst the most influential people in European technology by *Wired UK* and is a regular broadcaster. According to the about section on his website, on which there are four biographies of varying lengths, he has been an advisor on start-ups to the British Prime Minister and the Mayor of London.

To co-opt the immortal words of Will Ferrell's Ron Burgundy in *Anchorman*, Butcher is 'kind of a big deal' and, as the editor-at-large of TechCrunch, somebody who wields considerable influence, particularly over technologically literate business owners.

In July 2015, Butcher wrote a blog entitled 'The Press Release is Dead – Use This Instead'. He begins by saying (capitals his) 'I'm UTTERLY SICK and TIRED of dealing with MILLIONS of tech entrepreneurs (these days there are a HELL of a lot of you) and (some) PR people who have ZERO clue how to pitch me/TechCrunch/the media.'

Tell us how you really feel, Mike.

He continues: 'Their pitches are long-winded and rambling. They ask if they could "send some more information", as if I care. I have no idea if it's interesting or not until you send it!'

In a 2014 conversation with another TechCrunch journalist, Anthony Ha, Buzzsumo asked him how many pitches he received by email each day. His answer was 'the last time I counted, it was around 80 to my personal account (well, that's emails, but most are pitches), and several hundred sent to tips@techcrunch.com and forwarded to all of us'.

The crux of Butcher's point is that, in his considered opinion and through years of professional experience, '"press releases" are written in the way a PR's client would write a news story. They are usually pretty rambling and designed to please the client (read: stroke their ego) rather than assist the journalist to get shit done, and fast.' He clarifies the title of the blog in light of the latter quote by saying, 'So, I think the press release format is DEAD.'

At the time of writing, this blog post is linked to by more than 1,700 different websites according to Open Site Explorer, a Moz tool that allows you to check for the domain authority, page authority, inbound links and more related to individual URLs. In the past year, the blog has been shared approximately 4,600 times on social media, according to Buzzsumo, a tool that allows you to see the volume of links from social media sites including Facebook, Twitter, LinkedIn, Pinterest and Google+. Two thousand, six hundred times on Facebook and 1,100 times on Twitter.

As any marketer who's dealt with similar metrics before will tell you – that's one popular blog. Without having access to the number of people the blog and its general message reached, it would be a fair guess to estimate that it was seen by a sizeable number of business owners, PR practitioners and other journalists.

The rapidly changing media landscape – and how it relates to releases

Around the time I entered the industry, social media marketing was still in its relative infancy. An interesting relic of the time exists in the form of the very first Facebook group – not page, group – started on behalf of takeaway website Just-Eat, on which I'm still an administrator.

Just-Eat is now what's known in business as a 'unicorn' – a company worth more than £1 billion – yet, just eight relatively short years ago, we were very obviously trialling various ways to market to an increasingly social audience. The group had literally... hundreds of members at its peak.

The post-recession media landscape, combined with the growing up of social media, has led to a rapid shift in not only the media we consume, but in how and when we consume it. More people than ever read news online, with many getting their daily news fix via social media. Supporting this shift, UK news brands 'drove 605.3 million social media actions' between January and August 2015, according to data collected by Newsworks. That figure doesn't include social media engagement such as liking, retweeting and following, citing it as 'direct activity from news brand URLs'.

This shift has meant a number of changes have occurred, or are in the process of occurring. Of the top 50 digital news websites in the United States, 39 have more traffic to their sites and associated applications coming from mobile devices than from desktop computers, according to Pew Research Center's analysis of comScore data, as detailed in the State of the News Media 2015 report. That same report concludes that 'financially, the newspaper industry continues to be hard-hit', with newspaper advertising revenue in 2014 down 4 per cent compared to 2013, to $19.9 billion – less than half of what it was in 2004.

Combined print and advertising newspaper ad revenue in the United States is at its lowest point in the twelve years of data highlighted by Pew Research Center's report, though digital advertising revenue has continued to increase, from $1.2 billion in 2003 to $3.5 billion in 2014.

Newsroom workforce numbers are still falling. According to the American Society of News Editors' Newsroom Employment Census, after falling 11 per cent in 2008 and 6 per cent in 2012, overall newsroom employment was down 3 per cent in 2013 – the most recent year for which figures are available – to 36,700, from approximately 55,000 in 2006.

In the UK, it's a similar story, with widespread redundancies occurring regularly. Anecdotally, I recently went through a list of journalists at national newspapers, correct less than a year beforehand, and at least a quarter had either gone freelance or left journalism entirely. 2016 saw the last editions of *The Independent* and the *i* paper printed as the paper was sold by owner Evgeny Lebedev to Johnston Press, becoming the first British national newspaper to publish solely online. *The New Day* was a British daily paper published by Trinity Mirror launched in late-February 2016. The target for regular circulation was 200,000, but after a drop in sales to 30,000 copies per day, the paper was abandoned – just two months after its launch.

I see (and have always seen) our role as communicating to and with our clients' target audience. It just so happens, in years gone by, the print media has been the best route in, with many PR professionals focused on gaining positive editorial coverage in titles read by that audience – otherwise under the banner of 'media relations'. Journalists and producers are no longer the gatekeepers to that audience that they once were, though. In 2012, Tim Dunlop, author of *The New Front Page: New Media and the Rise of the Audience*, wrote for ABC News Australia in agreement, saying that the public is 'no longer dependent on the mainstream media to interpret and explain important events', and that the gatekeepers of news have 'lost their keys'.

I'd argue this decline in revenue and consequently the overall workforce, combined with the public's disloyal approach to news consumption, has led, rightly or wrongly, to press releases being more prevalent than ever. There are no hard statistics to back this up, but, speaking from personal experience, the number of press releases we send that are reproduced verbatim (or near to it) has increased in recent years. National journalists in particular are time-strapped and click-conscious, a position public relations can benefit from, provided we give the media what they want in newsworthy, well-written stories.

Why press releases are not dead

Many people would say they work in PR, but do not have any contact with the media, instead communicating to a client's intended audience through the digital channels available to us. This has led to a belief among some that media relations is in some way no longer important.

'Press releases are over-used and often the wrong tool for the job', claims marketer Guy Bergstrom (2016) and, given the number of ways we can communicate to and with our target audience(s) now – be it through podcasters, YouTubers, social media platforms, bloggers, content marketing (and other owned content creation including video channels), email marketing and many other tactics – I entirely agree. Though perhaps our primary means of disseminating information a decade ago in PR, the media landscape today means it's never been easier to reach the public and, very often, traditional media relations methods aren't always the most successful.

Alex Aiken's comment that 'you should not start with three pages of A4, but a tweet, an infographic or a video' is not wrong – it just isn't absolutely right, either. For somebody in an influential role to state that a PR professional should straight away start with other forms of shareable content is to ignore the benefits of a well-written press release. Aiken and the government should know – similarly to Coca-Cola and the Canadian government, since his words on the 20 September 2013, there have been 12,219 press releases published on GOV.UK's website.

A press release in practice

My agency did some work in late 2015 with a fascinatingly quirky Canadian client called Nobilified. Nobilified sell hand-painted artwork – which you can have yourself inserted into – painted by classically trained artists around the world. Imagine your face staring back at you from a portrait of Henry VIII, the Mona Lisa or American Gothic. The site is especially popular with celebrities and business people as sales show, with many companies awarding staff with paintings in 'employee of the X' scenarios. All very funny and press-friendly.

Tasked with increasing sales, authoritative links and awareness within the UK, we got to thinking about celebrities the British press and public might like to see 'Nobilified'. One kept coming back to mind – controversial columnist Katie Hopkins. Once we'd found a suitably historic source painting, 'Christ Crucified', painted by Diego Velazquez in the 1600s, we pitched it to the client, who loved it and set in motion the work of art's creation. We settled on the idea of all profits from the print sales going to a charity for Syrian refugees, after mother-of-three Hopkins had claimed the picture of a drowned three-year-old Syrian refugee Aylan Kurdi was 'staged', amongst other controversial comments.

We did what you could call traditional media relations from here on in – we wrote a press release, sent it to our target media list and stoked the fire a touch with 'influencers' on social media, in the hope that it would reach Hopkins. Her response would add weight from a press perspective, we thought.

The spike on the left of Figure 4.1 is the traffic to Nobilified as a result of the story, having achieved coverage on the likes of *The Huffington Post*, and fuelled by Hopkins tweeting about it.

Figure 4.1   Traffic from PR activity

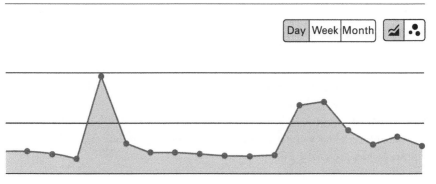

On the right, you see another recent bump – thanks to something far, far less time-intensive that the client already had in the pipeline. It's the result of being highlighted in a just-about-safe-for-work video by the creators of a YouTube channel called 'SimplePickup2'.

Again, sales comparatively increased – and traffic remained elevated for much longer than the Hopkins story – not surprising given the here today, gone tomorrow nature of media coverage and audience exposure/interest.

Two traffic and sales increases from two different tactics – one using a press release, the other through the client having had a quick email conversation with a content creator. In terms of time taken, the Hopkins story undoubtedly took much longer and, though successful from a link-building perspective, it was only marginally more successful in terms of traffic and sales. Although not quite right as a primary tactic for the client, you can see how continued activity in communicating to audiences through video content creators, without so much as going near another press release, would still achieve a number of its aims.

But, just because there are other ways to communicate to and with our target audience, as I'm aware I keep saying, that isn't the same as the press release being 'dead', redundant or obsolete, in the same way a cassette player is. As a tactic, the press release has stood the test of time and continues to deliver results, but, with a host of new tactics at our fingertips, there's simply more choice now in terms of how we achieve those results.

The stance of William Comcowich, CMO (Chief Marketing Officer) of CyberAlert LLC, is, without having to resort to adding to the number of 'press releases are dead' comments, a far more enlightened and reasoned one. He says 'communicating through content marketing, visuals, videos and social media has become the new norm for PR' and that 'while writing press releases is certainly still PR's responsibility, PR specialists must also leverage multimedia assets, write content, plan and implement events, and track/measure results'.

Further reading

Bergstrom, G, 2016. Top 10 myths about public relations. *The Balance*, 12 August. Available at: <https://www.thebalance.com/top-myths-about-public-relations-2295838> [Accessed 2 September 2016]

Butcher, M, 2015. The press release is dead – use this instead. *Mbites*, 1 July. Available at: <http://mbites.com/2015/07/01/the-press-release-is-dead/> [Accessed 2 September 2016]

Coca-Cola Company, 2016. Press releases. *Coca-Cola Company*. Available at:
<http://www.coca-colacompany.com/press-center/press-releases/> [Accessed 2
September 2016]

Dunlop, T, 2012. The gatekeepers of news have lost their keys. *ABC*, 10 October.
Available at: <http://www.abc.net.au/news/2012-10-10/dunlop—mainstream-
media/4305220> [Accessed 2 September 2016]

GOV.UK, 2016. Announcements: Press releases. *GOV.UK*. Available at: <https://
www.gov.uk/government/announcements?keywords=&announcement_filter_
option=press-releases&topics%5B%5D=all&departments%5B%5D=all&
world_locations%5B%5D=all&from_date=20%2F09%2F2013&to_date>
[Accessed 2 September 2016]

Magee, K, 2013. 'The press release is dead,' declares the government's comms chief
Alex Aiken. *PRWeek*, 23 September. Available at: <http://www.prweek.com/
article/1212883/the-press-release-dead-declares-governments-comms-chief-alex-
aiken> [Accessed 2 September 2016]

The New York Times, 1995. Edward Bernays, 'Father of public relations' and
leader in opinion making, dies at 103. *The New York Times*, 10 March.
Available at: <http://www.nytimes.com/books/98/08/16/specials/bernays-obit.
html> [Accessed 2 September 2016]

Newsworks, 2015. *Slideshare*, 16 January. Available at: <http://www.slideshare.net/
newsworks/newswhip-charts-jan15%20/%20_blank> [Accessed 2 September
2016]

Wilson, M, 2014. Canadian government kicks traditional press releases to the curb.
PR Daily, 13 January. Available at: <http://www.prdaily.com/Main/Articles/
Canadian_government_kicks_traditional_press_releas_15894.aspx> [Accessed 2
September 2016]

Wing, H, 2014. How to pitch to journalists: expert tips from Techcrunch, NYT
and more. *Buzzsumo*, 31 March. Available at: <http://buzzsumo.com/blog/pitch-
journalist-tips-techcrunch-ny-times/> [Accessed 2 September 2016]

Working, R, 2013. Coca-Cola digital chief: 'Kill the press release'. *PR Daily*, 2
December. Available at: <http://www.prdaily.com/Main/Articles/CocaCola_
digital_chief_Kill_the_press_release_15656.aspx> [Accessed 2 September 2016]

- MYTH 5 -

THE MEDIA IGNORES GOOD NEWS

'For most folks, no news is good news; for the press, good news is not news.' So said political pundit, American journalist and columnist Gloria Borger.

Another quote I found in relation to this topic is the slightly more indelicate 'if it bleeds, it leads', the origin of which is uncertain, but noted by journalist Eric Pooley in a 1989 *New York* magazine article entitled 'Grins, Gore, and Videotape – The Trouble with Local TV News'.

Negative or shocking headlines and bulletin-leads are seen to be the bulk of the media we consume. I'm writing this in mid-2016, after possibly the heaviest and most doom-filled roll of news I've ever witnessed. We've had Brexit – following Britain's decision to leave the EU. We had Prime Minister David Cameron resign, with a short-lived mudslinging battle for Number 10 Downing Street preceding it. There have been far too many senseless and devastatingly upsetting terrorist attacks for me to want to depress myself counting. Divisive chasms opened between left and right in the United States as businessman Donald Trump defied the odds to win the Republican nomination. Video evidence of unarmed black men killed by US police officers was followed by a gunman killing three police officers in Baton Rouge, Louisiana. There's also been (what's felt like) a never-ending parade of high-profile celebrity deaths, including musicians and icons David Bowie and Prince, comedians Victoria Wood and Ronnie Corbett, TV presenter Terry Wogan and actor Alan Rickman.

Selfishly speaking, it's been impossibly difficult to secure client coverage in the national newspapers at times, obviously not helped by the fact that those working on news desks are stretched thanks to widespread redundancies as a result of publisher profit pains. During times of pitching difficulty, I tend to adapt and work up proactive stories that both relate to the client *and* will be of interest to journalists working outside of the daily news in the secondary sections like health, beauty and fashion, with more populist pitches at the earlier end of the summer falling on deaf ears. It's not been the case that the press has been ignoring good news, but that there's been so much of the bad; this powerful tidal wave of negativity, that good news has rarely managed to find a way through. Calls to the national newspapers were pretty much futile for a period, while journalists I have a closer relationship with confided that they were drowning under the weight of it all.

Now... there was a gleamingly bright light nobody had anticipated. In the future, this will, I hope, put a smile on readers' faces. I genuinely believe that the torrent came to rest thanks – in small part, I add to cover myself – to Pokémon Go and the all-encompassing way in which it was swept up gratefully by the press. As many will recall, it wasn't just the gaming media, either. Silliness is a great antidote to depressing real world stories and, for the most part, the augmented reality app has provided the light relief the media and public were looking for. I realize people might think I'm over-egging this, but a look at Google Trend searches in the first half of 2016 demonstrates something truly remarkable – even during the US election primaries and weeks after its release, Pokémon Go was being searched for at least three times more than either Hillary Clinton or Donald Trump. At its peak in mid-July, for every person that searched for Hillary, despite it being a controversial and much-debated election year, there were 100 searches related to the game. To further put it into perspective, for every Gangnam Style search in late 2012 when at the height of its popularity, there were 10 for (Pokémon Go developer) Niantic's blockbuster in its mid-July heyday, in what's been a perfect combination of nostalgia, technology and hype.

Taking much of 2016 aside, news 'has long centred on negative things because it engages our fear reflex and hence is generally more attention-grabbing', according to Tom Stafford, lecturer in psychology and cognitive science at the University of Sheffield (Oliver, 2016). 'It suggests there is something worth worrying about – something which might mean we should change course, or react in some way. That's why we're attentive to bad news, it means things aren't going well, so we might have to act.' This is why 'good news is not news' – because we are receptive to the bad, and what we're receptive to, the press will focus on.

As a PR person, there is a huge professional advantage in being aware of what's being said in the news – not just in client trade media, but in the wider media too, primarily in case of there being something we can react to. This constant exposure has its downsides though, as too much news can often create 'a choice between perpetual vigilance (and anxiety), or tuning it out', according to Stafford, the latter rarely being an option for many of us.

Anecdotally, I can attest to using this leaning towards negativity in order to gain client coverage. The power of a good controversial story cannot be overstated, and it's commonplace to come up with angles for stories that are essentially there to rile readers or viewers up. The thinking here was that anger is a strong emotion that leads to social sharing, and can aid us in our job of trying to reach the right audience. It was almost a case of reaching potential customers and users by proxy, while still heavily geared towards link building.

This entirely human public attentiveness to negative stories has given life to the feeling that the press doesn't just 'centre' on the negative, but that it almost entirely focuses on it, to the exclusion of good news. I've heard everything from conspiracy theories about the press being funded to keep us in a state of moral panic to the much more plausible 'bad stories simply sell more copies than good', but the fact is the media doesn't ignore good news. We just haven't traditionally consumed it in the same volume or with the same degree of interest.

It's not that those within the media don't recognize the negativity themselves. 'An important factor in what is driving the bad news bias is that we are hard-wired to pay attention to threats and alarming information, and the media capitalises on this,' said Seán Dagan Wood, the editor of the magazine *Positive News*.

Charlie Beckett, former editor of Channel 4 News and director of journalism think-tank POLIS, discussed the topic of negative reporting on a programme called 'Good News is No News' on BBC Radio 4, and said that there 'is an ingrained belief in mainstream media that news has to be about something broken, violent or disturbing', which 'runs so deep that it's almost the unconscious of the craft'.

The reality of the world is that not all can be positive, but prominent calls for it to recognize happier stories have been being made for decades. In 1993, Sir Martyn Lewis, the ex-BBC news presenter that broke the news of the car crash that killed Princess Diana (interrupting a funeral scene in French film *Borsalino*, fact fans), publicly demanded that journalists paid more attention to less 'gloomy' news. In extracts of speeches Lewis gave in the United States, featured in *The Independent* (Lewis, 1993), Lewis highlighted questions he claimed were asked with 'depressing regularity on virtually every occasion television people brush with viewers', opening with 'why is the news so gloomy, and why don't you give us more good news?' He argued that it was 'high time that we who work in television news started treating the accusation seriously' for 'seldom can a complaint repeated so freely, frequently and vehemently have generated so little discussion and debate among those against whom it is directed'.

Lewis said that the print media was less to blame than its broadcast cousin on account of the fact that they have space to 'ensure that their readers' diet is seldom unremittingly bad'. He also said that despite good stories being memorable on account of their rarity, they existed but were low priority. He said they were often bumped in favour of news editors across the world stressing the need for young reporters to hunt for conflict and criticism. 'It is always the good news stories that are demoted or dropped if there is pressure on time or space. Judgements on the relative value of news stories have, on the whole, come to be based on the extent to which things go wrong. The bigger the tragedy, the greater the images of the disaster, the more prominence it acquires.'

Lewis specifically brought PR into the debate too, stating that he wasn't 'arguing for us to be blinded by the artificial shine sometimes placed on stories by public relations teams' and nor should the media 'succumb to the skill and blandishments of the spin doctors from the world of politics', but that the press's 'proper desire not to fall victim to PR has developed into such scepticism that it makes us overly dismissive of positive stories'.

Spoilsports.

Anyway, Lewis was criticized and said his job was on the line for speaking out. He claims to have been misunderstood (Calahane, 2012). He said that people within the media believed he wanted good news at the expense of real news, but argued that not to be the case, restating that he wanted 'a more balanced news agenda' that treats good newsworthy stories in the same way as negative stories. He called the practice of relying on bad news 'lazy journalism', claiming that bad news stories land on the lap of journalists with stories that could 'lift and inspire' uncovered.

A changing tide?

As mentioned, decades have passed since Lewis' claims, and the way we consume news has changed irrevocably. The media is now more fragmented than ever, and far from only having a select few TV and radio station news programmes and a handful of national newspapers from which to consume the news, we as the viewers, listeners and readers have the power to influence the direction taken by journalists. Not entirely, of course – bad things happen and will continue to happen that we can't help but be drawn into, but we are able to decide who and what we mute and ignore more than ever before. Dagan Wood, *Positive News*'s editor, believes we've reached 'peak negativity in the news', claiming the 'overall narrative that the media creates is no longer serving us and it's increasingly at odds with our evolving sense of who we are, what works and what's possible'. With the industry turned upside down by digital technology, Beckett said in the BBC Radio 4 'Good News is No News' programme that 'journalists are questioning the fundamentals of news itself'.

My personal feeling throughout many of the earlier years of my PR career was that the press didn't ignore good news – we just failed to care enough about it as consumers to warrant their time in covering it. Running in direct contrast to this, though, Arianna Huffington wrote in 2015 to say good news stories on *The Huffington Post* are more likely to be shared than other stories. Jessica Prois, an executive editor, said a visitor to a good news piece is 'twice as likely to share or comment versus an average *Huffington Post* article. Sharing solutions-based stories creates a "we're all in this together" movement, especially at a time when countless studies tell us that technology and Facebook make us feel more isolated and lonely.' This has been backed up by research by Dr Denise Baden, an associate professor at Southampton Business School at the University of Southampton, which found that the more negatively people feel after consuming bad news, the less likely they are to voice an opinion or take action.

Two interesting statistics to note: in the 1990s, murder coverage increased more than 500 per cent – despite homicide rates dropping more than 40 per cent, according to the Center for Media and Public Affairs, and as highlighted in that same post.

Arianna Huffington believes the landscape is changing. 'New technologies have changed the way people share stories and the stories they gravitate to. But journalists? They are the ones brought up to think that positive stories are "soft" stories. We need to change the way we look at journalism.'

In 2013, Jonah Berger, a social psychologist at the University of Pennsylvania and author of *Contagious: Why Things Catch On*, along with colleague Katherine Milkman, released the findings of research into people's social networking habits, analysing the types of content people share most, with whom, when, and why. During the course of their study, they looked at thousands of *New York Times* stories to see which were shared by email the most over the course of six months. They found that stories that aroused emotion – especially positive – in people were much more likely to be shared.

We are now able to curate our own feeds and, to some degree, our own exposure to the news. Our disloyalty as news consumers means we hop between outlets, and at our fingertips is the ability to mute both profiles and types of social media updates we want to see less of. Clicking the little X in the corner of a post on Facebook and selecting 'see fewer posts like this' puts more power into the hands of the public, and although there's no evidence to suggest this is happening on a widespread level, I think we as PR professionals and journalists should at least consider the fact that there are people out there no longer content to wade through negativity to find the odd pearl of good news.

Social media has, quite frankly, changed everything. As a trustee for The Superhero Foundation, a charity that helps families raise money for treatment not available on the NHS, and having worked extensively on charity stories, I feel it's changed the game.

When I first started helping Jamie McDonald, the guy that ran across Canada dressed as a superhero and raised hundreds of thousands of pounds in the process in a bid to give back to the charities that helped him as a sick kid, I was met with media indifference – but this was to be expected. Crazy people do crazy things for charity every day of the week and there has to be some kind of filter. It was only through protracted social media effort and carefully prioritizing certain aspects of the story that I think we knocked on the door too many times for them to ignore us. I was concerned that the story would be seen as too worthy for mainstream outlets, no doubt incorrectly informed by the misconceptions I've written about. The story wasn't too worthy by any stretch – it was simply a case of whether or not the story would find an audience and, once it was proven through our social media efforts that there indeed was a large audience that cared, the media cared. But, and this isn't to detract from the power of the press, they were rarely the reason donations were made – analytics showed us that social media was easily responsible for a good three-quarters of everything we raised. In subsequent stories I've worked on, again, the press interest is worth its weight in gold, especially as subconscious social proof of a story's worth to the public, but it's not for the outcome it creates.

I don't believe that the media ignore good news. I think – and this sounds so ridiculously simple and dispels any notion of some kind of journalism conspiracy to keep us unhappy – that they just ignore stories that won't find an audience. So, I started to approach charity communications in the same way I would consumer PR clients and, by finding relatable angles and a way to grab people, you can draw both journalists and members of the public into a cause and/or story.

We'll always have the light-hearted 'and finally' ending to our evening news bulletins, but, given the media agenda allows it, and we as PR professionals do our bit in crafting the message in the right way, I think good news will continue to infiltrate the headlines and we can do away with this ridiculous notion that journalists ignore it. Again – they don't, they simply care about reader, listener and viewer figures and now, more than ever, we can help them here.

I hear faint cries of 'but what if we don't have PR support?', to which I'd say hold on for the next chapter. I think you'll find plenty to help with communicating a message freely and with reach in mind.

'You won't read about this in the media, but...'

There's an odd strain of public belief related to what the press do and don't cover that extends beyond a good/bad–happy/sad division, and it's to do with issues that generally don't directly affect the audience they're hoping to reach.

In November 2015, social and new formats editor for *The Guardian*, Martin Belam – somebody I've never met but strikes me as an incredibly switched-on bloke – wrote an exasperated *Medium* post. In it, he included a tweet from online prankster Jack Jones, which appeared to be the straw that broke the camel's back. 'No media has covered this, but RIP to all the people that lost their lives in Lebanon yesterday from Isis attacks', Jones wrote, along with a photo of an explosion angrily ascending above a busy skyline. At the time of writing, more than 55,000 people have retweeted it, which is to put it in relative terms, Justin Bieber levels of sharing. It clearly struck a chord.

'I've been watching with first amusement and then frustration as tweeter after tweeter claim the media aren't covering things going on in the world that they really, really are covering', began Belam's understandably irate response.

'But it's just blatantly untrue. Search Google News and you will find pages and pages of reports of the attacks in Beirut. Pages and pages and pages. Over 1,286 articles in fact – lots of which pre-date the attacks in Paris', referencing the coordinated November attacks in Paris that left 130 innocent people dead.

It turns out that the image Jones used was from an entirely different incident nine years earlier, but in his virtue signalling hunt for retweets; in for a penny, in for a pound, I guess.

Belam said that there was absolutely 'room for debate about the proportionality of coverage of an incident like this compared to something like the Paris attacks that happened on Friday, but to say that the media don't cover terrorism attacks outside of Europe is a lie', but that 'if you look at [traffic] analytics, people don't read them very much'.

As I say, it's not quite the same as the half-true accusation that the press has ignored good news – at least they had a legitimate business case for doing so before the advent of widespread social media use showed us all what we actually wanted – but important to highlight given the insinuation is similar.

Further reading

Belam, M, 2015. 'You won't read about this in the media, but…'. *Medium*, 15 November. Available at: <https://medium.com/@martinbelam/you-won-t-read-about-this-in-the-media-but-b275d46fd51f> [Accessed 2 September 2016]

Calahane, C, 2012. Martyn Lewis: 'Media should report solutions'. *Positive. News*, 11 September. Available at: <https://www.positive.news/2012/society/media/8386/martyn-lewis-media-report-solutions/> [Accessed 2 September 2016]

Huffington, A, 2015. What's working: all the news that's fit to print. *The Huffington Post*, 8 April. Available at: <http://www.huffingtonpost.com/arianna-huffington/whats-working-all-the-news_b_6603924.html> [Accessed 2 September 2016]

Lewis, M, 1993. Not my idea of good news: at the end of a week of horrifying events, Martyn Lewis, BBC presenter, argues for a change in news values. *The Independent*, 25 April. Available at: <http://www.independent.co.uk/voices/not-my-idea-of-good-news-at-the-end-of-a-week-of-horrifying-events-martyn-lewis-bbc-presenter-argues-1457539.html> [Accessed 2 September 2016]

Oliver, L, 2016. And now for the good news: why the media are taking a positive outlook. *The Guardian*, 1 August. Available at: <https://www.theguardian.com/world/2016/aug/01/and-now-for-good-news-why-media-taking-positive-outlook> [Accessed 2 September 2016]

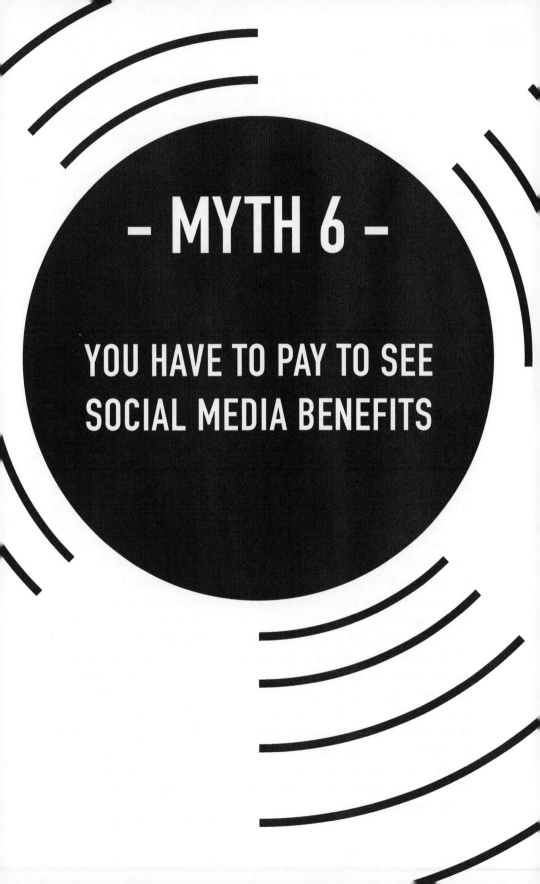

– MYTH 6 –

YOU HAVE TO PAY TO SEE SOCIAL MEDIA BENEFITS

I'm often asked what the difference between PR and advertising is. I always put it like this: public relations is to marketing as football is to sport. It's a discipline under an umbrella term. Advertising is another sport entirely, characterized by the fact that any exposure through advertising is paid for and, therefore, controlled or 'owned'. Success in PR is 'earned'.

Social media marketing has, for much of its existence, worked in much the same way. You can pay to advertise your brand on social media platforms – allowing you targeted control over who (to an extent) sees your advert and what that advert says (again, to an extent – varying rules apply platform-to-platform on what can and can't be advertised). You can also choose to communicate to and with your target audience using social media without paying. Of course, the big social media channels – Facebook, YouTube and Twitter – are among the best-used in the West; QQ, WeChat, and Weibo in China would much prefer you paying to reach users you'd like to turn into customers and/or communicate with.

There's been a Church and State convergence in the last few years, though, just as there has been for perhaps longer between SEO and PR, leading PRs typically tasked with achieving free or earned exposure to dabble with paid promotion of client messages. This chapter is going to assess whether or not social media has got to the stage where you have to pay, and what you can do in an increasingly busy digital landscape.

The undeniable decline in organic reach means the probability that people that 'like' your page see your content is bottoming out. That's a head-ache but also a surmountable challenge for page administrators. A study from 'news feed optimization service' EdgeRank Checker (acquired in June 2014 by Socialbakers) found that between February 2012 and March 2014, organic reach for the average Facebook Page dropped from 16 per cent to 6.5 per cent (Constine, 2014). They found this figure, which has no doubt changed in the time since, by assessing the organic reach of 50,000 posts by 1,000 pages.

In June 2014, and possibly in relation to concerns cited shortly after EdgeRank Checker's report, complaints from marketers prompted an offi-cial response from Facebook's VP of Advertising Technology, Brian Boland (Facebook Business, 2016). Boland said 'Over the past few months, I've read articles and answered questions from many people who are concerned about declines in organic reach for their Facebook Pages. My colleagues and I at Facebook understand that this has been a pain point for many busi-nesses, and we're committed to helping you understand what's driving this change so your business can succeed on Facebook.' He goes on to say that the reason is twofold:

1 'More and more content is being created and shared every day.' He cited that there were, on average, 1,500 stories that could appear in a person's News Feed each time they log on, and for people with lots of friends and page likes, 'as many as 15,000 potential stories could appear any time they log on'. Obviously, this is incredibly high.

2 So, understandably, 'Rather than showing people all possible content, News Feed is designed to show each person on Facebook the content that's most relevant to them.'

Boland tackles the obvious thought head-on. Under the question 'Is organic reach dropping because Facebook is trying to make more money?' he simply answered to say, 'No. Our goal is always to provide the best experience for the people that use Facebook.' In my opinion, the actual truth is that it's both things. It's to make money and keep users happy with just the right amount of relevant content. Of course, Facebook's goal is to provide the best experience for its users – because, without them, there's nobody to show adverts to. It follows then that, with a large engaged audience as the carrot at the end of the stick and a decreasing organic reach, businesses will turn to paying to reach them because they assume there's no other way.

A decrease in organic reach is simple supply and demand economics

This problem (or revenue opportunity if you're Facebook) isn't unique to Mark Zuckerberg's giant. Boland insists that 'many large marketing platforms have seen declines in organic reach', citing online search engines as the original businesses to see diminishing returns for businesses and websites that previously ranked highly in search results, in light of less competition. As SEO became a full-time job for businesses, making the market ever-more competitive, this only became truer. Google Adsense and other rival products stood out as the paid product response and alternative to trying to rank organically – and by this point, I say 'organically' lightly given the notoriously sneaky and 'black hat' ways search marketers have gone about influencing search engine results over the years.

I haven't found clear and recent evidence in the same vein as the EdgeRank Checker report to suggest the organic reach issue is happening to users of Twitter, Instagram or any other leading platforms, but the smart money would be to say it is. It just makes sense, especially given Instagram is owned by Facebook, as is the less obviously monetizable WhatsApp.

It should come as no surprise that Google, which also owns video social network/discovery platform and ad monster YouTube, is the second largest internet company (Wikipedia, 2016) in the world by revenue ($74.98 billion in 2015) – and the biggest by market cap, at $493.2 billion at the time of writing. The market cap, in a bid to keep this book as an easier read for newbies, is a simple equation: the price per share in any given company multiplied by the number of shares 'outstanding', which really just means the number of shares currently held by all shareholders.

If this was a conversation, this would be the point at which I'd ask you to guess as to the second largest company by market cap. That's right – it's Facebook, valued at $332.1 billion (again, I hasten to add, at the time of writing market cap fluctuates as share prices rise and fall, and as companies release more shares). Facebook was the fourth biggest earning internet business in 2015, with annual revenue of $17.93 billion. You'll forgive me for thinking that Facebook's commitment to 'helping you understand what's driving this change so your business can succeed' will rarely point anywhere other than in the direction of its main method of monetization.

Are social networks strictly pay-to-play now?

On to the point of the chapter. There seem to me to be three types of client approaches when it comes to social media. The first is the client that has stars in their eyes. They've been bombarded by friends and the media with just how huge the opportunity is to reach a big audience, and they want a piece of that pie. The second are ones that come to us, perhaps initially only for media relations work, with a belief that social media is best handled by social media agencies otherwise dedicated to account growth and management. Thirdly, there are clients that have been scared off by the 'organic is dead' headlines and are under the assumption that social media is too hard an area to see any benefit from without paying – if they consider there to be any benefits to their business using social at all.

As I've said, my belief is that social media marketing can and should fall under the remit of PR, in exactly the same way media relations does. Social is a channel in much the same way as media relations is, but without the, dare I say, often pesky and fickle media in the middle, no longer the gatekeepers and kingmakers they once were. Social media is, organic reach issues aside, a much more democratic way to reach an audience. There are a number of ways to use social media for clients. I'll run through a few now.

Day-to-day management

As highlighted at the beginning of this chapter, there are, at any given time, more than 1,500 items that could appear in somebody's Facebook News Feed. That will vary social network to network, of course, and is also dependent on the number of friends you have/people and brands you follow. That's an incredible amount of information to process, even after being algorithmically trimmed for relevance. And what do we want to go and do? Well, we want to insert our clients in front of the scrolling masses, as if they didn't have enough to contend with. Of course, we can pay to do this, but that comes with a few issues. Firstly, that it costs money. Secondly, as with advertising since the dawn of time, the fact that it's forced on you and you know it only exists exactly because somebody has paid to force it on you, it doesn't carry the same weight as something somebody you trust has shared.

The obvious and, for me in the majority of instances, preferred alternative is to come up with posts that tick a number of boxes:

- The messages need to befit the medium, which sounds simple enough, but every day I'll still see people sharing Facebook posts automatically to Twitter and Instagram that just don't translate. For instance, you'll see 100-word-long Facebook page statuses instantly copied across to Twitter, which leaves it looking half-finished. I'd be surprised if anybody ever clicks the link to read more unless the poster is a Mega Famous.

- Facebook gives higher organic reach weighting to visual updates – that is to say, images and videos. Add that to the fact that social media updates are typically only ever improved with images and it makes sense to consider what visuals you'll be using. Not only do images and videos make tweets stand out, but YouTube, Instagram and Snapchat are obviously all visual mediums first and foremost.

- Any and all updates should be for the eyes of your target audience only. In fact, if it doesn't make sense to people that wouldn't be interested in your client, you're doing well. You can't be all things to all people and the same is true of your social media efforts for clients (or, as I have to keep reminding myself so as not to forget in-house workers, your employer). This is as important a tip for small businesses and individuals as it is global brands. Incredibly niche example this, but if you worked as a kitchen fitter and had just installed a beautiful kitchen with an incredibly happy customer, that's well worth sharing. So what if it only gets three likes and one comment? One of those four people might be a customer. You can start to see where money can be made, especially when you can actively direct your audience to a buying or enquiry page.

- Following on from that point then, anything you do say can and should relate to your client's aims to the best of your ability. Not every message should say 'hey you, buy our stuff', but calls to action you can measure make this exercise worthwhile – otherwise you might as well head down the pub with your client or employer's money and talk to kindly strangers about cat memes and the news stories of the day. This is admittedly difficult to do all of the time – and there are certain instances where brands will publish seemingly nonsensical things. Later in the chapter I'll talk about ways to game social media algorithms, which will help you make sense of exactly that kind of thing.

- The internet is already one big echo chamber. It's a social media cliché now, but 'push' marketing rarely works. When we manage social media for clients, the aim is to either start or add to a conversation our client is in the position to have with its audience, and work to reach that audience through relevance and, ideally, being of interest. When adding, this could be a wider conversation within their industry or the media, or a topical story that relates well enough. PRs are perhaps expected to be more up to date with what's happening in the world than any other professionals barring journalists themselves, so it stands to reason that while we're considering news within our clients' fields to react to on their behalf through media relations, this does translate across to social, too. It's important to remember that, as a brand, you are an interruption. It's not that you don't deserve a voice, it's just that as an interruption, the least you can do is be an interesting one.

Content creation

The rise of online phenomena like early noughties blogging legend Maddox, David Firth's peculiar but brilliant dystopic video series *Salad Fingers*, short-lived man-meme Dan Bilzerian and, more recently or at least more enduringly, vloggers Zoella, KSI and PewDiePie was all possible without mainstream media support or paid promotion. These people have created unique or commentary focused content and used technology and the online channels freely available to them to share their voice and build a following, to varied financial success. Brands like Dollar Shave Club, with its 'Our Blades Are F***ing Great' video, proved you can reach a profitable audience through digital 'owned' content, too. Having been viewed more than 20 million times on YouTube, the promotional video starring CEO Michael Dubin was a key element in the brand's ascension. Dollar Shave Club was bought by Unilever for $1 billion in July 2016.

This is an exciting time for brands and especially talented individuals. It actually appears to be the case that, in our click-based online media economy, these people serve to bolster the profile of the media that feature them at least as much, if not more, than the reverse is true. Putting aside the older names highlighted in my short and off-the-top-of-my-head list, it remains to be seen which of these can maintain their prominence (I'm at pains to say 'celebrity'), but the same is true of the generations of musicians, actors and artists before them.

Of course, these are all examples of content creators who've hit on output that resonated with an audience without having to spend a fortune. When working with brands, there might not be the talent, interest or budget in doing this. In any case, as it's become easier to create content, we're inundated with it. Going back to an A Level sports studies lesson I recall, there was a participation pyramid used to demonstrate how the more people there were playing a sport, the better the standard at the top. It's the same with content.

Although you can cheaply create content, the likelihood of it 'making it' is similar to the chances of a player coming from a disadvantaged background without help becoming a professional. Sportspeople, especially those with opportunities, provisions and the esteem to dedicate themselves, get a leg up when talent is spotted in a variety of ways – financial support, the best consultants, advisors and influential people around them. Of course, there's still no saying this will be enough given how competitive things get and, if I've not laboured the point too much, you can hopefully see the parallels here with content creation. There aren't statistics to support this, but it follows that you're more likely to succeed working with people that can advise based on experience, create great-looking content and have an influential network with which to promote it. Even with all of that, though, I've seen expensive campaigns fall flat. The most important element, as with the talent of an individual, is the idea itself, whether that's a video, great image or a message that gets spread far and wide – or, if it's working properly, to the intended audience.

Customer relations

Another aspect worth highlighting is that customer relations, or what I've come to consider *genuinely* public relations, is something PRs have had to learn about as the conversation has become decidedly two-way. This is something that doesn't cost brands a penny beyond the time of the person or team dedicated to doing so. While some brands separate social media management into proactive and reactive communication to the relief of some more traditional agencies, no doubt, unless said brand is experiencing a significant amount of online conversation in its direction, I see no reason we can't manage that. Speaking entirely anecdotally, the majority of big brand 'community managers' I know started out in PR, anyway, proving it lays a great foundation. For a start, communicating to our client's audience is what we're paid to do – social media is simply another channel through which to achieve this. Listening intently to what's said in return or perhaps first is well within our remit as communication professionals too, and acting on that with our client's key messaging and/or goals in mind should be second nature.

Building an audience

I realize that everything I've touched on so far is all well and good, but there's the small matter of having people to actually share day-to-day messaging, interesting content and the like with. When you first start out on social media, it can be frustrating. It's a noisy place and if you simply throw yourself into it without paying much attention to who you're speaking with, I can't imagine you'll stick around for long.

A strong social following, according to a few definitions I've read, is one that 'is made up of people that cross geographical, political and social boundaries to pursue mutual interests or goals'. It comes back to the not being all things to all people point I made. The web is an incredible place where, no matter your niche interests, you can, in all probability, find a like-minded crowd. As marketing agency imFORZA wrote in 2013, 'a community that can openly communicate with one another, whether it's from your company to your audience or your audience to each other, is one that tends to grow quickly and organically'.

While my main recommendation is that you simply get involved, observe etiquette and have fun, here is a more in-depth list of tips for both finding and building a social media following. The caveat here being – while many of these tips are applicable across platforms, they do relate to the bigger players like Facebook, Twitter and LinkedIn. Modify them for use on newer or more niche services:

1   Social networks (and even their older relatives, online forums) tend to have great search functions. These can be invaluable when starting out and finding the right people to follow, especially on Instagram and Twitter. Type your area of interest into the search bar, such as 'PR', and you will find a large number of accounts that write about or have named/tagged themselves with that search phrase. Follow these people/connect with them, get to know what they share, how and why, and get involved by sharing their content, tagging and mentioning them. If flattery gets you everywhere, social media appreciation isn't too far behind.

2   Similarly, you can find influencers in your business niche or area of interest using freely available online tools such as Buzzsumo and Bluenod.

3   After working out the general etiquette of social networks, which varies platform to platform but tends to revolve around the mantra 'don't be a d***', I quickly realized that original and relevant content is important. If, after you've taken the time to get to grips with the landscape, all you do is retweet others' tweets, you may as well stop wasting your time. People will want to follow you, not the person you're most influenced by. If they wanted to keep reading their tweets, chances are, they'd follow them and cut you out. A good 95 per cent of what I tweet about @RichLeighPR is PR related, because that's what people have likely followed me for.

4   Follow your competitors' followers. Really simple one, this, and one that works nicely, provided it's clear that your client/accounts are in a similar space to the rival account. Just as tools like Bluenod enable you to visualize how certain people are influenced by others, this can be a quick way to build an initial audience.

5   Direct friends, in-store and/or online customers, users and any other interested parties to your social media accounts. By encouraging email subscribers and your business card recipients to follow you on social media, you're preaching to the half-converted. Cross-promoting your presence on other social networks works well too, provided it's not constant (eg 'connect with me on LinkedIn where I write about X' style messaging).

6 Similarly (and this is a quick one people completely forget about), link to your social media accounts from your site – especially your contact page.

7 Share posts you feel are likely to be well shared, by being a source for 'breaking' stories within your space. The more relevant to your niche, the better. A cynical tip, but something I've definitely used alongside posting original content. For instance, before it became packed with clueless One Direction fans claiming that every clothing choice they made was an intentional ploy of some sort, I used to regularly search 'PR stunt' – speech marks included – on Instagram and Twitter most mornings, in a bid to be early to content for PRexamples.com and/or social sharing, which leads me on to...

8 Write original guest content on blogs and titles that appeal to your target audience. I've said it before and I'll say it again – I'm a teenage dad from a city not exactly renowned for PR, that dropped out of his A-Levels, with no real qualification nor experience to speak of before entering the world of communications. Early on, I started approaching titles with ideas for features, columns and reactions. Given every title uses social media to promote its content, if you highlight your social media profile in the content if possible, or simply say 'hey, it'd be great if you could @ me in the messages you send', you'll be promoted directly to their audience in a way that appears to be social-proof. It also gives you something to then share.

9 Write or create original content for your own blog. It's never been easier to freely publish your own writing, images or videos on a platform you own and control, whether you choose to use Medium, WordPress, BlogSpot or any other site to do it. As soon as I'd built something of an audience on Twitter and LinkedIn using the above methods – choosing those networks intentionally for the audience I wanted to reach – I quickly realized my own online real estate would mean I could post unfiltered and head in whichever direction I chose. It's all shareable and helps to build influence.

10 Search hashtags relevant to your intended audience. For instance, if you are (or your client is) a fashion retailer, check out popular hashtags like #fbloggers, used by – you guessed it – fashion bloggers. Get to know who uses them, follow, interact and build from there. I've always used hashtags sparingly and feel that, on the whole, people have either forgotten or never quite grasped how to use them. If you've ever seen a post with every word hashtagged, you'll know what I mean. They are used for grouping social media messages based around one topic or interest – with the number of people actually clicking through to search messages within that grouping surprisingly small. On some networks, Instagram especially, people actually pay small amounts to have bots automatically 'like' posts tagged with certain things and/or follow the person that shared it, so there is a potential follower benefit there, but not enough to spam everybody's timeline with ugly #s, in my opinion. Hashtagify and Hashtracking are two services I've used to see who shares what in the past.

11 Get involved in or create your own 'chat' related to your interest. If you or your client runs, say, a virtual reality content business – what's happening across social media related to this?

12 Run competitions and prize draws. An early Facebook audience-building winner, this, until Zuckerberg and company decided to limit what you could and couldn't do (with limits like 'share this post to enter' since lifted and re-allowed). Competitions provide a great cross-platform reason to use calls to action like 'enter your email address here', allowing you to data grab, or 'follow and retweet to enter', allowing your audience to grow. There are a couple of potential issues here, namely a) the prize should be of interest and ideally only of interest to your specific audience and b) competition enterers tend to be the least loyal 'followers' I've ever come across. They might help to boost numbers, but if point a) isn't adhered to, they'll often be one of the stay-at-home types that quite genuinely just search social media to see what free stuff they can win.

13 A related tip is to incentivize audience-building by giving away free product samples to the first X people to do something specific, or offer product or service discounts. I wouldn't recommend this often, but it's a good way to actually highlight what it is your business or client does or sells.

14 Be sociable – if spoken to, speak. It's a conversation after all. I don't mean engage in 'aren't we so cool and subversive!?' overtly conversational speak, but humour and an identifiable personality goes a long way. For those old enough from the UK, you might remember how Innocent Drinks' packaging spoke to its customers as if the packaging was human. As quirky as it was when they did it, well, that got old fast as soon as every old jar of peanut butter started getting matey, didn't it? I try to keep my social media profile professional... ish and, for the majority of clients, have found this works well.

15 Maintain consistent social media usernames. Nice and simple, but something far too many forget. I listen to one podcast where the wrapping up takes about five minutes because their Snapchat, Instagram, Facebook, Twitter and Reddit subreddit names are all different. It's confusing and cuts down on the chance of people taking the time to search for and find you.

Why should you bother?

Although this is being said right in the midst of the chapter, my first question to clients when it comes to social media is – why bother? It's an intentionally abrasive initial standpoint, but it cuts right to understanding just what they're hoping to achieve by having a presence on social media.

If you find a channel on which your potential customers are, or where you can listen to what customers, users or stakeholders are saying about you and your brand, then that's great. Just like trying to pitch a video game to Vogue, though, and much like the tip that the message should befit the medium, you shouldn't waste time and energy somewhere just because everybody else seems to be doing it. Apple famously doesn't have a branded Twitter account, so my question to clients really relates to the point: does your small business really need a Facebook page?

More or less, the answer is that there is indeed something for everyone, dependent on not just following the herd, or trying to be the first to shout 'look, we're an early adopter!' by registering to use the Next Big Thing, before dumping it for the next and leaving behind a digital reminder of fickleness. There are enough platforms, some with varied and even niche (as in the case of video game streaming site Twitch) audiences that one can generally find a route to a client's intended audience and goal if you consider your options carefully. We don't need every business flocking to Snapchat, which is especially unfriendly and rarely useful to brands at present anyway.

In researching this chapter to find niche examples of businesses using social media (seemingly) successfully, I found a page belonging to a company called the Cardboard Box Shop, from Brisbane, Australia. If you need proof yourself, head to facebook.com/CBBoxShop. There, by scrolling down, you'll see what appear to be customer queries being answered by an administrator that are actually leading to sales. It's about as unsexy a business using social media as I've seen, but if I was running that page, lack of regular updates aside, I'd be fairly happy with how that was going for the comparative effort being put in.

Ways to game Facebook's algorithm to build a free audience

Before I get onto instances where paying isn't necessarily such a bad option, I wanted to highlight simple ways you can increase profile and page reach, getting around Facebook's bid to force you to pay for ads – um, sorry, I mean – show each person on Facebook the content that's most relevant to them. This section is obviously Facebook-specific, but some of these tactics will be transferable.

To the issue at hand. A few years ago, I was talking to a senior big agency professional. This person worked as the lead on a household name brand's Facebook page. They had the words 'social media guru' in their biography and subsisted on a diet of skinny pumpkin spice lattes – you know the type. We were talking about social media changes, when they asked, 'Why, when I post a photo, does it have a bigger reach than when I post a link?' It dawned on me both just how much to learn there was in social media, but also how naïve and keen bigger brands have been to offload the responsibility of communicating to a large audience. The reason for the different reach is, as touched on, Facebook's algorithm.

In old parlance, it was referred to as 'EdgeRank'. In the spring of 2009, when Facebook released its first iteration of the News Feed, it was unrestricted, and displayed everything posted. This was before, as was highlighted, things got altogether too busy. Before we started adding people we met once out of politeness, and before we 'liked' quite so many pages. The Facebook powers-that-be realized they'd have to find a way to control the flow of content, before users started to become bogged down with information and updates from people and brands we barely knew or cared about. An overwhelmed user won't stay a user for long – so a way to ensure relevance and interest had to evolve. That way was ranking algorithm EdgeRank, announced at the 2010 f8 conference at the San Francisco Design Centre.

EdgeRank was based on a huge number of unknown factors, as well as some that were known. As highlighted on Sprout Social's EdgeRank guide (Patterson, 2015), there were three main factors that contributed to the likelihood of a user being shown relevant content: affinity, weight and time decay. We don't need to get too deep into the woods on this, given Facebook hasn't used the word EdgeRank internally for years and says a number of factors are now considered equally as important as these, but I'll briefly explain because they still have a bearing on reach.

Firstly, you are likely to see something if you are close to the person post-ing. This is the affinity part. As explained in Sprout Social's guide, 'if you frequently interact with the person posting, have several mutual friends, or are related, Facebook is more likely to give that content a higher weight'. So far, so understandable.

Secondly: weight. There are two aspects to this. Your action in relation to previous content from that person or brand will affect your likelihood of being shown it, as will the type of post itself. 'Not all actions are considered equal in the eyes of Facebook's algorithm. For example, a friend creating a status update would carry more weight than someone simply liking a status update.' Again, it makes sense – if you're commenting on a post, you prob-ably care about it more than if you spend longer-than-average looking on it before scrolling, something I've been told is counted, though that could be little more than a rumour. The second aspect when it comes to weighting is what type of post it is – and this is a big one. We'll get onto this in terms of ways I've used successfully for clients for years to beat the algorithm.

Thirdly, time decay. 'As a post gets older, it's more likely that it has already been seen or that it is no longer as relevant. Facebook remedies both of these problems by taking the age of the post into consideration.'

So, how do you beat this? Well, breaking those important factors down, as well as considering aspects such as the time at which your posts are best shared, you can ensure a higher reach. I'll run through some things you can do in your next update to improve the chance of your content reaching an audience without paying:

- Imagine a sliding reach scale for post types – you have links, where you copy and paste a link into an update and Facebook drags through a photo from said link, text updates and photo/video visual updates. It makes sense that Facebook wouldn't want you to send people away from its own walls, so it assigns low weight to posts that link out of the platform. It wants to keep users using (subtle dependency connotation intended…!). So don't use links. The same with text updates: they're boring-looking and easy to miss. You'll want to focus almost-solely on images and videos. 'But what if I want to post a link to a product, a bit of coverage or any other external page?' I hear you ask. Easy: one way to get around the fact that links don't reach very far is to trick Facebook by uploading an image first and then including a link in the written part of your status.

- Post content you know will provoke a reaction, or… quite literally ask for it. If you're running a competition, gone are the recent rules that prevented you from asking people to share, comment or like to enter.

Alternatively, and this works especially well when used sparingly for personal, small businesses and charity clients I've worked with, simply ask people to 'click the share button below', or 'tag friends you think might be interested!' The difference in reach by asking people to share and tag can be staggering. I usually like to add a reason – 'whether you're donating, commenting or even sharing using the button below this, every bit of support you give us really does help', or if a small business, I play on that in an audience-specific way. 'We're trying to make a difference in <insert sector here>, so if you know of any friends that might be interested, please do feel free to share or tag them in below – as a brand new/small business, any support makes a huge difference to us.' It sounds crass when I type it out like that, but hey – it's all about reaching the right people, while building a loyal, appreciative and appreciated community.

- Not a tip I like to make use of much, but, for some of you, this will explain a lot. You know when you see a business post memes – Monday moans, Friday funnies, inspirational quotes, cat pictures – those sorts of things? There's a reason they're doing that – and it's because it's content that, as incongruous as it might be that a pizza company is posting catLOLs, will get people clicking that like button. As we've learnt, if you interact with content you're more likely to see that page's future content when it comes to them wanting to highlight business-specific posts that might well lead to revenue so... that's why they do it.

- A lot is made of the time at and frequency with which you post updates and for good reason. Great and/or shareable content will do well anytime, especially if the page posting is incredibly popular, but the same can't be said for a small business page. Stick to posting at the times you assume Facebook (and this is applicable to all other social networks) will be busy. Lunchtimes and particularly evenings work best. Holidays and the weekends, as I've thankfully found when handling client crises, are the worst time to reach an audience, putting aside Saturday nights when X Factor or similar is on.

Finally, should you ever pay?

There's a reason this is one of the longest chapters in the book: building and communicating with a relevant and beneficial audience takes time, commitment and can involve a small degree of trial and error. Clients and excitable bosses don't often like to hear this.

If you'd prefer to avoid the hard work and autodidacticism, there's one thing you can do to help build an audience... you can pay. Of course, there are sites you can use to pay for fake likes, channel subscribers, comments, followers and more – these aren't as expensive as you'd imagine but are obviously utterly useless beyond vanity metrics.

As I touched on, there has been a convergence of a number of previously split digital professions; or, at least, there are now shared tactics across disciplines. Link building is increasingly handed over to PRs. Advertising agencies are trying their hand at PRing content, and PRs are ever-more likely to consider social and native advertising for clients when the time is right – with traditional advertising still reserved for causing offence or shock through PR, as in the instance of New Zealand's Hell Pizza, which controversially created a billboard made up of rabbit skins to advertise its Easter-themed rabbit pizza. Gone are the days we as an industry turn our nose up at paid advertising entirely; though there's still a feeling that 'earned' tactics should be our primary effort.

There are a few instances where I've recommended social media advertising from the off, alongside the tactics recommended in this chapter. The most recent example was a regional sporting start-up – a new fun league, aimed at getting individuals playing again, as well as introducing younger players to it. Being a local and niche league, our target audience was very well defined and Facebook was undoubtedly the platform on which to find and communicate to this audience. However, the client had next to no time with which to launch, having been struck by a number of site delays, on which visitors had to sign up. The client was panicking that, with a minimum number of teams of a minimum number of people as the goal, all their hard work would be for nothing if they couldn't reach those numbers. So, we used many of the media and social media tactics you'd imagine, confident the messaging would hit home – but, alongside those, we boosted a number of call-to-action posts in a bid to speed the process up, too. Over the course of a month, we spent just £250 on carefully boosting posts to a target audience, refining this after reviewing the insights and results for the first couple, and ended up with one very happy and relieved client. Not only had we filled every team spot and built an incredibly passionate army of followers, there was a waiting list too, which meant the client could expand to another venue almost immediately. I don't believe we'd have had the same results without paying, given the time frame.

We've used paid advertising across Twitter, LinkedIn, Instagram and Facebook for bigger clients with deeper pockets, too, especially when they've had stories or releases that we wanted to reach a very specific audience with and spare budget to spend. As niche magazines die out, paid social makes more and more sense if money is available and where the call to action is time-sensitive. Of course paid works when properly targeted. I've promoted my own agency's case study content regularly on LinkedIn, resulting in client enquiries from posts targeting marketing directors and the like, but, as with all marketing, this result isn't guaranteed.

The nature of digital advertising means you have an element of control and the ability to review success metrics, but it is by no means the only nor necessarily the best game in town. If you want to succeed using social media, you can do so without spending a single penny.

Further reading

Cardboard box shop, 2016. [Facebook]. Available at: <https://www.facebook.com/CBBoxShop/> [Accessed 2 September 2016]

Constine, J, 2014. Why is Facebook Page Reach decreasing? More competition and limited attention. *TechCrunch*, 3 April. Available at: <https://techcrunch.com/2014/04/03/the-filtered-feed-problem/> [Accessed 2 September 2016]

Facebook Business, 2016. Organic reach on Facebook: your questions answered. Available at: <https://www.facebook.com/business/news/Organic-Reach-on-Facebook> [Accessed 2 September 2016]

imFORZA, 2013. Growing a social following from scratch. *imFORZA blog*, [blog]. Available at: <https://www.imforza.com/blog/growing-a-social-following-from-scratch/> [Accessed 2 September 2016]

Patterson, M, 2015. EdgeRank: a guide to the Facebook News Feed algorithm. *Sprout Social*, 26 January. Available at: <http://sproutsocial.com/insights/facebook-news-feed-algorithm-guide> [Accessed 2 September 2016]

Wikipedia, 2016. *List of largest Internet companies*. Available at: <https://en.wikipedia.org/wiki/List_of_largest_Internet_companies> [Accessed 2 September 2016]

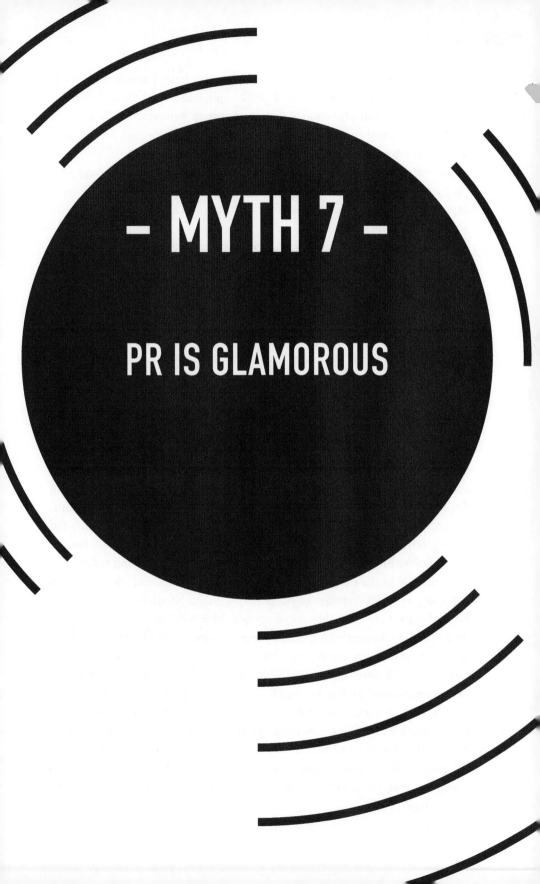

– MYTH 7 –

PR IS GLAMOROUS

In the chapter 'PR is all spin, smokescreen and lies', I touched on some people within our industry that I think contribute to the myth that PR professionals tell fibs for money and/or are pretty heinous people. There is, of course, fictional representation of PR to touch on too – and, for the most part, it isn't good.

It's not manipulation I wanted to talk about in this chapter, though, but the perception of PR as one big party. Public relations is routinely fictionally depicted as being a glamorous and/or hedonistic career, full of people with questionable ethics.

In film, TV and books, PR and communications are portrayed in an almost entirely unflattering light. In 2014, I asked for examples of fictional portrayals of PR on Twitter and, besides *The West Wing*'s press secretary, C J Cregg, all other responses could be seen as negative.

The best-known portrayal in a novel of somebody in a role closely associated with public relations is perhaps Nick Naylor, the charismatic protagonist of Christopher Buckley's satire *Thank You for Smoking*, released in 1994 (and adapted into a 2005 movie of the same name, starring Aaron Eckhart).

Naylor is the chief spokesperson for the fictional Academy of Tobacco Studies, a tobacco industry lobbying firm promoting the benefits of – but more often than not, defending – cigarettes. Although intelligent and quick-witted – as is shown to be necessary when dealing with the press and politicians – he's characterized as an emotionally absent father with a questionable moral compass, who even at one point says that his job 'requires a certain moral flexibility'. Along with two other members of the MOD (Merchants of Death) Squad, comprised of spokespeople from the alcohol and firearms industries, we're given an insight into the various methods used to 'spin' facts and figures, the trio more often than not relying on emotional arguments and reason.

In the UK in the nineties, millions watched the BBC's comedy *Absolutely Fabulous*, in which Jennifer Saunders played Edina Monsoon. Rachel Gilley, Bite's deputy managing director, described Monsoon as 'a heavy-drinking, drug-abusing PR agent who spends her time chasing bizarre fads in a desperate attempt to stay young and hip' in a PR Moment article entitled 'Why *Ab Fab*'s Edina is my PR hero' (Gilley, 2016). Monsoon was partially based on Lynne Franks, according to Franks herself, whose eponymous agency established itself as one of the leading fashion PR agencies. Franks is said, by a former boss of mine who got his start there before working his way up to managing director (the creative and financial wizard that is Graham Goodkind), to have led communal Buddhist chants. Asked by PRWeek how Lynne Franks would remember him, he quipped, 'As the little boy who staunchly refused to take part' (Magee, 2007).

Similarly, around the world throughout the noughties, millions more watched as *Sex and the City*'s 'try-sexual' (as in, she'd try anything once) PR agent Samantha Jones partied her way through all six seasons. The show's crime wasn't Samantha's wild oat sowing, obviously, but that it gave starry-eyed and impressionable teens the notion that the PR industry was all rubbing shoulders with celebrities, events, glitz and glam. The number of people I've spoken to that say *Sex and the City* played a part in their decision to become a PR person is depressingly – and amusingly – high (in a *Schadenfreude* kind of way).

I can't think of many other career choices that can influence society as much as PR does that are as rarely and inaccurately represented. (It's important to say that I realize we're very often only a conduit for that impact. However, taking a campaign like, say, Sport England's 2015 initiative 'This Girl Can', credited with encouraging 150,000 women over the age of 16 to exercise and participate in sport following a downward post-Olympic trend, you can see how social change can be brought about thanks to messaging. This wouldn't have been achieved without a great communication strategy.) I digress.

In 2012, Krystal Lin, a then-intern at Weber Shandwick Seattle wrote a blog, in which she admits that her first impression of a public relations professional came 'from watching Samantha Jones from *Sex and the City*'. She continued: 'PR seemed like it was all about attending star-studded events, dining at the hottest and newest restaurants and going to the most glamorous parties. It made me think, "Wow, being a publicist certainly seems like all fun and no work!"' She was quick though to state that she wasn't attracted to that particular lifestyle.

But of course, public relations is nothing like that and, just as boss Daniel Cleaver misguidedly tells Bridget in the 2001 film version of *Bridget Jones's Diary*, there's certainly more to it than 'swanning in in your short skirt' and 'sexy see-through blouse' to 'fanny about with press releases'.

In a PR Daily blog post from 2012 examining the myth that PR is all about party planning, Lorra Brown, an associate PR professor at William Paterson University said that public relations is about 'coming up with the best solutions to help clients meet their communication or business objectives' – an altogether less-sexy but truer interpretation.

As long as this myth of PR as being one big party is allowed to prevail, young people around the world are making the decision to spend years of their lives and varying sums of usually-borrowed money on their education to embark on a career that looks nothing like they think it does.

In case this sounds like I'm creating a bunch of straw men to make a point, Matt Ragas, an assistant professor in the college of communication at

DePaul University, said in the same 2012 PR Daily article that 'many of his students hold these misconceptions about the PR field', but 'quickly grasp the reality and realize that party planning is just one tactic in the PR professional's arsenal'.

So, if not glamorous, what's it actually like?

There are numerous 'day in the life of a PR' posts online and, despite every day being different, especially in an agency where you're balancing multiple clients, there are certain tasks that crop up in near enough every recounting I've read and role I've worked in.

In 2012, I asked Caren Davies, the then-head of publicity for the UK versions of *The X Factor* and *Britain's Got Talent*, to run me through a typical day for her, which was then featured on PRexamples.com's 'Off the Record' section. As the head of publicity for two of the most popular TV shows in the UK (in fact, the final of the series of *Britain's Got Talent* Caren talked about working on in her post was the highest-rated UK TV show of the year to that point, averaging more than 11 million viewers), Caren's job would no doubt qualify as a 'dream job' for many, but her day sounds remarkably similar to one most PRs will be familiar with.

Caren said that she would start a typical day checking through press coverage on her mobile as soon as she woke up, ensuring she'd read or watched any breaking news. In her words, 'I think every PR does that'.

Her day while working on *X Factor* was then split between meetings to ensure the overarching communications strategy was being adhered to and to no doubt divide tasks up between the team. Jobs included proactively arranging interviews and photo shoots for contestants and the judges; responding to media enquiries: 'with a show of this size there is a never ending stream of calls into the office and a lot of issues to deal with. ... at times, things happen that are out of our control and my day will be shaped by those events'; approving content (in Caren's case, she was proofreading three Winners Books, only one of which would obviously be released); having catch-ups with teams and other stakeholders and ending her day by checking in with any news she might otherwise have missed.

Planning, proactive pitching, organizing, reacting, writing, proofreading and reporting. A far cry from the way Samantha Jones glides through the industry, but all too recognizable a template for most people working in PR.

The always-on nature of PR

Caren's account, in which she mentioned her working day starting the second she woke up, tells of a long, mentally straining day – and again, this is something many working within in-house and agency roles will be familiar with. She tells of 5.30 am starts to accompany people to morning breakfast shows and of never being home before 8 pm, despite 'normal' hours being 9 am–6 pm, of being on call 24 hours a day and working until 1 am if media calls are still coming in. Long hours in PR – often with no set start and finish times for your day – are commonplace.

And this is something worth touching on. The hours are often long, or at least unpredictable, in that clients will happily blur the lines between work time and private time if you allow them to, or aren't in the position to dictate. The work can be cerebrally strenuous, results-orientated and pressured. Obviously, a career in PR is a world away from toiling on an oil rig and nowhere near manually taxing in the way a labourer's day is (a fact my much-more-manual-than-me family don't let me forget), but it's a job in which you rarely switch off.

I always remind myself that I'm in a fortunate position and that as my brother likes to remind me, when I've had a tough day 'there are people that would do anything to have had your bad day'. However, that's why people that actually work in the world of PR can't relate to shows like *Sex and the City* and E!'s short-lived 'reality' TV offerings *The Spin Crowd* and *The Spindustry*. Their sanitized version of PR just doesn't look anything like the reality we know because, well, as most industries and professions would, the aforementioned shows need the sheen, faux-conflict and celebrity-invasion to be anything more exciting than watching deadline-weary PRs writing pitch emails to journalists.

This red carpet-tinted view of what PR will be like sits uneasily with the reality that, according to 2015 research from the PRCA and PRWeek of 1,500 respondents, 34 per cent of the PR industry has suffered from, or been diagnosed with, mental ill health. It's difficult to find a like-for-like basis for comparison, but statistics released by the Office of National Statistics (ONS) in 2013 show that 23 per cent of people in paid work reported they were experiencing mental health issues. This, alongside 2016 research from CareerCast that named PR the sixth most stressful job in the world, only less stressful than enlisted military personnel, firefighters, airline pilots, police officers and event coordinators.

While neither I nor any rational person would believe a PR person's job to be comparable in terms of stress to a midwife's or a paramedic's, to name just two roles that spring to mind where life or death situations are sadly part and parcel of those professionals' careers, it adds to a picture of a career that is undoubtedly stressful.

The PRCA and PRWeek research found that a combined 60 per cent of those surveyed wouldn't feel comfortable talking to colleagues or line managers about their mental health, with a similar combined number – 61 per cent – stating that they felt the PR industry was either not very accepting or very unaccepting of people suffering from mental ill health. Respondents listed stress, pressure from clients, levels of support from management, workload and career progression as issues which have impacted on their mental health. Some of the mental health issues experienced by respondents included bulimia, depression, anxiety, panic attacks and post-traumatic stress disorder.

At the time of the research, PRCA Director General Francis Ingham pointed out that industry growth during the recession prompted 'a major effort by the industry to deliver more and prove value' in the face of increasingly ROI and budget-conscious clients. Ingham believes the cost of that to practitioners has been 'pressure and long hours' with a 'resultant increase in stress-related mental health issues'.

Using the findings as a point on which to talk about PR and marketing professionals' 'always-on' culture in an article for The Drum, Stephen Waddington says he believes the issue in marketing and PR is that 'there's no longer a clear distinction between work and play, day and night'. He, informed by the results of the 2016 CMI (Chartered Management Institute) Quality of Working Life Study, places blame at the door of 'digital presenteeism', with 61 per cent of the 1,574 management-level respondents agreeing that technology has made it difficult to switch off from work. More than half of respondents, 54 per cent, said they 'frequently check' emails outside normal working hours, with 21 per cent checking emails 'all the time'.

Another aspect that affects the time and stress-levels of PR people and other professionals the world over is this strange unspoken admiration for employees desperate to be the first in the office and the last to leave. This certainly isn't unique to PR and other marketing disciplines, but does set in place subliminal expectations that future employees tend to follow, much like senior professionals taking their work home with them. Waddington points out that this 24/7 dedication fails to 'set a good example for colleagues, especially junior colleagues that feel the need to follow suit in order to prove themselves'.

This chapter paints a bleak picture of a career doing much the same as everybody else in PR, of long hours, stress and an inability to switch off – which tells a partial story. What those studies don't tell us is that public relations can be an incredibly rewarding career choice – creatively, socially and in terms of actually being able to have an impact on the brands, organizations and individuals worked with. Glitzy events, parties and photo opportunities with the rich and famous can and do come under the remit of a PR professional, depending on the agency or company worked for, but to study for or attempt to craft a career based on the fictional representation that those things form the basis, as opposed to being the exceptions of an industry, is to set oneself up for a fall.

I can't think of a better way to finish this chapter – tackling this enduring belief that PR is some doss of a career – than in the words of a man that took a very public public relations career break. I'll let him expand on it, but here's a first person account of a man once at the PR helm of one of the country's most popular supermarkets and, from the outside looking in, the break appeared to be a much-needed reset. Dom Burch held various communication roles at Asda since 2002, heading up its corporate and consumer PR strategy and going on to specialize by leading its social media strategy, before he left in February 2016.

The subject of the email Dom sent to me including this analysis of his time off was 'Career break, or break down?'. That might give you some idea of just how it fits in, but more than being specifically about PR, it speaks to any career in which you might allow yourself to be a professional first, human being second.

Here's Dom's account:

CASE STUDY

Five years ago I took a six-month career break.

The relentless pressure of working in a busy PR department for nine years at Asda had started to take its toll.

The little red light on my work BlackBerry serving as a constant reminder that a mini crisis was always around the next corner. Like a dripping tap or a ticking clock, it was a constant distraction; one I became addicted to feeding from the minute I rose to the minute I laid my head down at night. Sixteen hours a day, seven days a week.

Having made the decision to take a career break I immediately experienced a strangely liberating feeling. I started to approach life with a different head on, knowing that an escape from the rat race was in sight. The spell had been broken. The mere thought of leaving the dreaded BlackBerry behind put a bounce back in my step.

In spite of having three months left at work, I was less stressed out by things from that point onwards. And I hadn't even had any time off yet. I started to enjoy work more than before, perhaps because I knew the end was in sight. It prompted me to get my house in order, to get my team organized, to prioritize and plan like I have never prioritized and planned before.

I was conscious of not wanting to be forgotten, daft as that seems. So before I went I wanted to deliver two or three big things that had impact – so that people sat up and noticed, as if to say 'look what you're going to miss'.

Ironically, the fast approaching deadline played to my strengths. It focused my mind to ensure I delivered. I actually enjoyed the pressure and the challenge.

My wife and I had talked about going travelling again but never quite got round to it. There was always a good reason not to. Paying for a wedding. Moving house. Bringing up kids.

But now we had no real excuse.

Once the decision was made, the die was cast.

I accept not everyone is as lucky as me and is able to afford a career break, and most employers probably wouldn't be as accommodating as mine at the time. But consider this – if something terrible happened to you or your family, somehow you'd cope with whatever was thrown at you. In fact, you'd probably triumph in the face of adversity.

I've seen it happen time after time with people who have lost their jobs, or who have experienced a serious illness. Once over the initial set back they come back stronger, more fulfilled, with a healthier perspective on life. Taking stock is hard to do though when you are working every hour god sends, and looking after a family and dealing with all the usual issues.

But when you are forced to get off the treadmill, things can become remarkably clear.

At the time, I remember reading about a pension dispute by 40,000 members of the University and College Union (UCU). It led to academics 'working to contract'. By sticking tightly to their contracted hours each week, suddenly there was no more working on the train or late into the evening or at weekends.

The results in less than a month were apparently staggering.

People began to realize just how much the extra hours they put in affected their lives, and not in a good way. As one academic told *The Guardian* newspaper: 'Sticking to my contracted 35 hours has shown me that work was almost taking over my whole life. If you're conscientious, what inevitably happens when you've too much work to fit in is that you take it home. I haven't taken lunch breaks since I can't remember when.

'It's a bit of a cliché, but working to contract has been like having a weight lifted off my shoulders. I've still got the same amount of work to do, but it's just getting that breathing space that makes the difference: you begin to look at what you have to do and prioritize it, instead of feeling that everything has to be done as quickly as possible and feeling guilty when it isn't.'

When your circumstances change it's amazing how adaptable you really are. Therefore, if it is possible to overcome adversity when it is thrust upon you I reckon it is not just possible, but desirable to insert some positive events into your own life to disrupt the linear journey you are on.

I'm still benefitting from my career break five years on. It was the single best decision in my working life to date. Why not take a few detours – after all, we all end up in the same place in the end.

Further reading

Gilley, R, 2016. Why Ab Fab's Edina is my PR hero. *PRmoment.com*, 13 April. Available at: <http://www.prmoment.com/3406/why-ab-fabs-edina-is-my-pr-hero-by-bites-rachel-gilley.aspx> [Accessed 2 September 2016]

Lin, K, 2012. No, real PR is not like Samantha Jones' PR. *Weber Shandwick Seattle*, 17 July. Available at: <http://www.webershandwickseattle.com/2012/07/no-real-pr-is-not-like-samantha-jones-pr/> [Accessed 2 September 2016]

Magee, K, 2007. PROFILE: Graham Goodkind, chairman and founder, Frank PR. *PRWeek*, 14 November. Available at: <http://www.prweek.com/article/766684/profile-graham-goodkind-chairman-founder-frank-pr#mTY0YUf71rlhihxe.99> [Accessed 2 September 2016]

PR Daily, 2012. 'PR is all about party planning' – and other misconceptions. *PR Daily*, 27 December. Available at: <http://www.prdaily.com/Main/Articles/PR_is_all_about_party_planningand_other_misconcept_11791.aspx> [Accessed 2 September 2016]

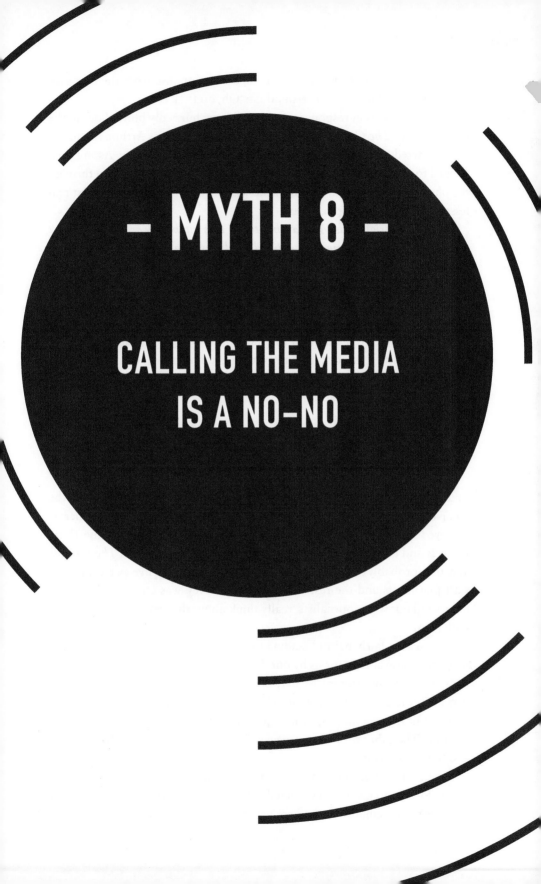

- MYTH 8 -

CALLING THE MEDIA IS A NO-NO

Within my first month in the job, the agitated response from the first ever journalist call I made was a resounding: 'Oh, do f**k off'.

This poetry was in response to a pitch I'd just hurriedly blurted out to the then-editor of *The Guardian*'s technology section, Charles Arthur. Arthur, as many scarred-for-life PRs will know, didn't suffer fools gladly. As my boss giggled to himself, having likely heard the sound of the phone slam through the phone's earpiece from across the desk, it dawned on me that my first real lesson in PR had just been given.

(If you're intrigued as to what the story I was pitching was – well, I won't lie to you, it's an odd one. You can still find it online, though – just Google the title 'Rest in peace thanks to unique new website', including the quotation marks. You'll know when you find the release.)

There's a dread attached to picking up the phone to journalists and producers to talk through a story, so much so that many senior PR people I know wouldn't even entertain the thought of doing so. Firstly, I'd like to look at the issues associated with how we communicate with journalists, and then get onto why I think that many PRs are missing a trick by believing in and bowing to this myth.

The stats

In 2014, DWPub – a UK-based PR service supplier (DWPub, 2014), the company behind media request service Response Source, amongst others – surveyed more than 400 journalists, from national titles such as the *Daily Express* and the *Financial Times* through to trade titles such as *The Lawyer* and the (probably) peerless *Concrete* magazine. Eighty-five per cent were staff journalists and the rest freelance. The survey was commissioned in a bid to find out what journalists 'really think about the ways PR people work with them'.

It makes for fairly painful reading for PR types – as pretty much every bit of advice I've ever read for us by our deadline-conscious, pitch-weary friends does. At first opportunity to bat, an underarmed throw of a question – 'Do PR professionals understand what a journalist needs?' – was met with 50 per cent of respondents stating, quite simply, that 'no', we do not. So far, so good. The other 50 per cent was split between 'not sure' – 26 per cent, and 'yes' – 24 per cent.

A handful of questions later, we arrive at this multiple-answer question, 'How do you prefer to be contacted?' The vast majority – 89 per cent – of journalists said email was the best way to contact them with story pitches.

The second best-preferred way for the respondents to receive story pitches – and this is far more positive-sounding than is reality – was by phone... with 18 per cent. Even bearing in mind respondents were able to select more than one answer (surely removing the inference of 'preference', no?), it doesn't bode well for the likelihood that the journalist you call will be pleased to receive your call. The third best-preferred method was via Twitter, with a whopping five per cent of votes. Email is the clear and obvious winner.

The next question was 'What are your greatest frustrations when dealing with PR people?' Though the most-cited grievance was of 'lack of understanding of [their] publication and subject area' – at 80 per cent; 'unwelcome phone calls' ranked highly with 53 per cent of nods.

Looking at the two responses above – we can surmise that:

a) journalists don't much like to be contacted with client pitches in ways other than email; and

b) we pitch ignorantly and too often by phone.

A similar white paper by news release distribution service Business Wire in 2015 (Loechner, 2015) of 400 US, Asia-Pacific and South American journalists found much the same. Well, I say that – it wasn't multi-answer, so respondents could only pick one 'Preferred Method For Receiving Breaking News From An Organization', and it was worded much more promotionally than DW Pub's. For instance – and remembering that Business Wire is a service that companies and their agencies pay to place news releases on – the best-preferred method, selected by 67 per cent of journalists, was an 'email alert with link to full press release' – odd phrasing all theirs – and the second best-preferred method was found to be 'newswire press release', with 21 per cent. Just 2 per cent said they preferred a telephone call.

In short, journalists prefer to be emailed. Shocker. Call *The New York Times* – or, perhaps don't.

What do journalists say?

'I never want to be called by a PR person unless I am expecting the call. Especially for cold pitches. Email is the best way to pitch me. If I don't respond to the email, it's simply because I don't have the time to say "no" to the hundreds of pitches I receive each week. I hit silent on every single call that comes to my phone', said Steve Kovach, Senior Editor at Business Insider, reported in a post entitled 'How to Pitch Respectfully (Put Down the Phone)' (Zitron, 2013).

This post, written by Ed Zitron – the founder of public relations firm EZPR, ex-journalist and author of *This Is How You Pitch: How to Kick Ass in Your First Years of PR* – highlights a truth: 'Many PR people are told by senior people to make call-downs – calling everyone who hasn't emailed you back – and reporters despise it.'

That happens in agencies and in-house teams all around the world, every single day. If you are a journalist and writing for an outlet of any prominence, chances are, your name is on a call sheet somewhere most days of the week. And if that is true, then in a column beside your name; sorted by outlet alphabetically, by readership or possible SEO-usefulness, a note will get written that, the author hopes, will appease his or her manager, and that said manager hopes will appease his or her director, who in turn might or might not use this as proof to the client that time was spent to that end.

I'm not saying that it's right, I'm saying that it happens – and Zitron, described as 'the world's most self-loathing PR person' (Schonfeld, 2014) has made something of a name for himself, especially among journalists, by pointing out what should be obvious: that calling a time-strapped journalist with an irrelevantly targeted pitch is the professional equivalent of calling the emergency services to tell them about an out-of-date Pot Noodle. It's no wonder journalists take such a dim view of PR calls when they're often little more than a cell in a spreadsheet to pick a colour for.

I think what we've seen is a result of the PRs that cried irrelevant press release – something I can't pretend I haven't been responsible for, like every other one of us. Running down a list and having a stilted 15-second chase call with the people that pick up, where you mumble your way through an introduction before uttering the six words every journalist rolls their eyes hard at, 'Did you get my press release?', is 'still far more commonplace than you'd think, even from the big name agencies', according to a journalist that asked not to be named.

As ex-journalist Alex Singleton, now a public relations practitioner and the author of *The PR Masterclass*, says, the release chase call 'is annoying, and journalists (who are bombarded with these calls) suspect that the person ringing is a junior member of a team ringing a long list'.

Singleton went on to say that, having worked on both sides of the room in magazines, newspapers and digital titles before working in PR, he'd 'admit that there's something media relations teams sometimes do that is less effective than making irritating calls: it's having a silent office where no journalist is ever rung. Done right, phone calls definitely work.'

Whether you define it as 'spray and pray' or the practice of throwing enough s**t at the wall and hoping some will stick, it's this blanket box-ticking approach that undoubtedly contributes to this enduring myth that the phone should be avoided. 'Interns doing the ring-round for bus-fares' is how former PRCA chairman Adrian Wheeler described this approach in the comment section of Singleton's piece, and many readers will know just how accurate that statement is, particularly at big city firms – that's if they even bother to pay the bus fare.

What we've been left with is a sea of journalistic complaints our industry bodies point to as examples of bad practice. The virtuous professionals then believe that to stay on the right side of the media, which for a large percentage of us is still important to our jobs, they should simply never talk to them. This could not be more wrong (imagine the stress in that sentence as if Chandler Bing were saying it).

If you are a young professional, a student hoping to enter the world of PR after you graduate, or even somebody eyeing up the industry, please know this: phone calls work and are an essential part of being more than just somebody that presses the send button. (Meetings work better – I've still, after countless meetings, never had a sit-down with a journalist, with or without a client there, that hasn't resulted in something positive for my clients.)

The agreed best way to pitch is to know what a writer or producer will want to hear about, and one thing every good PR person should do is make it their business to know. You can do this with Googling – your media database might show recent stories or using services like Journalisted where you see what that journalist has written about, but there are a couple of issues here. Firstly, the media is changing, quickly. I mean that both in the sense of media real estate – what publications still exist now and might still exist when this book is in your hands – and in the sense that journalists move between roles now more than ever, at their current outlets and in jumping ship. In 2016 so far in the UK, these being only the ones I can recall off the top of my head, *The Independent* went online-only, a new national called *The New Day* launched and was then axed just two months later, *Vice* laid off a large number of its staff in the United States and the UK, BuzzFeed 'reshuffled', Mashable cut two dozen staffers and The Telegraph Media group made a number of writers among its senior journalists redundant, including staff on the features, culture, picture and foreign affairs desks.

Secondly, that information only tells you what they've previously written about, not what they will write about. Of course, you use it to inform but, supposing you have a client or story that's absolutely perfect for a journalist or title, but they've ignored your initial email and perhaps a second 'is this of any use?' email has gone without acknowledgement too – well, what then? The most important thing is to be sure your client or story is as perfect for that person as you thought it was, both in terms of relevance and it actually being newsworthy. Be sure it is (the latter harder to fix than the former). There are only so many times you can send client feedback that glosses over your being ignored, and it usually comes down to one of these two things.

We have a job to do and no response isn't quite good enough, especially if the client or story is (and again this will always be subjective on both sides) both newsworthy and relevant. I've always focused on getting a yes or a no from journalists I'm sure are right for stories. If I get a no, I try to understand why – and ask instead what's useful to that person in the future. Sometimes, this even leads to an opportunity to pitch something you might have coming up... that's always nice. I've found that communicating that you only want to be sending relevant stuff over opens that person up, because it's not something they'll be used to. You're wasting your time and theirs with otherwise ill-targeted work, so taking that extra hour or so with the raw media contact list before you pitch and asking these questions either over the phone or email can save a lot of effort and rejection in the future.

Email tracking

Given the working time constraints on both parties – something I feel PRs understand much more than the journalist that calls and demands information there and then – I agree that the phone should be used when appropriate to talk to the people whose audience you believe your story fits for. Technology helps us, here.

Email tracking is a contentious issue, and a thoroughly modern one, that in the near future may have either become common practice or could entirely fall by the wayside. If you've never heard of it, email services are available that tell you when your recipient opens your email and/or clicks a link. A handful of press release distribution services offer varied degrees of reporting, while stand-alone services like HubSpot's Sidekick and Yesware work by connecting to your email programme of choice, inserting a one by one pixel into sent messages. Email marketing services like MailChimp offer in-depth and live reports that highlight recipient information and have done for years – something I've never heard referenced negatively, but journalists have louder voices than your average e-newsletter recipient and might well not appreciate said tracking.

Ed Zitron, the small agency owner I referenced earlier, touched on email tracking negatively in a recent Medium post aimed at reporters he called The Definitive Guide to PR People. Zitron wrote that PRs now 'know when/ where you clicked said email. I do mean *when and where*, as they'll know the time *and* the location. How creepy is *that*?' In response to that, I'd point out that the 'where' is irrelevant, and not something I've ever even seen from my service of choice, Sidekick, or particularly care about. I simply couldn't care less where most journalists are, anyway other than to know their audience is relevant. Add into this the fact that you have been able to pinpoint the location of people for years, whether through Google Analytics, social media location tagging, link shortening services like Bit.ly and many other methods, and it seems like a non-issue. Also, if a journalist thinks email tracking is 'creepy' (you can probably tell I really don't), I bet they'd sooner that than 'Did you get my press release?' follow-ups.

I'll explain as best as I can both how email tracking ties in to making calls and why PR and the media should embrace it. My team has been using it for a year or so and, though conscious of the link format, we're mostly of the mindset that it helps to know which emails have been opened and when.

Every PR person that hasn't been put off speaking to actual real life humans by doom merchants (and I've met a lot of these) has heard the line 'I haven't received that release', or 'yeah, I read it and it wasn't for us'. Tracking helps, here. I'm not saying that you still call every name on the media list and confront a journalist when they aren't truthful or have probably forgotten your message. I'm saying that you instead shift attention to the journalists whose names don't appear in the 'opened' column. Again, if you've targeted relevantly and your email should be of interest, it being unopened certainly isn't going to help you get that yes or no you'll need to keep clients happy and informed. This is where I'd call, ask to speak to that person, or if they're not available, their department, and make them aware of the story.

When an email is repeatedly opened, especially over the course of a short period of time, that's very often a positive sign. It usually either means it's been forwarded, or that writer or producer is re-opening because they're using it. Sometimes though, if that recipient is a national news journalist and time starts creeping towards the end of the day or end of the story's half-life, calling can push it over the line. I've lost count of the number of times I've spoken to a journalist the day after a story went out that's said the story is old news and, as such, unusable – which makes sense given our quick-turnaround 24-hour news cycles – so anything you can do to get feedback before it's too late is beneficial. A repeatedly opened email shows interest, so if you haven't heard or seen anything as a result and time's

getting on, call. Ask if there's anything else you can help with, be it information, an interview or images. I'd say that, in the vast majority of times this
has happened to me or my team, it's been a query we've been able to quickly
help with, or we've been able to offer clarification of something the recipient
was unsure about.

So... when should you call?

Throughout this chapter, I've taken pains to point out that journalists are
time-strapped, and that relevant targeting with good stories is the most
important aspect of good PR. I'm going to put aside assertions from people
within the industry that you never should, because I entirely disagree and
have happy clients and good relationships still with journalists to prove it
works. This is nothing to do with box-ticking, or running your cursor down
a spreadsheet like a press release-sending zombie – this is to do with being
useful to both your clients and the people you believe your story works for.

Lindsay Goldwert is a New York-based former 'media professional', who
balanced her time between PR and journalism. At the time of writing, and
according to Goldwert's Twitter biography, she's now a writer, stand-up
comic and 'ex-breaking news person'. In an article entitled 'I'm a PR Pro.
Should I Call a Journalist?' (Goldwert, 2015), Goldwert said, 'Even if you've
been handed a media list with a journalist's phone number on it, I would
advise strongly that you never, ever use it'. That said, and utilizing her time
on both sides of the fence, she cites four rare exceptions to that advice:

1 You have a personal relationship – as in an actual friendship or mutually
   beneficial relationship.
2 You've worked successfully together in the past – where if 'the journalist hasn't told you "You are the only PR person I don't despise" or the
   equivalent' you shouldn't consider calling.
3 You have huge news – of the 'is Apple about to buy Google?' variety, as
   opposed to 'a new app of some kind' or a 'Kardashian wore a certain
   brand of jewellery to an awards show'.
4 You're pitching radio/TV – where some still rely on the phone.

Now, as begrudging as all that may sound, we're getting closer to the truth –
and it certainly isn't that you should refrain from ever hearing the voice of
a journalist, lest you be turned to stone.

I'd add a few more numbered points to this list:

5 When a journalist (for whom you haven't received an out of office) hasn't opened or responded to a release that is, in as unbiased a way as you can possibly muster, objectively right for their audience. Journalists and the great and the good of PR can disagree all they like, we have clients to keep and if a call to the journalist or their department is what it takes to highlight the story or client, it's a minute well spent.

6 This depends on the journalist's or producer's niche and, as such, the immediacy of action normally on their part, but if a journalist has repeatedly opened your release, you've received no reply and there's been no coverage, politely email to ask if the story could work for them. No reply to that? Give them a call.

7 If you have an unusual offering – a feature idea you want to get immediate feedback on and are sure they'll like, or an idea for an exclusive media partnership – call. Have a conversation. For instance, I was recently introduced to a transgender builder registered to a client's local services website, and was sure the focus would make for an incredibly interesting feature. I first emailed a contact in business at the BBC with the bones of an idea, asked if they had five minutes to chat, called them and had a 10-minute talk about this builder, her background and her willingness to tell a positive story of acceptance within a typically macho industry. Call me old-fashioned, but this was cause for a conversation, not a heavy pitch.

Calling tips

Journalists and producers are busy people, not helped by shrinking newsrooms as a result of an ever-more fragmented media. Check public social media accounts to see what that person's been saying today, if anything. If obvious they're busy, then don't call. If your media database of choice says 'doesn't want to be called' – don't call. If not urgent, exclusive or easier to explain as part of a back and forth conversation and you haven't tried emailing yet, don't call. Right, all that should appease those perpetuating this myth. Here are my tips:

1 Call at a suitable time; 9 am is not a suitable time for most journalists. It's harder to make a generalization for when it's a good time to call a journalist than it was five years ago, but early in the day and lunchtime tend not to be great for either party. Many journalists are always

'on-deadline' now, but we've found the afternoon is more fruitful. There are topical times where a call is a terrible idea, too – it could be the Chancellor's Budget, an industry-specific announcement or a tragedy that's just occurred. Exercise common sense.

2   Don't call mobile phones. Unless you're best friends, just don't.

3   Don't call to ask if they got your release. You'll be laughed off the phone and for good reason. In any case, if you're using tracking and haven't received a bounce-back of some sort, you'll already know – after all, we really should trust in technology's ability to ensure an email is delivered, no? Assuming you know they haven't opened it, I've found that telling a journalist I have a story in their area of interest and wondered if they'd be interested in seeing it works. You'll likely get a chance to give a quick overview and they'll say something like 'sure, send it to X'. Perhaps they're working from a new address, or it just got quickly buried in their inbox. I invariably have the story ready to send again, anyway, and send the email while I'm on the phone. They might then open it and give you a response on the spot. Again, the point is to not only be useful, but get a yes or a no for your client.

4   Be personable, but there's no reason to fall into faux-friendliness. Unless I know the journalist or producer well, I don't much care how their weekend was and they don't much care about telling me. Get to the point, which ideally turns out to be something useful for both parties. Friendliness can come with time and a mutual respect.

5   It can be tempting, especially if you haven't done it often, but try not to read from a script. If you know your story or client well enough, go in with a couple of key points, but otherwise simply make it about ensuring they get to see the email pitch in instances you know they haven't.

6   A phone call is a conversation. Just like I remind clients that a broadcast interview is essentially a chat with a mic and/or a camera there, there's no need to overcomplicate things, and I've seen otherwise social people lose their ability to speak like a human when calling the media.

7   You're just one person doing your job speaking to somebody else doing theirs – if your story gets rejected, it isn't personal. At the beginning of the chapter, I explained how my first pitch went particularly (comically) badly. I've always had pretty thick skin so this isn't necessarily an easy tip to take on if you haven't, but get used to rejection. It'll happen a lot.

8   If you've a number of calls to make, have made one call and they didn't answer, that isn't job done. That can't be the sum of all your effort

because, frankly, that won't cut it with clients. Try another journalist; call reception, ask for the department that person works in and offer the client or story (where relevant, obviously) to that person.

9   If you're struggling with calls, ask your manager or another colleague to show you how to do it. Given in many agencies there's traditionally pressure from above for execs to make the calls, these bosses should be able to walk the walk and support you through the stages. Listen and take notes. Another tip for the shy is to go into another room if you have access, it's understandable that you wouldn't want to make your first few calls with the entire office listening. In no time at all, you probably won't much care.

10 Further to point six (it's a conversation), I've found another successful and relationship-building tactic can be to ask what that person prefers to receive from PRs. You should already know their area of interest, but I mean, do they prefer stat-based stories, exclusives or a specific slant? They'll usually tell you, and journalists I've known since the start of my career still remember me paying attention to getting things to them when and how they like it.

Further reading

Goldwert, L, 2015. I'm a PR pro. Should I call a journalist? *PRNewser*, 30 September. Available at: <http://www.adweek.com/prnewser/im-a-pr-pro-should-i-call-a-journalist/118237> [Accessed 2 September 2016]

Loechner, J, 2015. Journalism and media relations. *MediaPost*, 5 November. Available at: <http://www.mediapost.com/publications/article/261628/journalism-and-media-relations.html> [Accessed 2 September 2016]

Schonfeld, Z, 2014. A conversation with the world's most self-loathing PR person. *Newsweek*, 30 December. Available at: <http://europe.newsweek.com/why-pr-industry-conversation-ed-zitron-295589> [Accessed 2 September 2016]

Singleton, A, 2015. 'Did you get my press release?' *Influence*, 13 February. Available at: <http://influence.cipr.co.uk/2015/02/13/get-press-release/> [Accessed 2 September 2016]

DWPub, 2014. *What do journalists think of PR people? Survey results.* [pdf] Available at: <http://www.responsesource.com/content/uploads/2014/10/DWPub-journalist-survey-What-do-journalists-think-of-PR-people.pdf> [Accessed 2 September 2016]

Zitron, E, 2013. How to pitch respectfully (put down the phone). *Inc.*, 18 November. Available at: <http://www.inc.com/ed-zitron/how-to-pitch-respectfully-put-down-the-hone.html> [Accessed 2 September 2016]

– MYTH 9 –

YOU CAN MAKE
SOMETHING GO VIRAL

If there's one word I wish had never been invented, it's 'viral'. I don't mean to sound rude nor dismissive, but every single client that's ever asked me to help them make something go viral has in some way etched away at the core of my very soul. That's right, clients that read this – as you've sat across from me, both parties excited about working together, your throwaway and hopeful request has set my Death Clock back at least a full 24 hours. In a sentence sure to gladden the hearts of journalists everywhere, and as in *Peter Pan* when a non-believer declares their stance on fairy existence, every time the word 'viral' is uttered and isn't in relation to the spread of disease, there is a PR person somewhere that falls down dead.

The word *viral* is thrown around so often and so commonly in relation to marketing that I feel like it's beginning to lose all meaning, so I'll take a step back and, firstly, do the arduous job of copying and pasting the dictionary definition from Google (accessed February 2017):

---

viral *adjective*

1 of the nature of, caused by, or relating to a virus or viruses.

2 (of an image, video, piece of information, etc) circulated rapidly and widely from one Internet user to another.

As you can see, there are two common meanings – the second borne from the first. Viruses rapidly spread from one person to another, as can content – be it an image, video or piece of information. Over the years and as examples of online virality mount up, a misguided notion has emerged. 'If there can be so many instances of content having gone viral, surely we should be closer to being able to guarantee it? *Surely*, there must be somebody out there practised enough in the process of making content go viral that it's just a case of finding the right person?'

When somebody makes the assumption that virality can be in some way gamed or ensured, we're on the back foot, professionally speaking. This somebody might not be a client. It might be a manager, owner or any other stakeholder, each with the best of intentions but possibly none of the responsibility for ensuring the entirely finger-in-the-air objective of 'going viral' is achieved.

Like many half-decent PR-types that have been around the block, I've led or been part of teams responsible for creating both personal and brand client campaigns that have gone, as some might determine it, viral. The problem with the term is there are no set goalposts and, as such, a client video that reaches a couple of hundred thousand people might be gratefully hailed by them as viral while, in truth, it pales in terms of exposure in comparison to something that legitimately spread like wildfire. I don't believe anything that goes viral in a global, all-of-your-friends-definitely-saw-it type of way can be bought.

One head of PR for a well-known UK brand that asked to be kept anonymous agrees. She said, 'It's a pressure for in-house PRs as well, from bosses higher up who think you can buy a trend. To a degree, you can – with Twitter offering sponsored and Facebook letting you put things in front of eyes but ultimately it has to be good. And, while you can make an educated guess, it is ultimately just a guess – virality relies on far too many factors that you can't control. The *Star Wars* mask lady (who we discuss later in this chapter) as a case in point, on another day we might all have vilified her as a complete imbecile. It's completely capricious. Anyone who is immersed in social knows this, but it's hard to sell internally – particularly when you do want to take credit when things *miraculously* do go well.'

When considering why things go viral, there are many factors at play, one of which is the sheer volume of information we're dealing with on a daily basis, especially online. Just like charts were created to rank music in order to define popularity, there will now always be images, videos or pieces of information like social media updates that perform better than others, in our bid to find hierarchy in the noise. This analogy between music charts and the most prominent online content of any given week works when you consider that a 'number one' song might not always be technically the 'best' song – it's usually the one that experiences the biggest initial promotion, lending it social credence and, therefore, it becomes cool to like, download and/or buy it. Our individual response to art and media is subjective, but this pack social guidance is part of the reason otherwise arguably better things are ignored. We just don't have enough in the way of time to devote to everything, so combined attention leads the way.

Breaking virality down

Roger Wu is the co-founder of content distribution network Cooperatize. In 2014, he wrote an article for *Forbes* about two strategies his company believe create online virality. The first he dubbed the Roadblock Effect – 'a top down effect resulting in concentrated impressions in a short time period', and the second the Stagger Effect – 'a bottoms up approach that results in an equal number of impressions as the Roadblock but over a longer period of time'.

Wu believes the Roadblock is an instance of virality whereby you simply can't get past it. He gives the example of the Harlem Shake, a group dance craze in early 2013 that defies serious explanation. You couldn't move for the number of friends and 'we're crazy, us' brands hastily editing their own versions together and then, just like that, it was all over. A Google Trends search for the term shows us that it was first searched for in February, peaked in March and then fell off a cliff. The graph looks like a needle, spiking sharply up and then dropping just as quickly.

Another example of the Roadblock Effect is the ALS Ice Bucket Challenge from August 2014. Not quite as popular as the Harlem Shake, but a viral hit that raised more than $100 million for the ALS Association, and more for other charities. In a 2015 *Time* article about the challenge, Tim Gamory, the acting COO of Charity Navigator (a US-based independent charity evaluator), said 'searches for ALS went up a ridiculous amount, from around 500 to 68,000 in August. And then it went right back down.'

Wu's second strategy, the Stagger Effect, describes a marketing strategy more than an accidental hit as we'd usually define viral content of the Roadblock variety. He says that this effect doesn't require the same intense co-ordination as the Roadblock, and although it 'still creates the same illusion that everyone is talking about you' it is accomplished in a staggered manner. He cites 2013's Gangnam Style by South Korean K-Pop singer Psy as an example of this kind of viral hit, having taken around three months to peak and more than a year to drop back to relative obscurity. The song is still the best-viewed YouTube video ever, with two and a half billion views.

Though useful to have terms to describe two different types of content, examples of both of which can undoubtedly be found, I don't believe that they are strategies so much as simply definitions.

Andy Barr, head of 10 Yetis Digital and my first boss in PR, created a report in October 2012, called 'How Gangnam Style went viral with a strategic marketing campaign from YG Entertainment' (Barr, 2012). He surmised that Gangnam Style's success was the result of a 'well-structured and meticulously executed campaign by the South Korean label company behind the song: YG Entertainment'. Barr broke the staggered promotion of the song down into three key points. He first described how YG primed its existing audience and created artist partnerships. Secondly, he believes the content was intentionally created in a universally relatable way, with bright colours, simple-to-learn dance moves and simple language. Thirdly, he says YG pushed the song using more typical PR tactics, relying on its extensive seeding network and media coverage of both the song and pre-founded partnerships.

It's rare I disagree with anything Andy says, but since Gangnam Style was released, its success is yet to have been anywhere near replicated, leading me to believe it has far more to do with a confluence of unknown factors than preparation and intent.

One thing we need to remember with truly viral hits, or success of any kind in any area of art or business, is that they are notable because they are the exception and not the rule. I'm sure Gangnam Style was analysed by the brightest commercial and productive minds in the music world in a bid to develop another global phenomenon, but nothing has even come close. Millions of musicians must release millions of tracks every year, especially now the barriers to reaching and communicating with an audience directly are next to non-existent, but because we rarely hear about the ones that don't make it big, there's an assumption that success is easier or more common, somehow.

CASE STUDY

The happy Chewbacca

We don't have to go far back to find an example of what can only be described as truly viral content – of the 'roadblock' variety. In May 2016, a lady named Candace Payne used Facebook Live to stream a video of her trying on a *Star Wars* Chewbacca mask to her friends. Thanks to some lax privacy settings and Payne's incredibly infectious laugh and personality, the original video itself, automatically saved post-stream, has been watched more than 156 million times at the time of writing. It's been shared more than 3 million times. These figures make it the most-viewed Facebook Live video of all time, with many millions of views elsewhere. To put it into context, the 'sneezing baby panda' many readers will be familiar with has had 220 million views, and Psy's 'Gangnam Style' music video has had 2.5 billion views.

The conveyor belt of fleeting online fame transported the video and its star in the now-familiar way, with light-entertainment presenters such as Ellen and British export James Corden scrabbling to be the first to snag 'Chewbacca Lady' and thus a few million views themselves. It's been estimated that Payne has received $420,000 worth of gifts, including a trip to Disneyland, $2,500 worth of gift cards from Kohl's, the store that sold the *Star Wars* Chewbacca mask and even full-tuition college scholarship offers from Southeastern University to Payne and her family, valued at $400,000.

As the owner and overall editor of PRexamples.com, a site housing thousands of examples of PR stunts and campaigns, I'm often one of the first cynics to narrow my eyes and consider a marketer's involvement in something being conveyed as otherwise organic. Like a magician watching for sleights of hand, I look for the mechanics of a campaign or stunt, but can't see anything tell-tale in this example. That, though, doesn't mean the named brand – American department store retail chain Kohl's – hasn't walked away from this in a better and happier position than it was beforehand.

Thanks to Payne, Kohl's was put in front of at least 150 million people, though many more when you consider the media coverage, duplicate videos and the brand's own subsequent marketing efforts. That compares to the 34 million people that watched the Oscars in February 2016, for which Kohl's was the exclusive department store sponsor. According to data from Amobee Brand Intelligence (McGee, 2016), 'digital content engagement' related to Kohl's increased 101 per cent from 18 May to 22 May compared to the previous five days.

Opportunities for the public to be exposed to the brand is one thing; financial gain in the form of revenue and share price is another altogether. Although Kohl's sold out of the mask itself in the days following the video, it's unclear how much this unexpected bump was worth. What is clear is that it did little for the brand's share price, but, sales aside, one can only assume that the five-to-one reach in comparison to the Academy Awards global audience was well worth the cost of a $2,500 post-exposure gift card.

With so many examples, why can't we learn and replicate?

While Payne's video has and will no doubt be joylessly analysed by students, professionals and armchair experts in case studies (ahem, like this one) until the next example comes along, I firmly believe that viral success cannot easily be distilled and marketed in any repeatable way – more's the pity. We can look at her clip and other hits from a human psychology level, on which it's easy to understand why the video would resonate, but would still likely come up short if we tried to piece these elements together. Everything from being a parent treating herself with something so simple to her childlike excitement as she demonstrates the mask and its ability to make the famous Chewbacca growl is relatable but almost entirely unreproducible.

BuzzFeed's editorial director Jack Shepherd has previously written three tips to help make something go viral and they're as close to the answer as I think we're going to get (well, two of them are, anyway). He says that the 'first thing [BuzzFeed] learned about viral content is to never, under any circumstances, say the words "viral content"'. BuzzFeed's content receives more than 7 billion monthly global views as of early 2016, and more than 200 million people visit the site every month, so it's fair to say they know a thing or two about what people like to share (Shepherd, 2014).

Secondly, and more relevantly, Shepherd says that the things people like to share the most are things about themselves. 'Sharing something about yourself is often a statement about what you believe in, what causes or values you align yourself with, and what, in particular, you love and identify with.' As well as BuzzFeed's frankly odd but shareable personality quizzes, this theory lends itself to the rise of 'virtue signalling', a phrase *The Spectator*'s James Bartholomew claims he invented in April 2015, a term used to loosely define people that say or write things to indicate that they are virtuous or good people. I've taken advantage of this a good few times with PR campaigns, including the time my agency had controversial British columnist Katie Hopkins 'crucified' in an oil painting you could buy prints of from an online client that specializes in reproducing personalized and updated works of art. In light of some intentionally provocative statements Hopkins made about refugees, offending many, we ensured that profits went to a Syrian refugee charity when the public bought a print.

Shepherd concluded by saying, 'the third thing that we've learned about viral content is that people are more likely to share something if they have a strong, positive emotional response to it', highlighting a 2010 study of *The New York Times*' 'most emailed' list, which found the articles that people are more likely to share fall into one of four categories: awe-inspiring, emotional, positive or surprising. I'd add 'angered' to that list from my personal experience of stunts but agree that, on the whole, these are the emotions you're hoping to tap into.

The two main takeaways from Shepherd, then, are that people respond well when the content reflects well on them if they share it, and that you're always trying to elicit a positive or negative emotional response.

To dispel this myth that you can make content 'go viral', especially in the Roadblock Effect sense, I think you only need to look at the number of campaigns that marketing professionals produce which break through in a way that reaches people of multiple generations, no matter their profession. I'd argue the majority of output lives and dies over the course of a few days, by which time it might have picked up a few million views if you're lucky. After that it's typically only people within the industry that remember it.

I compile a monthly and yearly list of the best stunts and campaigns on PRexamples.com, ranked based on the number of unique reads each post on the site receives. Feel free to go back and search each of the years' top 20 lists, starting from 2012 until today, and check to see just how many of those you recognize or remember – chances are, it'll be very few of them, and members of the public will recall even fewer.

Further reading

Barr, A, 2012. Case study: how Gangnam Style went viral with a strategic marketing campaign from YG Entertainment. *The Drum*, 30 October. Available at: <http://www.thedrum.com/news/2012/10/30/case-study-how-gangnam-style-went-viral-campaign-yg-entertainment> [Accessed 3 September 2016]

Google Trends. Available at: <https://www.google.co.uk/trends/explore#q=harlem%20shake%2C%20ice%20bucket%20challenge&cmpt=q&tz=Etc%2FGMT-1> [Accessed 3 September 2016]

McGee, M, 2016. Chewbacca mask viral video drives sales for Kohl's, others. *Marketing Land*, 23 May. Available at: <http://marketingland.com/chewbacca-mask-viral-video-drives-sales-kohls-others-178268> [Accessed 3 September 2016]

Shepherd, J, 2014. How to make something go viral: tips from BuzzFeed. *The Guardian*, 16 March. Available at: <http://www.theguardian.com/media/2014/mar/16/how-to-make-something-go-viral-tips-buzzfeed> [Accessed 3 September 2016]

Wolff-Mann, E, 2015. Remember the ice bucket challenge? Here's what happened to the money. *Time*, 21 August. Available at: <http://time.com/money/4000583/ice-bucket-challenge-money-donations/> [Accessed 3 September 2016]

Wu, R, 2014. Will you go viral? Here's a way to predict. *Forbes*, 3 January. Available at: <http://www.forbes.com/sites/groupthink/2014/01/03/will-you-go-viral-heres-a-way-to-predict/#36e62d6521e1> [Accessed 3 September 2016]

– MYTH 10 –

YOU HAVE TO BE AN EXTROVERT TO SUCCEED IN PR

Google a variation of 'introverts in PR' and you'll see that many people either question their potential suitability or feel the need to defend their position. There's an assumption, not helped by media portrayal of PR people – something I touched on in the chapter, 'PR is glamorous' – that you have to be a certain type of person to succeed, or even work, in PR. This is absolutely not the case.

The words introvert and extrovert have grown in prominence since schools, businesses and sectors started to assess the personalities of pupils, employees and potential employees using the Myers–Briggs Type Indicator test, created by Katharine Cook Briggs and her daughter Isabel Briggs Myers, building on the work of Swiss psychiatrist Carl Jung. There is a misconception that PR professionals have to be charismatic extroverts, most comfortable when attending launch events, rubbing shoulders with the rich and famous or persuading the media. We can dominate client ideas meetings and there is truth in the notion that extroverts are much more likely to shout loudly about their successes than our more subtly minded colleagues, which can be insufferable. As Gini Dietrich, founder and CEO of Arment Dietrich, said (PR Daily, 2012), 'being an extrovert or a people person does not automatically make you good at communications'.

I am, by nature, an outgoing person. I'm sociable, unduly confident in new situations, often outspoken and... sometimes an idiot. I've quietened down over the years, but to give an example, a couple of years into my career, I thought nothing of drunkenly pitching a motoring client's product to former *Top Gear* presenter Richard Hammond. It didn't end particularly well. It turns out he was fairly tipsy too and, taking offence at my talking shop, it escalated to something of an altercation that meant we both spent the remaining hours at that event on opposite sides of the event. In my mind, I was taking advantage of a situation I knew I wouldn't be in again for a client. In my employer's mind and probably those of everybody else there, I was being an insufferable drunken idiot. What they don't know is... I would have done the same sober.

See – unduly confident. I told you.

While being outgoing doesn't hurt when tempered properly, there's nothing to say you can't be slightly more reserved and still succeed. Catherine Fisher, LinkedIn's corporate communications director, wrote about the assumption people that knew her had, who asserted that she had to be a 'people person' to be in communications. In response to that she said, 'It's my job to tell stories, deliver the message, and help connect the dots for people. It's *not* my job to be the life of the party' (Fisher, 2015). John Priestley, the head of PR agency Wolfstar London and a self-confessed introvert makes even more of a distinction, clearing up 'a common misconception' by saying 'introvert and misanthrope are not the same. The former is someone who feels refreshed by the company of a few select friends. The latter is someone who has no friends and likes to spend their time in a darkened room' (Priestley, 2015).

It's difficult to write this chapter without falling victim to attributing certain stereotypes, but there might well be a number (he hopes) of students or young PRs reading that might question their place in communications as somebody that perhaps tends to be that bit more reserved. If there's a chance to highlight to them that although we are all different, there's room for them to succeed, I'd like to take it.

One of the key characteristics when defining introverted people is that they prefer to unwind and recharge by themselves rather than by socializing. That says very little for the way they can contribute professionally, to me. The term according to Dictionary.com, introduced by Jung, describes a person 'whose motivations and actions are directed inward'; people that tend to be 'preoccupied with their own thoughts and feelings and minimizing contact with others'.

You can see how a career in PR, especially the PR that people believe exists as a result of aforementioned glamorization, might be thought to be a bad choice for introverts. Having worked directly with teams big and small, my personal experience is that the room divides somewhat neatly into the two camps – and companies are all the better for it. A third of the population are introverts, according to former corporate lawyer-turned-author Susan Cain, whose 2012 book *In Quiet: The Power of Introverts in a World That Can't Stop Talking* argues that modern Western culture misunderstands and undervalues the traits and capabilities of introverted people, leading to 'a colossal waste of talent, energy, and happiness'.

Traits introverts bring to the table

In researching this topic, I found a 2015 Reddit thread from a small PR agency owner, who admitted that the networking side of the business was a struggle. Calling out to other Redditors in the /r/PublicRelations subreddit, the original poster sought to find people of a similar mindset. 'I enjoy engaging in conversations with small groups of people, and that's how I've always approached media relations – as a conversation', the anonymous poster said. Given a large part of consumer PR, in my experience, is still in and around media relations, working well within a small group or in conversation with one journalist at a time is essential. The opportunities to swan around a packed client party air-kissing strangers with nice teeth are few and far between – a lot of our time is spent on the ground... well, in the office, emailing, using social networks and on the phone.

This brings me to a point a couple of my friends in the industry mentioned before I set out to write this – that not all PR people do media relations. Some haven't pitched a story or client to a journalist, producer or influencer for years, if ever. This is because, as I've otherwise touched on, public relations is more about reaching the right audience to achieve the intended client goal – through the best available channels – than it is specifically focused on the media. The media is one channel in a sea of a few. Coming up with, creating and communicating about clients (or, if in-house, the business you work for) using social media is commonplace and might well suit people that prefer to be in their own company. If managing the social media accounts and/or the creation of content for clients or your employer, you might struggle if you're the kind of person that can't go an hour without a chat.

Here are a handful of traits so-called introverts might tend to display, and how these might help those who process things more internally bring real value to an organization:

1 Listening: One of the most common traits associated with being introverted is an ability to listen more than you speak. That obviously isn't to say that I and my fellow loudmouths refuse to listen, but simply that our tendency towards talking can be a drawback. Introverts might catch something a client or journalist says, or a throwaway idea in a meeting, and run with it.

2 Creativity: I've often found introverts are much less likely to voice ideas, although they might be holding on to an excellent one. We all had that one kid in school that never talked to anybody but drew brilliantly vivid and imaginative scenes, or could photo-realistically reproduce celebrity faces – this kind of talent exists in silent people all around us. Creativity obviously isn't exclusive to introverts, but the manager that recognizes it in the person hiding at the back of the room will undoubtedly benefit. Though of fewer words, of the teams I've managed, there have been individuals who make those words count.

3 Work ethic: As the saying goes, hard work beats talent when talent doesn't work hard, and by being satisfied with or seeking self-approval as opposed to craving it in external validation, introverts can make great and fastidious workers. Success is best achieved with a combination of personalities, and without worker bees selflessly putting in the hours for the hive, we won't get there as quickly or efficiently.

4 Don't seek the limelight: If you've worked in a PR team for even a short length of time, you'll have been in a creative meeting. It's in these you are able to identify the extroverts within a couple of minutes – because there'll be those that dominate proceedings. Ideas aren't necessarily better because they're shouted out excitedly, but that doesn't stop us. I've lost count of the number of times where I've had an ideas meeting, only for a quieter member of the team to email an idea over when we're back at our desks that blows everything else out of the water. This obviously isn't to say – again, giant generalizations be here – that introverts don't enjoy external validation, but that they won't derail a meeting simply to be seen as contributing.

5 Can work alone: Contrasting with the apparent feeling of security in numbers among big city PRs, not every agency or business can afford a large PR team or department. I've come to know the sole PR manager for a successful and well-regarded online business we'd all otherwise assume had a large team, and she's proof that introverts can take the reins and simply get things done without constant approval. We spend a good deal of our time writing in PR, be it press releases, media pitches, new business proposals, messages to clients and stake-holders or social media posts, meaning there'll be silent periods. I often find myself apologizing for these and trying to rush to a point where we're all talking again, whereas a more introverted person might appreciate the space to think. Self-confessed introvert Andrew Pelesh expanded on this in a 2015 News Generation article he wrote entitled 'Introverts in PR: An Unexpected Success Story'. Pelesh called small talk 'a distraction' that can provide stress relief but is some-thing introverts shy away from. He said this is 'why [introverts] are good at getting to the point. In the era of scrolling newsfeeds and 140-character limits, capturing attention and saying a whole lot with only a few words is more critical than ever.'

This chapter was always going to be something of a short and punchy one, but hopefully I've touched on the reasons why the misconception only gregarious professionals can succeed is untrue.

As an industry, we take pride in every day being different – in a multi-tude of talents being important. This is exactly why we should welcome people from all backgrounds, of all personality types, to the table. From a cool and collected response to crises – when clients might be otherwise losing their heads, to preparing pitch documents quickly and accurately in the face of competition, there are a myriad of circumstances in which being the bullishly outgoing person doesn't necessarily work in your favour or indeed works against it.

There's a place in PR for everybody. Don't let anybody tell you any different.

Further reading

Fisher, C, 2015. The introvert's guide to working in communications. *PR Daily*, 2 January. Available at: <http://www.prdaily.com/Main/Articles/The_introverts_guide_to_working_in_communications_17014.aspx> [Accessed 3 September 2016]

Pelesh, A, 2015. Introverts in PR: an unexpected success story. *News Generation*, 20 March. Available at: <http://www.newsgeneration.com/2015/03/20/introverts-in-pr/> [Accessed 3 September 2016]

Priestley, J, 2015. Opinion – Why introverts make great PROs. *PRmoment.com*, 1 June. Available at: <http://www.prmoment.com/3064/why-introverts-make-great-pr-people.aspx> [Accessed 3 September 2016]

PR Daily, 2012. 'PR is all about party planning' – and other misconceptions. *PR Daily*, 27 December. Available at: <http://www.prdaily.com/Main/Articles/PR_is_all_about_party_planningand_other_misconcept_11791.aspx> [Accessed 3 September 2016]

/r/PublicRelations, 2015. Do you have to be an extrovert to succeed in PR? *Reddit*, 9 February. Available at: <https://www.reddit.com/r/PublicRelations/comments/2vcoyv/do_you_have_to_be_an_extrovert_to_succeed_in_pr> [Accessed 3 September 2016]

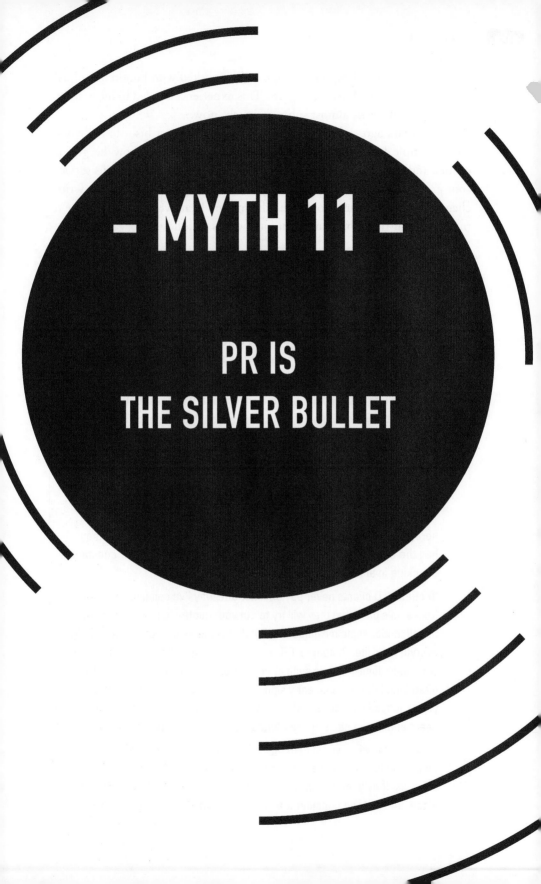

- MYTH 11 -

PR IS
THE SILVER BULLET

As I've touched on elsewhere, I've probably worked with hundreds of businesses and individuals over the years. This experience has led to me banding clients in a few ways, almost subconsciously, now.

A few years ago, a friend of mine was talking about his job. He works with multiple businesses at any given time. He told me how he groups clients, and how that literal structure has helped him to improve his service, spot potential issues and also to steer clear of nightmare clients. He writes client names into columns on a whiteboard and he moves them from time to time. His four-tiered banding technique works as follows:

'A clients': these are the ones you want. They pay on time, without a fuss. They trust in your abilities and respect your methods. They listen to reason, don't tend to micromanage, and understand the importance of flexibility – ultimately appreciating that, although we're not technically a part of their business, we care about achieving their aims.

'B clients': much like As, but with a few differences. They might be a few days late with payment, or they might query the cost before paying. They trust in your capability, but will question your methods until they've got used to them. Most people tend to be B clients.

'C clients': Cs rarely, if ever, pay on time. When questioned, it'll be for an inexplicable reason – or, sometimes, they will try to hold payment like it's a reward rather than compensation for time spent or being spent. They barely trust you and, though I could be entirely wide of the mark here, I feel like they think they could be doing a better job 'if only they had the time'. They want to be updated at every turn and their constant checking in and rigidity tends to hamper progress.

'D clients': D clients never pay on time. One way I've come to spot Ds from a mile off is that they will try to cut your quoted fee by a margin from the off, under some misguided notion that successful people negotiate for everything in life. Of course, PR is a service industry based on the selling of people's time – and as such, there's often wiggle room. However, I've often found this to be an early sign of a disrespectful person – that what you've judged your skills and time to be worth, no doubt in line with your peers and on the basis of experience and ability, is worth little.

D clients will never sign things off, or water them down to the point there'll be little in the way of success. Then, if and when there's little success, they'll forget that you advised against the changes in the first place, and instead consider it a failing of yours. They'll want to know absolutely everything, absolutely all of the time, micromanaging in between the seemingly daily progress calls. In the end, they'll blame your lack of effort/creativity/knowledge/insert other unfair assessment here and sack you off, with overdue invoices, in all probability. If this sounds familiar, you've either had to suffer at the hands of one of these clients, or are one of these people, in which case, you probably won't like what I have to say.

There's a reason I highlighted my friend's grouping method (which I've subconsciously adopted) – and it ties into this chapter's misconception nicely. Some people come to PR agencies under the assumption that PR is the silver bullet. What I mean by that is, it's the shot that will propel their business or themselves to dizzying heights of fame and popularity – and if that doesn't happen, it's because the agency wasn't quite good enough. The problem is never closer to home.

I don't know how well the saying 'you can't polish a turd' will resonate with international readers, but it certainly stands up within PR. A nicer way to expand on this is to say that PR is brilliant at shining a light on things – magnifying what makes a business or individual good in its many ways. Conversely, though, you can 'roll [said turd] in glitter' – with creative ideas that tend to draw focus away from an underperforming client, but no matter what you do, quite often it will still always be a turd.

'C' and 'D' clients tend to come to PR with higher expectations than their friendlier cousins. I don't feel it a cop-out to suggest that a business's products or service, or an individual's talent, drive and/or personality, need to actually be worth the reputational support PR offers. I've worked with more than a handful of clients that came to PR way too early, didn't have a particularly good business or the talent to succeed in my humble opinion, or placed an undue emphasis on their business's success married to our efforts. These clients tend to be one-man band/bootstrapped types. There's nothing wrong with being frugal, especially if you're a start-up and have a limited amount of investor money or your own savings tied up in your success, but hired help like PR agencies tend to be put in a position whereby you're asked to wear multiple hats. 'You don't mind helping me out with this, do you?' they might say early on – and though that 'this' could have little to do with PR, helping once then becomes the beginning of the end.

Another type of prospective client that comes along and immediately slots into the bottom two types is the fame-seeker. Usually, this person has been so ineffaceably entranced by the Siren-lure of celebrity that the fact that they have no marketable talent or skills is little more than a nuisance they try to gloss over. They seem to Google 'personal PR' or 'celebrity PR' and ask questions later, assuming the only thing stopping them from red carpet invitations is a publicist of some stripes, preferably one that doesn't much enjoy being paid. I've said it a number of times before, most PRs of average ability can help you become famous – depending on your measure – if you like, but it won't necessarily be for the right reasons, be particularly enduring nor maybe even for reasons you like. In fact, it could be by entirely exaggerating or even manufacturing a personality. Again, it's unlikely this'll work out well in the long term.

The telltale signs of a silver bullet seeker

I talked in the chapter 'PR can't be measured' about the importance of monitoring outcomes such as back links, search engine performance improvements and sales where possible. Highlighting our experience and belief in measuring more than simply output (like press coverage, or a tweet from a celebrity) has undoubtedly won us business. It's usually music to the ears of every margin-conscious client because, despite decades of industry measurement talk, it is still a rarity. There's a downside to it and a post-credit crunch shift to return-on-investment-focused supplier relationships, though. The issue comes when that client clings to this, and moves from these metrics being 'good-to-knows' to metrics by which you are absolutely and sometimes prematurely judged. I'd probably be one of these people if I was client or boardroom-side, too. 'You can measure enquiries in as a direct result, you say? Well, in that case we want X enquiries per month, or to be page one, number one by the end of the first three months.' If you don't add the caveat early on that PR isn't direct sales – that we can only push people to the door and convince to an extent before an automated or personal sales process has to take over – you're in for trouble.

I had a client when freelancing that, very quickly, made it known they'd only picked me instead of the others pitching because of my keenness on measuring the outcomes of our press office and creative work. I can actually recall the moment, two weeks in and having just learnt about my friend's banding method, that I said to a friend that I'd place this client in the A banding. It was going that well. Not many reside there, as you'd imagine. One short month later and they were undoubtedly a D client for exactly this silver bullet reason. Previously approved ideas, creative campaigns that were excitedly received initially, started to get vetoed. This was a foreboding sign of things to come – if only I'd seen it. They had high expectations of PR and, after delivering a shedload of early coverage and placing significant emphasis on blogger relations, they'd started to see a good increase in the number of sign-ups (I'm keeping this purposefully vague).

We sat down for a chat at the six-week mark and it was decided that, despite the purchases and newsletter subscribers as a direct and provable result of our work, the sign-ups in particular just weren't the right *kind* of sign-ups. Just not of the right calibre, I was told. It must be the messaging that's not working – 'yep, that's it'. Some of the press mentions didn't highlight supposedly key information (because journalists aren't there to shill but find and report newsworthiness) and I was even asked to go back and ask for a couple of journalists to edit the online pieces despite there being nothing fundamentally wrong with their interpretation of the client. Of course, I didn't – stating instead that if you wish to exactly control the message, you can pay for advertising, which is less trusted than editorial and for a comparable spread a damn sight more expensive than my retained fee. A bit deflated, I puffed out my cheeks and went back to the drawing board, not quite sure where to start.

In the time I was taking to formulate something of a change of direction, despite doing everything I'd said we'd do from the off, an email dropped into my inbox: 'This isn't working.' Of course, you're only getting to hear one side of this, but I immediately translated that to 'this isn't working in exactly the way we thought it would and we're not sure why not – so we're going to save ourselves some money while we look at why this is'. Putting aside the fact that it was incredibly early to be deciding a committed-to service wasn't working, it boiled down to one thing for me – they thought PR was the thing that would propel their brand-new business to start-up stardom, rather than looking at the reasons within their own offering that the 'right' people weren't signing up. It appeared to me to be a case of being incredibly selective, which isn't necessarily a negative thing, but also that their process might be off-putting for the people they were after. I just can't imagine an early-stage Twitter blaming the process by which they gained new users for people failing to sign in for a second time after first registering.

I couldn't have anticipated this itchy-trigger finger response based on early communication with the then-potential client, but after getting to know them, and even appreciating their anxieties, I came to terms with the fact that I could have done little to please them. In hindsight, my fault was much more likely in failing to address expectations effectively early on. After all, you never want to start with what could be perceived to be a negative, especially when we're pitching against others, but in retrospect, you have to find a way to be candid.

Losing clients isn't an area you hear much about, despite my experience being that this is a ruthlessly competitive industry, where clients have about as much loyalty as Fredo did to the Corleones in the end. The coming and going of clients is an ever-present, especially as their budgets and priorities change. There are some client relationships that just work – both sides get what they want and you evolve together. I know of agencies who've kept the same clients for decades. Equally, as in my above example, there are some that just don't. In my first agencies, I took client loss incredibly personally – something that's hard to get away from when you care about the job you do for somebody.

Losing clients stings all the more when you know it's because they mistakenly assumed that PR was the puzzle piece they'd been searching high and low for, yet don't have the self-awareness to consider that they might need to be adaptable, too. As time's gone on, I've started to spot these earlier by way of a gut feeling, but as the latter half of the chapter is testament to, it isn't easy. The only thing I can suggest is that you communicate the benefits of PR as best you can, as clearly as you can and, although it feels counter-productive, highlight potential areas of conflict as early as they arise, even if that's in the pitch stage.

Examples of business success and the role PR played

PR is rarely anything other than a slow burn. Canadian comedian Eddie Cantor could have been adding a slide to a potential client proposal when he said 'it takes years to become an overnight success', but of course, nobody wants to hear this and instead fancies you as a money-grabbing chancer if you dare highlight the probability of an awful lot of ground work. It takes time to define a message, craft it, disseminate it, listen or pay attention to feedback and begin to influence opinion through whichever channels provide a route to your audience.

One of the first clients I ever worked on was MyVoucherCodes.co.uk, a discount website. Its young founder, Mark Pearson, sold it in 2014 for £55m, having started it eight years earlier in late 2006 with just a few hundred pounds in his bedroom. MVC fell into that rare bracket of just clicking with the media and public almost straight away. I say almost, because although I came to it a year or so after it'd launched, when it was already turning over six figures every month through affiliate marketing, I would still be asked questions about the legality of using online discount vouchers (or coupons, depending on where you're from). Journalists would still need convincing that brands were in on this, simply using discount marketing as a way to find new customers in an economic downturn where customer loyalty was second to their ability to save money. Mark and MyVoucherCodes.co.uk had a rare confluence of factors in its favour – a ruthlessly driven founder, a sunny recession in which to make hay by 'helping millions save millions' and a genuinely beneficial, top-of-its-game service for users. We used to take pride in telling people that the site did no marketing other than PR and SEO (which PR fed into through link-building, anyway), but it's clear that though our work was an aspect of its success, and though it was as overnight a success as I've seen, to say PR was a silver bullet would be disingenuous.

Contrastingly, and a year or so later, we started working with the now-omnipresent online delivery service Just-Eat, an account we handled for a few years. Given its prominence now – as the sponsor of prime-time TV shows in the UK, with its logo splashed on every takeaway shop's frontage and on TV and transport ads – you could be forgiven for thinking it used to be anything but. When we started working on it, it had a few hundred restaurants at most across the UK to choose from. Journalists, and this was a point at which the media was still really the only game in town if you wanted to reach the biggest potential audience without forking (pun possibly intended) out on ads, had questions and concerns. Firstly, a few hundred restaurants were hardly enough to excite national journalists, especially given the spread was concentrated in mostly big cities, as you'd imagine. Secondly, and similarly to MVC, there was resistance to the new digital order of things. I can recall phone conversations and lunches with journalists that started with the question 'Why wouldn't you just pick up the phone as we always have done [to order a takeaway]?'.

Just-Eat is a behemoth now, having amassed at least $88.99 million in investment according to Crunchbase, with one round undisclosed, so that total figure is likely to be much higher. It has acquired nine businesses in its bid to expand internationally. As mentioned previously, it's hard to believe that I still have access to a Facebook group – not a page, a group – we moderated, and incredible to look back and see just how far things have progressed from a social media marketing perspective. At its peak, I think that group had something like a few hundred followers, and though the group is now 'secret', meaning only administrators can still see it, it appeared to be a real proving ground, with now-defunct tactics being used, tab testing, early-stage influencer relations evident and competitions that fell foul of Facebook's constantly evolving guidelines (before it switched back to 'like/comment/share to enter' as an approved tactic, again). Though Just-Eat used multiple marketing tactics and in fact switched its strategy up while we were working with them and after the first round of investment, I truly believe our efforts broke down the doors in terms of educating the press and, through them, the public and other restaurants in terms of the benefits and reasons you'd use the site (and later, the app).

My point in highlighting those two clients is as follows. One was as close to an overnight success in brand-terms as it's possible to be, but it still required a huge amount of effort, education and perseverance to make even a great service shine. The other is an example of a truly disruptive brand, for which success was hard-fought but now incredibly fruitful – 2015's revenue was £247.6 million. Both were market leaders because they created (or at the very least, popularized) the markets, and should stand as evidence to any start-up that to expect to be competing with industry giants or leading a field within a couple of months is as unlikely as it is hopeful.

Good PR can amplify a good business or a talented individual. That's where it is at its best. It can do the same for bad ones too, but neither side can kid themselves – you're only ever really papering over the cracks, and in either case, success is never immediate nor a straight line.

Further reading

Just-Eat. Crunchbase. Available at: <https://www.crunchbase.com/organization/just-eat#/entity> [Accessed 3 September 2016]

Just-Eat, 2016. *Just Eat plc: Annual Report & Accounts 2015.* [pdf] Available at: <http://je-ict-live-corpsite-assets-eu-west-1.s3.amazonaws.com/wp-content/uploads/2016/03/JUST-EAT-ARA-201516.pdf> [Accessed 3 September 2016]

- MYTH 12 -

GOOD PEOPLE AND PRODUCTS MARKET THEMSELVES

'Finally. Glad to see the media starting to take notice.'

That's a direct message one of my clients received after a BBC News inter-view early on in my career – and it annoyed me for days. I've often seen and heard similar since. In that sentiment, there's an assumption that undoes the hard work of everybody involved. It's an assumption that good will out – that all talented people and good businesses need to do is exist and success, fame, fortune, awards and adulation follow. It's rare, but occasionally clients come to us with the same assumption and attitude of self-importance. We're just there to press a button of some sort, after which their days of being unknown will be behind them.

Al Ries is a marketing and branding strategist and a best-selling author. Beginning his career in advertising at General Electric straight after gradu-ating from university in 1950, Ries went on to co-found ad agency Ries Cappiello Colwell in New York in 1963, which later evolved into marketing strategy firm Trout & Ries. In 1994, he co-founded Ries & Ries with his daughter Laura Ries. That's more than 60 years in advertising and brand strategy.

Ries wrote in industry title 'Ad Age' (2014), saying he believes that most chief executives are driven by the conviction that 'the better product always wins in the marketplace' and that 'marketing, and especially advertising, is an ego-building, waste of money', the budgets for which they approve because they might look 'foolish' if they didn't. Ries tells of a conversation from his GE days, when the head of the transformer department waved a pencil at him and some colleagues and said 'I can get more business with this pencil than you can get with all your advertising this year'. Of course, that was more than half a century ago and attitudes to marketing have changed, but I've seen evidence of this as recently as last week when a prospective client baulked at our fees, saying that once they'd launched they'd get by on the 'free' press they'd 'inevitably' get.

When people say a product sells itself, they mean that customers or users will flock to it without the use of advertising, PR, direct marketing, SEO, branding and all other marketing. That it really is good enough to break through the noise and push to be the best product in class by virtue of being there.

The interesting aspect of this misconception is the evidence that says otherwise, for brands big and small. For instance, Nike – the industry leader in sportswear and apparel – spent $3.3 billion on what it defines as 'demand creation' in its fiscal 2016 results, citing investment in direct-to-customer marketing, brand events and sports marketing. That spend was up 2 per cent on the year before. Revenues for NIKE, Inc. rose 6 per cent to $32.4 billion, up 12 per cent, meaning Nike spend $1 on marketing (demand creation) for every $9 earned. That's an incredible commitment to marketing what you might have otherwise assumed to be a brand that needn't sell itself.

To provide context, Adidas (2015 revenue of €16.915 billion – approximately $18.7 billion at the current exchange rate) spent €2.34 billion ($2.59 billion) on marketing – a comparatively higher spend as a percentage of sales.

Apologies for the flurry of figures, but they're important. A good few more coming up.

Looking at another global beast of a brand, fast food restaurant chain McDonald's made $25.4 billion in 2015. It spent $832.5 million on marketing in that same year, making its budget about 3 per cent of revenue. So, although McDonald's invests less in marketing than Nike on both an actual and comparative scale, according to restaurant industry research by Kantar Media research (Bhasin, 2012), $1 out of every $6 spent on restaurant advertising in America was done by McDonald's. Marketing spend isn't as affected by revenue as it is the market in which a business has to stand out and, given McDonald's already outspends, outnumbers and out-earns every other fast food restaurant chain in the world, it is clear that the business does what it needs to do to stay top, both in terms of figures and staying front of mind.

Coca-Cola had sales of $44.2 billion in 2015, with a marketing spend of $4 billion (Statista, 2016). Like Nike, the revenue to marketing spend ratio is around ten to one.

Those are three offline brands, adjusting to an increasingly digital post-recession world of bargain hunters. For as much real estate as the companies own and as likely as you are to see their logos while out and about, it makes sense that they might need to spend to stay front of mind. But, what about online leaders?

Well, Amazon, the biggest internet company by revenue – an astonishing $107 billion in 2015 (more than $30 billion more than second-placed Google) – spent more on marketing in the final quarter of 2015 than McDonald's spent in the entire year. In the final three months, leading up to 31 December, Amazon spent £1.75 billion. That's double McDonald's annual spend, for a brand that you might assume needn't market itself.

You could be forgiven for thinking a digital company like Facebook wouldn't need to market itself too, given its ubiquity and the viral way in which it should and does spread. But even Facebook, with a 2015 revenue of $17.93 billion, was supported by a $772 million marketing spend according to its fourth quarter and full year results.

These brands are all front-of-mind sector leaders. But does that make their products and services any better? Is Nike really better than Adidas? Is McDonald's better than KFC, or Subway, or any of the other fast food brands? Is Coca-Cola any more deserving of the top spot than Pepsi? It's obviously subjective, but I'd argue that while being sector leaders might have once been a result of quality, competitive pricing, innovation or some type of early-stage advantage, spending to ensure prominence is the only way to stay at or near to the top.

Where does this myth come from?

'If you build it, they will come' is a phrase most of us will have heard. I'm pretty sure I first heard it uttered by Kevin Costner's character in the movie *Field of Dreams*. In a business sense, it implies that the creation of something will be enough to draw a crowd. It ties in to the hopes of every business owner, that their product or service is so uniquely brilliant that, just by existing, it will find an audience and/or user/customer base.

As the internet has changed the way we shop, socialize and spend leisure time, this phrase couldn't be farther from the truth. 'If you just build it, good luck finding it anywhere other than page 12 of Google' is more apt. Spending little on marketing is a badge of honour for entrepreneurs. It says 'we're so great, we don't need to market ourselves'. In fact, and as touched on in the chapter 'PR is a silver bullet', we used to say exactly this in award entries for discount client MyVoucherCodes.co.uk, in a bid to make the company sound more impressive. 'With no proactive marketing spend other than on PR and in-house SEO, MyVoucherCodes.co.uk has managed to build...' It worked, and founder Mark Pearson cleaned up at many an award night. People are impressed by companies that seemingly explode and succeed without looking like they tried. It's like Usain Bolt's famously relaxed sprint finishes – it's all the more impressive because of the lack of apparent effort.

But, what we contributed to in doing that, and what many others otherwise forget, is that marketing doesn't begin or end with advertising and PR. In a world where a relatively small percentage understand the mechanics of public relations, it's understandable that the wider definition of marketing might get confused, too. Everything from referral programmes, branding, pricing in relation to rivals, customer surveying, discounts, competitions, customer emailing and even a quick message to friends and family to say 'hey, my business is live!' is marketing, even if it isn't immediately obvious that it is.

Newer businesses don't have the money or inclination to spend sums like McDonald's and Amazon do on marketing, and, as such, look for ways to reach a larger audience for less. It's entirely understandable and as a business owner, or individual in the early stages of your chosen area, you should absolutely look to save money in every way you can. Some of the marketing tactics I just mentioned can cost nothing up-front – and I think that's where the misconception that good products market themselves comes from. There are ways to circumvent paying for marketing, but show me a business owner that says they've never marketed their products or services and I'll show you a liar.

The internet has given people this incredible way to find and connect with audiences like never before, as discussed at length in the chapter 'You have to pay to see social media benefits'. We have this free pathway to fans, customers and users, should we want to take advantage. People are quick to forget that anything they do to proactively highlight themselves, their product or their service is marketing. The name a business chooses: marketing. The second a social media account is set up – that's marketing. I could go on.

The public as the product

Free products and services have exploded in popularity with investors and the public alike. From early-stage web services like Hotmail, WinZip and Napster to businesses like Skype, Spotify and Dropbox, free usage has led to a raft of household name brands. Millions of people will use these products every day yet have never paid a penny for their entry-level offering. In each case, these businesses have built a user base of advocates. People who'll use and spread word of these services by way of their design or usefulness. These services often appeal to a mass market, and by virtue of being free or at least offering a passably usable free service that will undoubtedly hector you to pay or upgrade at some stage, they pass under the radar of the public's cynicism. It is shadow capitalism – the digital equivalent of a drug dealer or (perhaps more likely, thinking about it), a supermarket worker offering a sample – keen to hook you on the product. In every successful case, the business has done an incredibly good job of creating something we all either need – for example, increased cloud storage – or want to use in an ever-developing bid to improve or streamline our lives.

People look at brands like Skype, and at social networks like Twitter and Facebook, and forget that just because they've never put their hand in their pocket to pay for them, they're businesses. At the risk of sounding all conspiracy theorist, if we're not paying for it, somebody else is, and we are obviously the product for advertisers that otherwise want our eyeballs, ears and attention. Businesses creating a product or service that its users will publicly promote on their behalf are at an immediate and obvious advantage. These public-as-product type companies lead us to the misconception, particularly among people spurred on by multibillion-pound valuations, that these brands have succeeded in the most unique of ways: without marketing. This, of course, couldn't be further from the truth. While it isn't a dead cert that a free-to-use service, site or application will succeed, the barriers to it are significantly lowered when compared to products you have to pay for from the outset.

Growth hacking

If a product or service looks like it's marketing itself, chances are it's been built in such a way that its users have been instrumental in its growth. This can be through referral tactics, subscription upgrades, discounts and many other strategies.

One of the pre-eminent marketing strategies used by early-stage digital brands is 'Growth Hacking'. It's a term often thrown around by entrepreneurial types with names like Theo. In the words of marketer and entrepreneur Sean Ellis, the person that coined it in 2010, 'a growth hacker is a person whose true north is growth'. Allow me to translate.

Growth hacking is a process by which business owners, engineers – as in, developers – and marketers experiment with ideas, quickly throwing ones that don't work out and building on ones that do. It doesn't just apply to marketing – it applies to the way that business is developed from the ground up, and at the core of the business are its users or customers. The idea is to find the best way to grow the business and, as hard a time as I and others like to give it, isn't a bad concept at all. It's a kind of meeting of worlds, where a coder can instil user and promotion-friendly aspects into the product or service itself.

Far from the sometimes painful process of marketing what's in front of you, business owners that subscribe to growth hacking principles tend to be people that will work with you and listen to your thoughts with relation to the core product or service. You might have ideas as to how fixing certain aspects will aid in your job of marketing it better and a receptive client or employer will consider options, filtering the good and the bad. It's rare, for reasons I appreciate, that a client or employer is this open, but when they are, it usually makes for a good relationship. Think of growth hacking like taking the time to build and rebuild a great snowman rather than just wrapping a Versace scarf around a shoddily constructed snowman's neck. To beat this ugly metaphor to death, growth hacking is a process that will then continue to look at the finely built (and dressed) snowman, looking for ways to still improve it.

Hotmail launched as the first free webmail service in 1996, and used a tactic now widely considered to be the first true example of growth hacking, despite the fact that the term wouldn't be introduced for another 14 years. After allegedly considering expensive traditional advertising options, founders Sabeer Bhatia and Jack Smith wrote one line that would change their fortunes: '*P.S.: I love you. Get your free email at Hotmail*'.

This message was at the bottom of every message sent from a Hotmail user, serving as an early form of signature that linked through to a simple sign-up page. Every sent email served to ask as promotion for the fledgling service. Within six months, Hotmail had gained more than 1 million members. A year after launching, in December 1997, Microsoft bought Hotmail. The simple yet successful decision to include that one line led to huge growth, with nearly 10 million people using the service by the time it sold for an enormous $400 million.

I feel almost ridiculous highlighting this as an example following such a shining and successful example, but I tried to use similar thinking with a business I co-created with my first agency boss, Andy Barr. Bloggabase.com is a searchable database of bloggers. In the same way Gorkana and other media databases are used to search for journalist information, we wanted bloggabase.com to provide a way for brands and marketers to connect with bloggers. The fact that bloggers were opted-in to hear from marketers was essential – and meant each blogger telling us a bit about themselves. At that stage, we were able to extract social media information and keep a tally of profile per cent completeness. The final stage to complete a blogger profile and achieve 100 per cent was to share that they'd signed up on social media. Simple psychology, perhaps – we're all prone to wanting to 'complete' things. This became by a long way our most effective method of blogger recruitment, and highlighted the service to brands and marketers nicely, too.

The founder of former sports nutrition client Myprotein.com attributed much of his and the business's early success to the referral programme. The scheme, which still appears to be popular today, gave every new customer a code they could share, entitling them and the secondary user a discount and points towards discounts, respectively. The business, started by Oliver Cookson in a lock-up using a £500 overdraft, sold in 2011 – seven years after launching – in a reported £58 million deal.

I wanted to touch on growth hacking as it uses often-invisible tactics many would otherwise ignore as marketing methods, which only adds to the myth of the products that market themselves. I'm by no means an expert though, and would suggest further reading of *Growth Hacker Marketing* by Ryan Holiday and quicksprout.com's 'Definitive Guide to Growth Hacking'.

To conclude, marketing is such an all-encompassing area that, the second a business owner considers the way their product(s) and/or service will be thought of, they're doing it. Of course, it never ends there. Friends and family will be told. Logos will be designed and colours will be decided on, based on the effect the creator hopes to achieve. Websites and social media profiles will be set up and 'about' sections will be pondered over for hours. Messages intended to provoke specific reactions will be agreed on far from the eyes of their eventual audience. Media and partnership lists will be compiled. Journalists will be contacted and… OK, you get the picture. As American graphic designer Alex Isley is quoted as having said, 'it takes a lot of effort to make things look effortless', but in doing so, we disguise our true value.

Further reading

Bhasin, K, 2012. This one statistic shows just how much McDonald's tries to entrench itself in everybody's minds. *Business Insider*, 14 March. Available at: <http://www.businessinsider.com/this-one-statistic-shows-how-much-mcdonalds-tries-to-entrench-itself-in-everybodys-minds-2012-3?IR=T> [Accessed 3 September 2016]

Facebook, 2016. *Facebook reports fourth quarter and full year 2015 results.* Available at: <https://investor.fb.com/investor-news/press-release-details/2016/Facebook-Reports-Fourth-Quarter-and-Full-Year-2015-Results/default.aspx> [Accessed 3 September 2016]

Nike, 2016. *Nike, Inc. reports fiscal 2016 fourth quarter and full year results.* Available at: <http://news.nike.com/news/nike-inc-reports-fiscal-2016-fourth-quarter-and-full-year-results> [Accessed 3 September 2016]

Ries, A, 2014. The better product always wins – and other marketing myths. *Advertising Age*, 27 January. Available at: <http://adage.com/article/al-ries/product-wins-marketing-myths/291305/> [Accessed 3 September 2016]

SEC.gov, 2016. Amazon.com announces fourth quarter sales up 22% to $35.7 billion. *SEC.gov*, 28 January. Available at: <https://www.sec.gov/Archives/edgar/data/1018724/000101872416000170/amzn-20151231xex991.htm> [Accessed 3 September 2016]

Statista, 2016. *The Coca-Cola Company's net operating revenues worldwide from 2007 to 2015 (in billion U.S. dollars)*. Available at: <http://www.statista.com/statistics/233371/net-operating-revenues-of-the-coca-cola-company-worldwide> [Accessed 3 September 2016]

Figure 7.1 – List of people and production-cost indicators

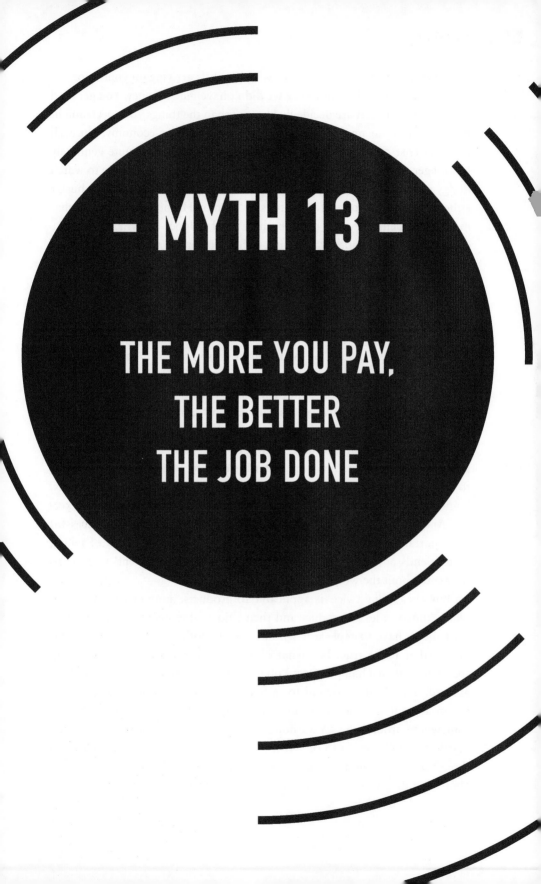

- MYTH 13 -

THE MORE YOU PAY, THE BETTER THE JOB DONE

Growing up in a house of five kids, where bailiffs arriving on your doorstep wasn't uncommon, it's fair to say we didn't have much money. You get used to owning items that are decidedly cheaper than the things your peers might have. Early on in my life, I realized the truth of false economy. Duracell batteries cost more, and do you know why? Because they quite genuinely last longer than a pack of twenty from the Pound Shop. Attempting to watch dodgy movies filmed at the cinema is no way to watch the latest blockbuster either. Oh, and not to mention bottles of 'Tommy Hil-finger' aftershave that made you smell like you'd had a bath in paint stripper (or whichever 'close enough' name the trader was hoping to fool customers with).

I felt like the worst and most ungrateful kid, conscious of the value attributed to everything we didn't have. At the risk of this becoming unnecessarily confessional, I grew up incredibly conscious of the phrase 'buy cheap, buy twice'.

It's natural for us to assume that the more money you spend on something, the better quality that something is. Luxury brands promote this ideal – products and services out of the financial grasp of many, made only more desirable as a result. We all assume a Ferrari is better built than a Ford Escort. Due to that assumption, their relative rarity and the exclusive club buying one seemingly gives you an invitation to, many are willing to buy one before they've even seen one in real life, let alone driven one.

It's certainly not an absolute truth, but it tends to be the case that the more you pay for something, the better the quality. Many factors contribute to this, including better workmanship, better design and better components. Sometimes though, it can simply be a case of better, shinier, louder marketing. And people spend more to make themselves feel better, more successful or important. I've come across people that clearly like the idea of telling their friends and family that they need to 'call their PR agent' more than they care about the work done, to a point.

'Buy cheap, buy twice' is applicable to products, more or less. Anybody who's known a lesser product and then enjoyed the finer equivalent, or at least didn't have to replace it within days, is both more appreciative and knows that to be true. But what about services? Can you really justify spending £40 on a haircut when Bob in his mobile hair caravan does, you're assured, 'a perfectly good cut for a fiver'? I've always thought about pricing in a 'by hour' way. The minimum wage when I was a child hovered somewhere around the £5 an hour mark, so even now, when I go to the hairdresser and spend £15 on a trim, I think about the fact that was at least three hours work for my mum when cleaning. You tend to be more cautious about spending when you consider things like that.

Fast-forward to starting a PR career: the fees you can command in this industry blew me away at first. I couldn't equate the relative 'by hour' cost fast enough, especially when I consider the agencies that won't so much as speak to a potential client for less than £5,000 a month. It's only as I learnt more about business that I understood just how different things are for people and businesses that don't see money in the way one who's had little might.

Services are a different kettle of fish, in my mind. Where a product might cost £X to make, therefore with labour and a margin to make it costs £Y to buy, services tend to rely less on the tools with which to do the job once initially bought, and more on the cost of the labour itself. Why can two different hairdressers with a decent pair of scissors each charge vastly different prices? Their experience is a big factor, of course, but perception is another – and sometimes, perception trumps everything. The aforementioned Bob, with his beer breath and his waiting line of Jeremy Kyle guest look-a-likes is unlikely to be able to charge quite as much as the pretentiously zen Philippe, with his soft shade salon and concoction of choking aromas – even if Bob is by miles the more experienced and adept. Maybe Bob's happy that way, but the fact that he'd be able to charge the same with direction and a few well-placed changes shows that, more than paying for a service, you occasionally pay far more for the prestige and experience.

Here's where, as a book aimed at tackling PR misconceptions, I want to bring it back to the industry and, more specifically, PR agencies.

I am told the eighties and nineties were flush times for public relations, advertising and marketing as a whole. I've spoken about these allegedly heady days with people that worked through them and the phrase 'champagne and cocaine in the boardroom' was quite genuinely mentioned on two different occasions by two different agency heads, who shall remain nameless. I'm pretty sure one of them was using it to describe the culture more than actual habits – and the other… well. It was a time when journalists had the time to be wined and dined, and the much-muttered 'we have a great relationship with X journalist' line most likely meant more than 'we've spoken on the phone a couple of times and well, she didn't shout at me, so yeah, we have a great relationship'.

These relationships were once worth something to clients. Now, these apparently halcyon days gone by, I'm not so sure. The assumption that paying more gets you a better service, especially in the service world of PR, affected as it is by the uncertain media industry, has never been more contestable.

Big city agencies

A number of factors have led us to a point where PR has become more regionally disparate than ever before. That's not to say that London doesn't still rule the roost in terms of fee income – it does; with just 15 agencies outside of London among the top 100 PR agencies, and only three in the top 50 (Suleman, 2016). It's that I genuinely believe those agencies have had such a head start that we won't see the penetration of those upper echelons by agencies outside the capital for some time yet. I can't speak for the United States, or big cities elsewhere around the globe, but times are changing, and clients, in a post-recession, ROI-conscious business landscape, care less about the name above the door or the swanky office than they once might have. There are a few areas we should look at.

Meeting with the media and clients

You could have made a valid claim even as recently as 2010 that being in a bigger city made meeting with journalists, producers and other influencers easier. You could have said that being in a bigger city, where the majority of clients with the majority of the money might have once been, made sitting down with them and doing business simpler. I don't believe you can make the claims anymore. There'll be people reading that disagree already, but one unarguable point is that, as the bottom continues to fall out of traditional publishing and ever-more cuts are made at outlets, the people we'd have once wined and dined just don't have the time for out-of-office meetings. It's difficult to so much as find the time for a coffee with journalists, or a quick chat at their desk these days.

It's still important, and you should still try to get face-time with them and, ideally, your clients would come too, but there's a marked difference in the ease with which you'll get a 'yes' now versus half a decade ago, especially with the nationals. As for press launches, a ye olde tactic that is insisted upon often by Steve Jobs fanatics, I can count on one hand the number of actual press launches I've worked on in the last five years. There's almost no need now outside of huge company announcements, and, as sad as it is to say, there are better things we can all be doing with our time. A few years ago, I was working on the invitation list for a swanky mid-afternoon affair, at an even swankier location, to announce the launch of a big-name client's new line. My colleagues and I had a guest allocation target, and were barely even a third of the way to filling it, deflated by 'sorry, I just can't make the time' responses. So, we started calling journalist friends in other sectors, considering ways we could both twist the release to fit for their audience and get some bums on seats. It helped a bit, having journalists we either knew well or that perhaps owed us a favour, but speaking to one, he said it had got to the stage that press events were decided on by the potential haul the journalists would be walking away from it with. In short – would they be getting much or any of what the client was releasing? And if so, that would much more easily sway the decision.

Press aside, the time you might be able to spend face-to-face with your clients could determine whether or not they chose you even a few years ago. At my first agency, 10 Yetis, where I worked between 2008 and 2013, a recurring question during pitches was 'How do you think being based outside of London affects you?' with the inference being that we might be at a disadvantage. We were able to answer with many of the points I'm making now, and had a good pitch win rate. My agency now is based outside of London and I haven't heard this question once in the last year, at least, despite the fact that 95 per cent of our clients are there. When a two hour drive or train is all that separates you from clients, and you can be in their office for 9 am, or Skyping them at any time, they care much less. I'm a people person, and absolutely love meeting, but technology has brought us together well enough that I've never even met some of my clients face-to-face, but can still have a great working relationship. In fact, we pitched over FaceTime to one, who answered from his beautiful house in Spain wearing only a towel. As disconcerting as that was at first – it's difficult to know where to look – the ease with which we can connect to clients and their intended audience, whether through the press or otherwise, means you can start a PR agency with little more than a phone and laptop.

Office costs

PR is a service business. We sell our time, and much like in my example of Bob versus Philippe, the variables are things like experience and perception. As much as we'd like to be able to prove otherwise, we all do much the same thing, but with varying degrees of creativity and success, dependent on the people in the business. When you're only as good as your last story, the agency world can be a cut-throat, loyalty-devoid way to make a living, as clients are ever-keener to shop around and make savings.

Does 'buy cheap, buy twice' relate to services, when the difference in price can be attributable to the difference in office space cost in a big city compared to the cost of working even 30 miles outside? I was speaking to one London-headquartered agency founder recently, who told me that a recent annual rent increase of three times meant they had to make 'hundreds of thousands more' a year just to stay in business there. Let's say a retained client is worth £60,000 a year to an agency, or £5,000 a month, which is on the higher side of average – that's at least a few of those before you're even paying staff or so much as turning a profit. That example sounds high, but using the online 'Find an Office London Calculator' I was able to find that even for a 10-desk short-term office, it was estimated that you'd have to spend between £49,000 in Waterloo and £99,000 in St James'. That doesn't include co-working spaces, the like of which become difficult to manage as a team grows. Staff figures per agency varied throughout 2015 in the UK, according to the annual PRWeek Top 150 (ordered by revenue), from 474 at top-placed Edelman to 9 at 148th-placed Field Consulting. London agencies charge more because they have to, whereas, to give a comparison, my office space in Gloucester is more like four figures a year, with room for 10 employees.

I'm conscious this is starting to sound like a pitch, but I'm stating facts – service costs are higher where the price to deliver that service is higher. And it's up to the client to work out just how worthwhile that cost is. More than assuming that I'm saying all clients should immediately throw their budget the way of agencies outside of big cities, I'm saying that change is afoot thanks in large part to technology and the constant inflation of big city real estate – and it'd be churlish to ignore it. In my experience, there's a snobbishness among London PRs about agencies not based there, but regional agencies are vying for the same pie that keeps them fed and increasingly capable of eating it, too.

Staff experience

Experience is often a deciding factor for clients. In proposals sent every day, you'll find examples, some shoe-horned in, some perfectly relevant, aimed at showing just why an agency is the perfect fit. It's common to lean on previous client work in the same sector, or an ancillary one. Specific people and teams within agencies are put onto client enquiries that fit with their experience.

In the interest of balance, there's a point well worth making about bigger city agencies. It's a fact that the talent pool outside of them is shallower, both by virtue of population and migration to them for work. Merely mention the fact that you're recruiting at a London agency, especially at an entry level, and a swathe of CVs arrive in your inbox, each hungrier than the last for an opportunity, fighting for your attention. Do the same outside and... well, that really isn't the case. It's not that you can't find staff keen to get into the industry – it's that the more experienced roles you recruit for, the fewer the choices.

Working in the same region as perhaps a dozen other comparable competitors at most, you get to know the people in the space pretty quickly. Where loyalty is hard to find in a more competitive big city job market, talent is harder to find elsewhere. As one would imagine, it appears to be consistent with population – the ease with which you can find staff with the experience and ability you need to deliver great work for clients gets harder the smaller the city. Manchester will have richer pickings than Bristol, which in turn is more bountiful than Gloucester (which, contrary to the geographical estimates of my former London colleagues, isn't 'up north'). To combat this regional recruitment issue, many have tried to turn to technology, working flexibly with out-of-office freelancers. This won't make me popular but, outside of one example, that hasn't worked for me; I much prefer having staff in-office.

There's an elephant in the room when it comes to agencies, especially the bigger ones – and that's interns. Unpaid ones. Clients are rarely aware that their story is being sold in not by the experienced team that pitched to them and they ultimately decided to go with, but by an eager young PR-in-the-making, who might be being paid travel, if they're lucky. Journalists, however, are acutely aware given they're the ones on the receiving end of said pitches. Everybody has to learn, but as Dom Burch, Why Social founder and former senior director of marketing innovation and new revenue at Asda said in a 2016 Drum article, unpaid interns 'are still common practice across the UK public relations, advertising and marketing sector', despite the fact that he presumed they'd died out years ago. 'In spite of being bad for business, and as I understand it, in breach of HMRC rules, many so-called employers still take advantage of grads looking for their first proper job', Burch embellished.

Unpaid interns exist because companies can get away with it and because people are desperate to get into the industry. They make agencies look bigger, do the work others often don't want to do – data work and the ring-around, for instance – and offset the cost of the expensive office, bumping up the margin. Googling 'internship PR agency London', I was met with an Indeed job page result. Looking at the 10 most recent agency ads, just three of them mentioned that they were paid, with another three highlighting the fact that travel and/or lunch was paid for. The other four didn't mention financial compensation of any kind. In line with this and as quoted in Burch's article, Sarah Stimson, former recruiter turned career coach, the founder of the Taylor Bennett Foundation and the creator of the PR Careers website said, 'Three agencies in the PRWeek Top 150 offered unpaid roles when I researched the market in January 2016. But a quick internet search will turn up numerous ads for unpaid roles.' She pointed to four that she was able to find immediately. This isn't to say that agencies and companies outside of big cities don't offer unpaid internships – they do. It's that those agencies are more easily able to get away with it on account of the increased interest in taking that first step on the ladder.

Unpaid internships hurt the industry. Senior and virtue-signalling heads will publicly decry the lack of diversity in the industry, while allowing their agency to take on young adults only able to work for nothing because their parents have the money to enable it. I think that, had I been born in or close to a bigger city, there's a good chance I wouldn't be working in PR today – I just wouldn't have been able to afford to.

Freelance and one-man band agencies

Self-employed professionals exist as a perfect alternative for companies looking for experts in specific areas and/or a lesser rate. Freelancers tend to be highly experienced individuals and, to entirely generalize, they are often ex-big city PRs looking for a better work-life balance. Ben Matthews, a freelance digital consultant and director at digital agency Montfort said that by going it alone, it meant he didn't 'have to do the 9–5 or the rat race and can theoretically work where and when [he] wants'. He also pointed out that many consider freelancing because 'you're good enough and you want the lifestyle it brings'.

I was freelance for a short period of time, but always knew I wanted to start my own agency and, as such, the second I had client workload enough to share it between other freelancers, I set about creating it. While solo though, the simpler things like being able to walk my kids to school far outweighed the stress of having to be your own boss, finding work and dealing with your own accounts. Having done it, I have the greatest respect for the tens of thousands of freelance PRs out there and would encourage all businesses looking for support to consider them. There are times when a client might prefer a team, but if looking for a flexible and sensible approach to public relations, there are many networks and ways to find them, not least Facebook groups dedicated to them where briefs can be advertised and specific people can be recommended by real people.

What can you expect to pay?

I've spent an entire chapter talking about paying for public relations, and not said much about how much it actually costs. In fact, I feel like it's something of a secret – an unspoken-of range that often wastes an awful lot of time, as business owners fish around for the answer, often courting agencies and freelancers with no intention of spending unless the price is rock-bottom. Besides incredibly rare cases, you won't find pricing on agency websites, because we don't want you to think there's a set price. As I mentioned before, PR is a service based on the selling of time, predominantly. The cost for our time then, between certain extremes, is inherently flexible. There is nearly always room for negotiation. While certain briefs do require far more time and effort, incurring a higher fee, it's a fact – the bigger the potential client, the shinier their shoes, the nicer the car they drive, the higher the price agencies will pitch in at.

This won't be definitive, but I'm going to go into typical pricing structures.

Agency

In 2014, *The Guardian* ranked public relations directors as the sixth-best paid professionals in the UK based on statistics released by the Office of National Statistics, with an average salary before tax said to be £77,619. Similar articles regularly rank marketers highly. With such high potential salaries – though very few people in agencies besides director-level types and up will be earning more than that figure – it's clear that client costs can be high.

There are a handful of options when working with agencies, from retainers, hourly rates (more commonly used during crisis communication work), project-based fees and, less commonly seen, payment-by-results. There are also often handling charges for disbursements, whatever the chosen relationship. These disbursements are usually invoiced for based on fees the agency might incur in servicing the account, from postage, third-party services necessary to service the account, and paid media spend. It's a way to reclaim those costs.

To keep things simple, it's best to explain that the majority of agencies work to a day rate. Smaller, boutique and often regionally based agencies – though not necessarily regional in terms of client rosters – can charge anything from £1,000 – £4,000 per month (more like $2,000 – $5,000 in the United States, according to 2014 analysis by media database Mustr) for a retained service.

Retained contracts mean that clients are typically tied in for a minimum or ongoing period. Retainers ensure that clients receive certain services during the contractual time, charged based on the estimated time taken to deliver the agreed services. As mentioned, I know of mid-sized London-based agencies that barely take client enquiries seriously for anything less than £5,000 per month, and larger ones will charge much more.

A 2013 Observer.com article highlights the approximate range of six US-based PR agencies, though I'll only highlight the extremes. According to Lloyd P Trufelman, founder and president of Trylon SMR, their average retainer costs $7,500 per month, ranging from $5,000 – $12,000. The $5,000 figure is the lowest mentioned by all six. Anne Green, president and CEO of CooperKatz & Company, Inc said 'to properly scope a client program and assign the proper team support, we feel $15,000 – $17,500 per month is a reasonable starting point'. Former Edelman CEO Mark Hass was quoted as saying that some clients paid '$100,000 or so per year, some pay us more than $100,000 per week and many clients pay us $100,000 or so per month'.

The cost of project-based relationships are harder to estimate, but they tend to be requested by clients interested in PR support for launches of particular services, products, events and campaigns. I've personally worked on projects ranging in budget between £800 for a simple release and £200,000 for an all-singing, all-dancing big brand campaign; the actual agency fee of which was around 20 per cent.

Freelancers

Ben Matthews, who also sells a seven-day email course on going freelance, wrote a brilliant guide to self-employed PR in the UK.

His guide, written in 2013, is targeted at professionals considering going freelance, but by co-opting it, it's easy enough to simplify and demonstrate the affordability in comparison. He recommends freelancers to start off with the salary last earned – and add a third to it. 'This is to account for the fact that you are doing your own HR, finance, sales, marketing, IT, office costs and anything else that normally is taken care of for you in a company.'

In England and Wales there are 252 working days in the year, assuming a five-day work week. Matthews then suggests freelancers subtract 20 working days from that figure, accounting for time off for holidays, sick days and quiet days.

In his incredibly useful example, if a freelancer previously earned £30k in their job – a salary that likely means they have a good few years of experience behind them – adding a third on equals £40k. Dividing £40k by 222 days equals just over £180 – which would become your day rate. With VAT added to this (20 per cent in the UK), £180 becomes £216.

Freelance prices vary widely dependent on their level of expertise and also the level of support and/or consultancy needed. I don't mind telling you that my freelance rate was higher than this. It also depends, of course, on the amount of time a professional might spend per month on an individual client; but three or four days a month coming in under £1,000, inclusive of VAT, is great value. It's incredibly rare to find an agency manned with staff and bogged down by overheads that will take clients on for the same or less.

In conclusion...

As with a more expensive product, you can really only go on personal experience and the learned opinions of others to make a decision as to whether or not paying more for a service like PR is worth it. Unfortunately, reviews don't really come into it in the same way with services – with awards and revenue rankings really the only external validators, perhaps besides asking for other client referrals. Of course, when going into a working relationship, you can also listen to that gut feeling of it being a good fit, helped by the agency's likely evidenced assertion that they're the right one for you.

When paying for an agency, the variables are: the time spent on an account; the actual services delivered, such as media relations, link-building, social media management etc; and both the number and seniority of the people assigned to the account. If working with a full-service agency, it's likely that a retained client will be handled by no fewer than two or three people, and rarely more than 10. Agencies typically split into teams by either number or expertise, so a 'team' could be 5 to 10 people that work on similar accounts, or split by experts within said agency. You can pay £3,000 for a smaller agency, or £20,000 per month, and this would still likely be true. Clients just need to weigh up whether the agency or individual can do the job for them in a way that either comes in within their budget, in a way that provides a return on investment, or ticks any other number of goal-focused boxes.

If I was a client, knowing what I know about the industry, I'd seriously question whether or not I needed to spend hundreds of thousands of pounds a year with such a talented, if fragmented, pool of experienced potential suppliers to choose from. Gone, hopefully, are the days where a big company or famous individual selects an agency based on the name above its door.

Further reading

Burch, D, 2016. Stop the slave internships still commonplace in communications. *The Drum*, 27 April. Available at: <http://www.thedrum.com/opinion/2016/04/27/stop-slave-internships-still-commonplace-communications> [Accessed 3 September 2016]

Ferguson, D, 2014. What are the highest paid jobs of 2014? *The Guardian*, 28 November. Available at: <https://www.theguardian.com/money/2014/nov/28/highest-paid-jobs-2014> [Accessed 3 September 2016]

Matthews, B, 2013. How to become a freelance consultant. *Ben Matthews*, 18 March. Available at: <https://benrmatthews.com/freelance-consultant/> [Accessed 3 September 2016]

Neale, B, 2011. *London office space and cost calculator*. Available at: <https://www.findalondonoffice.co.uk/toolbox/office-space-calculator/> [Accessed 3 September 2016]

Peltea, A, 2014. Show me the money – PR agency pricing structure fundamentals. *Mustr*. Available at: <http://getmustr.com/blog/show-money-pr-agency-pricing-structure-fundamentals-2/>]Accessed 3 September 2016]

Ryan, Ó, 2013. How much PR costs. *Observer*, 8 October. Available at: <http://observer.com/2013/10/how-much-pr-costs/> [Accessed 3 September 2016]

Suleman, K, 2016. PRWeek reveals the top 150 UK PR consultancies in 2016. *PRWeek*, 3 May. Available at: <http://www.prweek.com/article/1393421/prweek-reveals-top-150-uk-pr-consultancies-2016> [Accessed 3 September 2016]

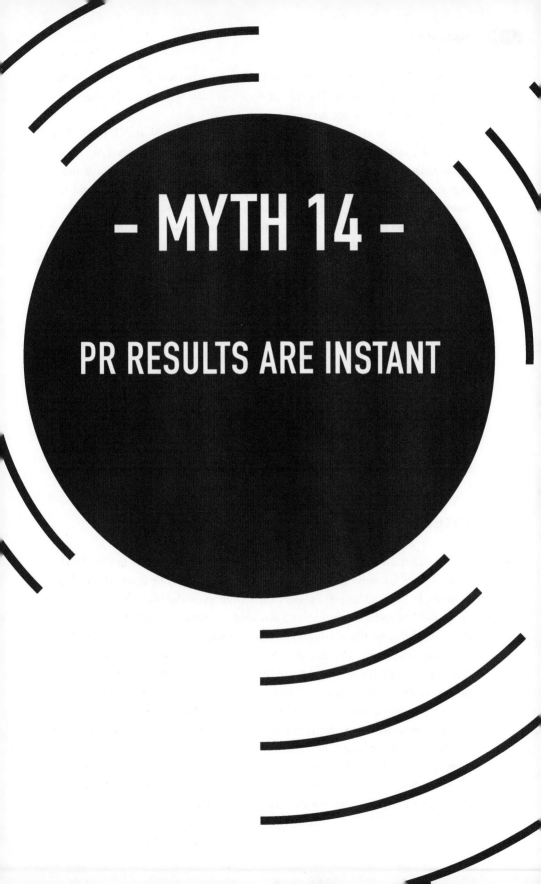

- MYTH 14 -

PR RESULTS ARE INSTANT

The ink on the contract has just dried. The team that will be working on the account has been briefed. The first invoice has been sent and... the client has already chased to ask for an update.

PR success is dependent on many different factors and I think I've laboured the point that media coverage in itself is not success, but more often than not, that's what it comes back to still. Unless they have prior experience with an agency or freelancer, clients tend not to understand the workings of the media well enough to know the process of achieving coverage, much less the work that goes into positioning them to achieve it in the first place.

This misconception is an unspoken one, but it's quickly evident when a client believes that all they need do is pay your invoice and results will come flooding in, because you'll be hearing from them day and night. Any PR person that's been day-to-day on a client before will have had one of these 'I want results yesterday'-type clients. These clients – and they come in all forms, from young entrepreneurs to hard-nosed big brand marketing directors – can quite literally make your professional and personal life a misery. Any initial enthusiasm on both sides goes out of the window, replaced instead by repeated soul-crushing status calls and terse exchanges.

I think it stems from three things – insecurity, poorly established expectations and ascribing the immediate and visible effects of other forms of marketing to PR.

Insecurity

This is often an issue with the company an agency or individual might be working for, far more than it is a problem with any work done or not done at an early point. There are clients for whom even the lower end of the fee range understandably represents a sizeable investment, which instantly puts those working on the account at a disadvantage unless they can come out swinging. The most insecure clients I've worked with have been the ones that, as touched on in the chapter 'PR is a silver bullet', stuff money into public relations in the hope it'll solve everything for them.

I once worked with a new business this was absolutely true of and the funniest thing was, they didn't even hide it. As soon as the highly scrutinized contract was signed, and the much-contested first invoice was paid, we were then and only then told that PR was expected to help sell a minimum of X of what they sold. Worse still, this client then went on to say that, unless this expectation was met, they'd have to not only pull out, but the business would fail, too, inferring that it would be pointless to chase damages because there'd be no business from which to retrieve them. It was a short-lived relationship and still one of few that I've ever suggested we walked away from. A week or so after our last exchange, I saw a tweet from an agency saying how excited they were to start work with said client. A friend that knows people at that agency quickly relayed to me how the situation had gone exactly as it had with us.

This insecurity doesn't always stem from the size of the investment for the client. Sometimes it's seemingly pressure the client is feeling from above or, in some cases, it's possible that it's the point of contact feeling out of their depth, which can lead to incredibly unreasonable demands. Third party suppliers are an easy scapegoat, so if things aren't going well in a business, it's always preferable to look at the people externally as the cause of or, at least, not the instant solution to the problem they once appeared to be.

Establishing expectations

The second factor leading to near-instant dissatisfaction is that of likely and reasonable expectations not being set and maintained. It could be the excitement of winning the client, consciousness of competitors or that you don't want to appear to be negative at the outset, but promising the world, or simply failing to walk the client through likely results, kills the relationship.

I couldn't begin to tell you how many times I've had client enquiries where a business or individual wants to 'give PR a go' for a month or two. To 'test the water', to gauge the results and see that it's delivering the returns the client would deem necessary for it to be worth carrying on with.

At times, and in part due to my own financial security as a freelancer and later, agency owner, I've said yes to clients like these. In the case of clients that would or should otherwise be retained, it rarely goes well. They've quite literally told you from the outset that PR has to deliver immediately, and that if it doesn't they won't be sticking around. One-off projects and the stunt-ier end of PR campaigns like this are fine, where perhaps there's a new product, service or update to announce, but going about the business of communicating with said client's target audience in a way that's in any way beneficial within a month is a tough gig. The only way to ensure both parties' sanity is to discuss, from the outset, likely results and how long it'll take to achieve them. This depends on a number of things of course, from the simplicity with which the client can be explained to the sector they operate within. If the brief is to educate potential customers on the merits of buying a new metal plating machine to improve corrosion resistance (NB: this is literally the dullest thing I could think of, and it took me long enough), then it's incredibly unlikely you'll succeed half as quickly as the PR person working on a sex toy designed by David Attenborough (that bit didn't take me nearly as long).

The problem is worsened when clients heap pressure on the connection between PR as a service and sales, or a definite return on investment. Of course, you hope that your work does lead to sales (which can be proven, as discussed when I previously wrote about measurement), but it's not a given, and certainly not before the second invoice is due, which is the time this particular type of client tends to get a bit jumpy.

With experience and, quite bluntly, a bit more money in the bank, I've started being as up-front as I can be. I will happily tell a potential client the truth – that even with one-off projects there's always a short period at the beginning where it doesn't feel like we're doing much at all – but this is where the groundwork is laid. It sounds hackneyed to put too much emphasis on the development of the right tone for messaging, and dilatory to suggest we need to spend more time speaking to journalists before we'll see results, but it's very often the case.

I'm confident we've lost out on potential clients to agencies that otherwise told them that results were assured, or worse still, guaranteed, but I try not to worry much about those now. As soon as an enquiring person asks how quickly we think we can get results, and if they don't appear too pleased with the response 'as soon as we're able to', I'm now OK with the fact that they might well go elsewhere. A month or two's stressed invoicing and chasing of payment just isn't worth the time you spend defending yourself. Anybody with a bit of industry experience will have had that feeling of dread before an update call, knowing your time would definitely be better spent actually working to the end you're about to be chewed out for not yet achieving.

Florida-based PR professional Margie Zable Fisher wrote a piece for Silicon Valley-based author, speaker and marketer Guy Kawasaki's website back in 2007, entitled 'The Top Ten Reasons Why PR Doesn't Work'. In it, she agrees, saying that 'PR folks need to better educate [clients] about how publicity works'. So, not just what PR can do, but the actual process by which we can achieve results. Zable Fisher says that when a client asks 'Can you get me on Oprah or the front page of *The Wall Street Journal*?' the answer might well be yes, 'but the process to get to the yes may take months or years, and may first include a series of smaller placements'. Nearly a decade on, and we're still talking about exactly the same issue.

Factors affecting PR results

Another aspect affecting expectations is that goals are often arbitrary, given the uncertain nature of what we do and the aforementioned issue with promising results. 'We expect X pieces of coverage' is an incredibly difficult target to agree to, but if you don't, you risk unsettling a new client, or failing to win a potential one.

The media agenda

At the time of writing, we've just had the EU referendum results, which were followed by the resignation of David Cameron and a short-lived leadership battle, an attempted leadership coup within the Labour party, an attempted governmental coup in Turkey, numerous high profile police shootings, Donald Trump's Republican candidacy and a shockingly regular series of terrorist attacks around the world, all spanning just a month or so. National journalists have been harder to get hold of and in front of than ever before, which has had a knock-on effect in terms of national pick-up for clients. A couple of weeks in, after a few stories had been ignored in favour of the craziest period of news I can remember, we decided that we'd have to find a way around it, and, as such, had to come up with story and feature ideas that didn't rely on those journalists, or the media full-stop. If we'd have contractually committed to a set goal or goals, there's little chance we or any other agency would have hit them this last month.

You just can't plan for this kind of media agenda. All you can do is use the time you're being paid for to do everything you can to achieve the agreed-upon client aims and communicate this all the while.

Time-strapped journalists

Tactics like content creation, content marketing, influencer engagement, social media communications and link building are becoming commonplace in PR, where our job might once have been solely media relations-focused. This is an important professional correction, not necessarily noticed by every agency out there, in the face of a rapidly changing media world.

In the UK, 300 local newspapers have been closed in the past 10 years, according to Press Gazette research (Ponsford, 2015). Before the financial crash of 2008 the Newspaper Society estimated there were 13,000 journalists employed in the regional press but the trade body, now called the

News Media Association, no longer keeps figures. Press Gazette researched Companies House figures kept by individual companies, and found that they suggest that the current total may be half that figure.

The latest employment figures from the Labour Force Survey for the year to June 2015, estimate that 64,000 people in the UK describe themselves as 'journalists, newspaper and periodical editors' (Press Gazette, 2015), compared to 83,000 PR professionals, as estimated by the PRCA's most recent PR Census (Greenslade, 2016).

Magazine launches are slowing – in 2015, 113 magazines launched, compared to 190 magazines in 2014, according to MediaFinder.com, an online database of US and Canadian publications. Magazine apps for tablets and paywalls have been a largely unsuccessful experiment.

Short and long lead publishing

If a client would like to promote a product launch over a short six-week period, that's fine – but they need to know that there'll be coverage (and other outputs) we hope will lead to outcomes many months down the line attributable to work we'll have done on the account.

For instance, and this is something you just wouldn't know unless you worked in and around the media, print publications are loosely split into short lead and long lead titles. Daily newspapers are short lead – their stories are written the day before. Online media is short lead, where news can be and often is published near instantly, as is broadcast news. Some weekly magazines, intent on having up-to-date celebrity 'gossip', are on the shorter lead end of the spectrum too. Conversely, there are longer lead titles. These are the monthlies – magazines like *Men's Health, Glamour, National Geographic* and the like. What the term essentially refers to are the deadlines to which the journalists at the publication work to, in order to have the issue ready to print. Some titles will be working up to five months in advance of publication. That means, if you want your client in front of their readers, you need to plan for it.

I've often heard the phrase Christmas in June (and sometimes, July), referring to PRs having to consider pitching Christmas stories, or clients for the annual Holiday Gift Guides, in the summer. It's absolutely true, and while the print magazine industry continues to die its agonizingly slow death, there are still certain audiences you can best reach through these titles. I would venture an educated guess at long lead PR considerations falling almost entirely by the wayside in the next five years, save for the most niche sectors, but for now, it's still important.

Even when you lay it out for clients – when you tell them that you're going to stagger activity so you contact the longer lead titles first, and the newsier outlets later on in a bid to have the coverage hit at roughly the same time – that initial few weeks can feel like you're doing absolutely nothing. It's happened, on occasion, where a client has been underwhelmed with results and decided to pack their bags, only for previously pitched coverage to land, exactly as originally intimated and do a good job for them. Again, for an industry that makes its money communicating, all we can do is properly communicate likely results, which becomes easier over time.

How long before SEO starts working?

Link building – or link earning as I heard it called the other day (we're all so desperate to be accurately defined, aren't we?) – is a key target for many businesses. Public relations is, as previously mentioned, in a strong position to be able to effectively achieve high authority links. However, the point in achieving these links, whether domain level or deeper into a client's website, is to affect the search engine ordering or prominence of that client. Sometimes with personal PR, we're briefed to help shift unfavourable results down the pecking order. Other times, as in the case of one current client, we're asked to ensure positive search results of *any* kind where an incredibly accomplished individual has otherwise ignored the media for decades and as such is being passed over for potential work as a result of having next to no digital footing.

Although I'm unsure the PR industry is in a position just yet to pitch for full SEO control of brands – I tend to partner up and leave the on-site and more technical aspects to search experts – we should be aware of the algorithmic workings of search engines, given that they're another incredibly important route to audiences we can affect to an incredibly positive degree.

Coverage for clients on well-respected online outlets will almost immediately rank well, so, for instance, a name search will return said article. The time to achieve this differs but can be comparatively quick. This is where pushing negative results down, or even establishing a presence on page one at all, can be helped. Equally, simple tactics like creating exact name public social media profiles tend to be visible fairly quickly.

In the case, though, of client website search engine performance – again something our work affects in a way that actually sends traffic and ideally sales to clients – results aren't as readily visible.

AudienceBloom CEO Jayson DeMers wrote 'the early stages of an SEO [focused] campaign usually require a significant investment with little payoff'.

He went on to say that 'rankings will probably either fail to cross the threshold of the first page, or will only apply to non-competitive, low-traffic keywords. For example, even if you move from position 89 to position 11 in the rankings for your most-prized keyword (a gain of 73 positions in the rankings) you shouldn't expect to see any traffic increase, because the keyword still doesn't rank on page one.

'Conversely, a ranking change from position 11 to position 5 (a gain of six positions in the rankings) would yield about a 5 per cent change in traffic for that keyword. A jump from position five to position two would yield a change of another 5–8 per cent in traffic, and a change from position two to position one would yield another 20–30 per cent jump in traffic for that keyword' (DeMers, 2016).

SEO success depends on a number of factors – ranging from how competitive your market is to the number of links earned. 'Many firms will tell you that it takes four to six months to start seeing results', said Josh Steimle, the CEO of digital marketing agency MWI, adding that 'success by any standard rarely comes within the first 3 months, even with a healthy budget' (Steimle, 2015). This wait is chiefly to do with the time it takes for search engine crawlers to pick up on new links and for that to have any positive effect on site placement. Unfortunately, there's no way to expedite this process, but with clear communication from the outset clients can be forewarned.

The visibility of other marketing disciplines

Another aspect that contributes to an expectation to see instant results within PR is that other marketing tactics, from paid media to direct marketing, are executed visibly. Something either exists in principle, be it an advertisement mock-up, an email template or a proposed leaflet design, or is visible almost immediately, like a pay-per-click ad. In what sounded like a less convoluted sentence in my head, PR suffers from being something that can't be seen until it exists, either in the form of output or audience action. Our contractual obligation to communicate our client's virtues to a relevant audience in a bid to achieve their target goal is really just empty words until its impact can be seen or felt. If working a brief to first survey and then attempt to shape audience opinion, you're going to be waiting a long time potentially until you can prove, usually by means of a follow-up assessment, that your work has made any difference whatsoever.

We've been conditioned to see marketing as a big shiny 'buy one get one free' sign at the supermarket. Every time we drive past a car dealership with a bright bunch of balloons, or spy a Google Ad atop every search we make, we're taking in marketing messages – it's hard to ignore. Buy me, notice me, they scream. PR is often silent and, while this invisibility enables us to manipulate (again, I say this aware of how negative it sounds, but hey ho), it often takes time to achieve – time clients might not be willing to wait.

There's nothing that can be done here or indeed to insure against that dreaded update call when you have little but vague interest beyond the point I've endlessly made – set expectations based on previous experience, under-promise and do what you know to work as well as you can do it. Otherwise, you'll become another in a long list of PR people and agencies spoken of to future suppliers of 'burned' companies as having delivered little beyond a bad experience.

Further reading

DeMers, J, 2016. How long does it take to see SEO results? *Inc.*, 29 February. Available at: <http://www.inc.com/jayson-demers/how-long-does-it-take-to-see-seo-results.html> [Accessed 4 September 2016]

Greenslade, R, 2016. Survey finds that PRs outnumber journalists by large margin. *The Guardian*, 10 June. Available at: <https://www.theguardian.com/media/greenslade/2016/jun/10/survey-finds-that-prs-outnumber-journalists-by-large-margin> [Accessed 4 September 2016]

Kawasaki, G, 2007. *The top ten reasons why PR doesn't work*. Available at: <http://guykawasaki.com/the_top_ten_rea/> [Accessed 4 September 2016]

MediaFinder, 2015. *Magazine launches down in 2015: MediaFinder reports that 113 launch in 2015 compared with 190 in 2014*. Available at: <http://mediafinder.com/public.cfm?page=pressReleases/MEDIFINDERREPORTSTHAT113LAUNCHIN2015COMPAREDWITH190IN2014> [Accessed 4 September 2016]

Ponsford, D, 2015. 6,000 drop in number of UK journalists over two years – but 18, 000 more PRs, labour force survey shows. *Press Gazette*, 9 September. Available at: <http://www.pressgazette.co.uk/6000-drop-number-uk-journalists-over-two-years-18000-more-prs-labour-force-survey-shows/> [Accessed 4 September 2016]

Steimle, J, 2015. How long does SEO take to start working? *Forbes*, 7 February. Available at: <http://www.forbes.com/sites/joshsteimle/2015/02/07/how-long-does-seo-take-to-start-working/#38b306c6ea65> [Accessed 4 September 2016]

Turvill, W, 2015. Johnston press closures mean more than 300 UK local newspapers have gone in last ten years. *Press Gazette*, 8 October. Available at: <http://www.pressgazette.co.uk/johnston-press-closures-mean-more-300-uk-local-newspapers-have-been-closed-ten-years/> [Accessed 4 September 2016]

– MYTH 15 –

CONSUMERS WANT CONVERSATIONS WITH BRANDS

It's hard to pinpoint exactly when it happened, but I think it's safe to say branding styles like Innocent Drinks' popularized this in the mainstream eye.

At some stage around the turn of the millennium, brands began talking to consumers like they were friends, lyrical monologues breaking the fourth wall on packaging of everything from smoothies to vacuum cleaners. 'Hold up there, chap or chappess, and let's have a chinwag about our gluten-free, super-duper yumlicious ingredients, shall we?' they all said, made-up words and portmanteaus crowbarred into every line with the subtlety of a brick to the face. In my mind, they all sound like Dick Van Dyke in Mary Poppins: 'Dearie me, me old mucker, we wouldn't want any of those naughty little chemicatrocities swimming their way down your speaking hole, would we?'

There was a time when it was just endearing enough that they could get away with it. Innocent was often charming, as the originators (or at least, popularizers) of such chummy copy. Know this, me old muckers, we allowed this to happen by emitting enough of a polite giggle that all brands within a 100-mile radius decided it was worth emulating in order to subtract cash from our bank accounts. Since then, social media has given every man, woman and brand a voice – and easier channels through which they can talk to us like five-year-olds, or at least like they have known us since we were five.

The ease with which brands can now communicate with potential and actual customers has led to this strange marketing approach: that of trying to become a friend to customers. It's common for clients to want to approach their social media marketing on this basis now – and because marketers, myself included, advocate a listening approach, that's been misinterpreted by many. There was a time when marketing was all one way 'push' tactics. Essentially, brands talked at us, barking their virtues from giant billboards and up at us from the pages of every paper or magazine we flicked through. Now, of course, we have the opportunity to speak back and, importantly, speak out. For clients, this is mostly brilliant. There are certain biases and strange behaviours at play that I'll discuss, but social media allows us to hear what customers and potential customers think of the people and businesses we work with.

Feedback only previously available through public polling is at our fingertips and happening all around us. Whenever we start working with clients, we filter through what's been said online in relation to them and the industry in which they operate, giving us a more complete picture of what people think, if indeed they think anything yet. It allows consumers a channel through which to somewhat publicly call companies out, as well as providing a valuable customer service route and even more importantly a way for businesses to improve themselves on account of honest feedback they otherwise wouldn't have received. The balance of power has shifted, where a business might have been able to effectively ignore concerns before, weeding people out with convoluted automated phone systems or lengthy letter-writing complaints procedures. In a world where one tweet can undo a company's reputation, clients often need to be vigilant, approachable and responsive. On the face of things, this might sound like a conversation, but it isn't really, at least not in the traditional sense. It's a transactional relationship where, as important as it is for the brand to be helpful, human and friendly with their audience, the public hold all, or at least many, of the cards.

As Matt Rosenberg, a senior vice president of marketing at 140 Proof wrote for Ad Age, 'there's a fine line between being helpful and being overbearing, especially when it comes to the "human" element' of brand communication, rightly pointing out that consumers 'are looking for help with a problem or information' (Rosenberg, 2014). Only the incredibly lonely could ever go looking for a conversation with a brand to pass the time of day, no? After all, every brand has an agenda and, more often than not, that agenda is to make money. It's always more about them than it is about us, something Rosenberg touched on well, having said that businesses can't be 'counted on to care whether I've had a good day, only whether I've inched closer to a purchase. To pretend otherwise is just awkward.' Insincerity in the way a brand conducts itself is painfully clear for all to see.

A brand should want happy customers or users and be glad of or at least receptive to the fact that there are and will now always be these channels through which members of the public can both contact and draw attention to them. What a brand shouldn't do is crave friendship. Loyalty can be engendered, but it'll never be the same loyalty as one might feel to a friend or family member. I think of it as I think of being a parent – do I care what my young children think? Absolutely. I want them to be happy and I'll do everything to ensure it. Do I have a desperate need that they see me as a friend, though? Absolutely not. Maybe some time in the future, but not right now. I'd be doing them no favours whatsoever and when I see parents thrusting their friendship on their own kids with statements like 'my son's my best friend' or 'we're always being mistaken for sisters!' I cringe. This is an odd and potentially controversial equivalence, I'll grant you, considering customers obviously aren't equal to our own kids, but the basis is similar. Neither need us to be their friends and we should all stop pretending that they do.

The problems with social media 'conversations'

Continuing on with my very own friend-making mission, I'll say it: people on the internet are very often idiots. They – well, we – will say stupid things for a myriad of ridiculous reasons and our behaviour online is very often different to the way we might act off it. In the same way that brands use schoolmate language and faux-intimacy but couldn't really care less about the conversation, members of the public don't much care for exchanges with brands that aren't on their terms either. Perhaps, rightly so. After all, a brand's reputation only exists, in the words of Stephen Waddington, 'as a result of the relationship between an organisation and its publics, typically customers... where any difference between our expectation of a brand and its behaviour will lead to a conversation on the social web' (Waddington, 2014).

This level of transparency and unparalleled access is incredible – and I mean that in a great, world-changing and a less positive 'Christ, we've given the chimp a pair of scissors' way. With the benefit of experience, my entire PR career having played out thus far while we as a society have worked out the ways in which social media can inform, alter and improve our experience as consumers, I've seen both sides first hand. The notion that consumers might want to have an objective discussion with brands is overshadowed by people that, after a lifetime of being marketed at, would sooner talk at brands, too. We have this disconnect, where both sides talk but very little is said. I don't believe that it is conversations consumers want, so much as swift resolutions or, at the very least, acknowledgement.

Room 101 is an off-again, on-again BBC television series based on a radio series of the same name. In it, guests are asked to discuss their pet hates, and given the opportunity to persuade the host to consign them to 'Room 101', inspired by the torture room in the George Orwell novel *Nineteen Eighty-Four* which is said to have contained 'the worst thing in the world'. If I was ever asked to appear on the show, dot @ing brands would be one of the first things to go. I'd guess that there's a good chance readers of this book will be among the more-than 300 million Twitter users, in which case, you've probably either done this or seen it done, and it really, really needs to stop. In case you aren't a user, or haven't seen it, 'dot @ing' is where somebody will write a tweet, but by putting a dot – as in, a full stop – at the beginning of the message before the username, ensuring it is visible to all of their followers. This 'hack' is to circumvent the fact that only users that follow both accounts will see tweets starting with another's username, otherwise keeping timelines clear of person-to-person conversations that could clutter up the experience with idle chitchat.

Dot @ing brands is a tactic users have taken to in order to ensure all of their followers see what is, more often than not, a needlessly passive-aggressive complaint. For example, '.@dogfoodmanufacturer, OMG by not even acknowledging cats your discrimination is plain for all to see. For shame. #catlivesmatter'. The aim is to highlight the complaint so that all can see it and the complainant can look morally superior or incredibly put upon, while putting the brand on the back foot. It's not a particularly popular phrase especially among the overwhelmingly liberal Twitter user base, but the term 'virtue signalling' – saying you love or hate something to show off what a nice person you are, instead of actually trying to fix the problem – fits perfectly here. These people do not want a conversation. In instances where dot @s are legitimate gripes, it's often a case of being the dullest, most First World Problem you've heard: '.@retailername, I ordered the superfood hamper and it arrived 20 minutes late with at least 8 per cent less avocado than last time. Disgusted.'

Of course I'm exaggerating for effect and there's an argument that people like me should be nowhere near company customer service channels with this attitude, but watching simpering community managers spend their working life trying to appease and cater to the whims of these eternal moaners is frustrating. Of course, you just get on with it, through gritted teeth and in deference to this new way of the world where, not only does the customer always believe they're right, they get to shout about you to whoever will listen too, rather than try to solve things amicably or let something slide. There are undoubtedly instances where complaints are valid and expedited by nature of being made public, but it seems to me, through my own experience, that a large number of social media messages to brands, across all public channels, are instances of venting far more regularly than they are cases the individual wishes to resolve. Ask any community manager to list the most stressful aspects of their job and this one-way entitlement will rank highly.

A survey by Forrester (Campaign, 2015) involving 3 million people concluded that less than 1 per cent engage regularly with brands online. This statistic is interesting because, not only does it show that it's irregular for consumers to talk to brands, but that the chummy tone taken by companies online is hardly resulting in actual conversation. If screamingly angry complaints are often more irritating than they are warranted – or indeed anything other than a needless expulsion of rage – the commonly colloquial effort by brands to befriend users is not only awkward but quite literally failing to provoke conversation.

Teen speak and 'brandter'

More than 168 brands — from McDonald's to Sprint — contributed to nearly 700 mentions of the terms 'bae' and 'on fleek' between January and November 2015, according to social media analytics firm Brandwatch (Dua, 2015).

If that sentence doesn't make you wince, perhaps you need to delete that scheduled post, immediately.

Burger King's 2014 classic – and I say that advisedly – 'If bae eats your burger, bae is not bae' tweet is exactly the kind of sub-par, lazy reach brands like to make in their bid to say something – anything – to make themselves relevant in the social media echo chamber. Marketing copy that started out in 1999 with Innocent's quaint and friendly tone has somehow evolved into a race to the bottom, with brands competing and seemingly putting in 'a great deal of effort in order to present themselves as a bizarrely "street" teen, when in reality, they are the opposite', as Nick Johnson, founder and CEO of The Incite Group agrees.

I can point to exactly one example of a brand using street speak and other colloquialisms in a funny and relevant way, but as a cursory check of Twitter profile @brandssayingbae will show you, it happens with frightening frequency. The one example, for clarity, was telecoms company O2. In 2012, whoever was running the account deemed a slang-laden tweet by a user called @Tunde24_7 worth replying to in kind. Tunde's advances – where he twice asked if the person managing the account was a 'chick doe' – were ignored, but he did at least receive some sensible advice regarding his mobile data.

Since O2's tweet was heralded in the way marginally funny things often are online, marketers have got steadily more confident in the way they communicate, not just with the public, but with each other. That's right. Buoyed by the success – because retweets and likes equal success, obviously – of O2's and other brands' efforts, fed up with the one-way anger often directed at them and the thousands of tweets sent with nary a reply, those tweeting for brands decided to talk to other people tweeting for brands. If you've never seen it, it's as odd as you can imagine and akin to that one old rambling man in the pub talking to himself finding another old rambling man to chat to. Quite sweet really, until you realize that this is actually a job real people are paid to do. This indictment of it might make me sound joyless, but wait until you hear the term used to define this – 'brandter'. A portmanteau derived from the words brand and banter, defining the act of two corporate accounts engaging in 'banter' on social media. It appears to have started around 2013 and has mostly died down now, but there'll be visible embers for a while yet, I'd wager. As soon as marketers realized that their social media messages made for an easily gained increase in reach and quickly assembled BuzzFeed-style 'you'll never believe what Oreo just did on Twitter!' articles, this odd tactic took hold.

'Brandter' can be as light touch as aftershave brand Old Spice referencing one of Taco Bell's products: 'Why is it that "fire sauce" isn't made with any real fire? Seems like false advertising' and receiving a reply from the fast food chain like '@OldSpice Is your deodorant made with really old spices?' It has been as ridiculous as two mobile phone brands participating in a rap battle, as O2 and Tesco Mobile did, with immortal lines like 'get out of our way, ya holding us back, oh, & your service is Jack' bandied about.

Sometimes it had and can have a bit more bite – as with Nokia's response to Apple's launch of its range of colourful iPhones. In an update that has received more than 36,000 retweets, Nokia's @LumiaUK account shared a photo of their previously released colourful designs, along with the words 'imitation is the best form of flattery' and 'thanks, Apple;)'. Arguably much smarter and more impactful a marketing tactic than a rap battle – instantly highlighting its previously released range to a potentially new audience – but your guess is as good as mine as to whether or not it had an actual business effect.

Having grown up in a world where Sega and Nintendo were arch nemeses, and the hatred between Coca-Cola and Pepsi was palpable, I think I preferred it when, as ex-deputy editor of Econsultancy Christopher Ratcliff said (2014), brands were 'bitter rivals, divided by capitalism, hurling rocks at each other from behind the safety of multimillion-dollar television ad campaigns'. This history makes Xbox's 'congratulations on your launch, Sony' tweet, also in 2013 and as Sony's PlayStation 4 console launched, all the more startling. Hilariously for us – and I say this as a PlayStation guy – this apparently kind approach, which of course was simply a way for Microsoft to ensure they weren't forgotten about in the consumer excitement about the release, forced Sony into the humiliating position of having to do the same thing to much less fanfare just one week later to mark the release of the Xbox One. I'd argue this was less a case of 'brandter' from Microsoft in the first instance and more a realization of the potential for free media.

In short, consumers care so little for conversations with brands that aren't either providing a direct service or solving an issue that we've seen social media managers talking to each other. I'd put money on the fact that it's gone further than that, too – the probability a bored and/or lonely employee took to having a conversation between two brands they managed in a bid for social shares is high.

So... what should brands do?

Given the proviso of this book is to tackle myths and misconceptions in one sewn-together 'a-ha, you see, you're WRONG, I'm RIGHT and here's why!' tome, I'm conscious of just how negative a read it could be. Where my standpoint has to be absolute and contrary, I'd like to offer the explanation that while I don't believe consumers care much (if at all) about conversations with brands in the way marketing directors wish they would, some brands succeed in creating a sense of online community in spite of this, in much the way I discussed in the chapter 'You have to pay to see social media benefits'.

For instance, the people looking after the social media accounts for camera brand GoPro both encourage the submission of and search externally for social media posts they can shine a light on, relying on user-generated content shot using their products as content. There's no pandering – they occasionally talk to the people behind the images and videos but, more often than not, it's to show the product off in a way that's been both validated by that third party and validating for them. This strategy is no doubt far more lucrative and community-building than any updates trying gamely to appear as anything other than financially motivated.

The fact is, consumers don't owe brands anything, and the sooner the transactional nature of marketing and customer service is not only accepted but embraced, the better.

Further reading

Campaign, 2015. *Should brands try to be our friends?* Available at: <http://www.campaignlive.co.uk/article/1351656/brands-try-friends#Sg3q6bW5U3CoJ6Oy.99> [Accessed 4 September 2016]
Dua, T, 2015. 2016 year in preview: brands will stop trying to be millennials' cool friend. *Digiday*, 16 December. Available at: <http://digiday.com/

brands/2016yearinpreview-brands-stahp-youre-totes-embarrassing-me/>
[Accessed 4 September 2016]

Ratcliff, C, 2014. What do we get out of brands interacting with each other on Twitter? *Econsultancy blog*, [blog] 26 March. Available at: <https://econsultancy.com/blog/64595-what-do-we-get-out-of-brands-interacting-with-each-other-on-twitter/> [Accessed 4 September 2016]

Rosenberg, M, 2014. Brands: consumers don't want to be your BFF in social (they want help). *Advertising Age*, 29 August. Available at: <http://adage.com/article/digitalnext/brands-consumers-bff/294726/> [Accessed 4 September 2016]

Waddington, S, 2014. #BrandVandals six months on. *Stephen Waddington blog*, [blog] 25 May. Available at: <http://wadds.co.uk/2014/05/25/brandvandals-months/> [Accessed 4 September 2016]

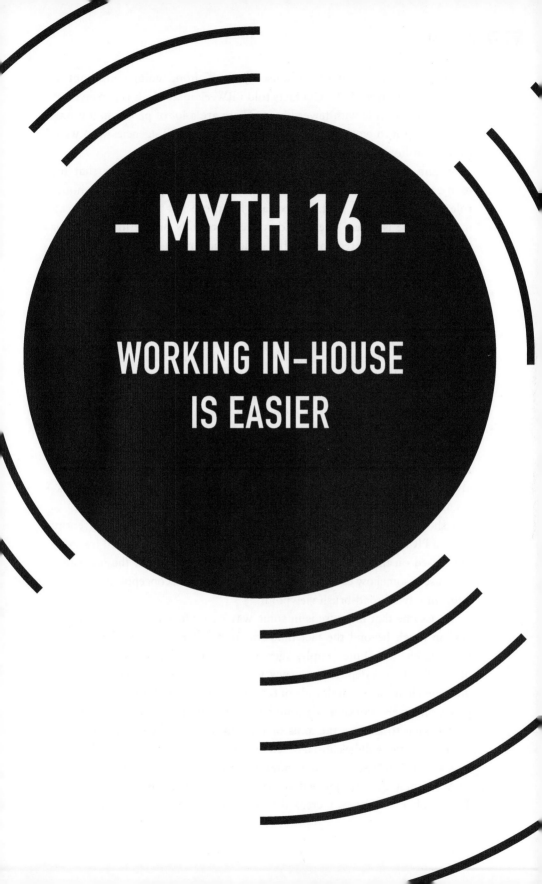

– MYTH 16 –

WORKING IN-HOUSE IS EASIER

'Everybody wants to work in-house,' Julia Walton, senior consultant at recruitment agency Media Contacts told PRWeek in 2011. 'It is perceived as being an easier role with fewer hours. There are a lot of people in journalism who want to work in PR and a lot of people in PR agencies who want to work in-house.'

Within a year or two of working in PR it was clear to me that for many, though perhaps not the 'everybody' Walton referred to, an in-house role was seen as the goal. To explain for those not yet well versed, an in-house role is where one would concentrate fully on the job of PR for their employer, whereas an agency role much more obviously involves multiple clients.

It appeared that PRs would commit to learning the trade in a fast-paced, high pressure and volatile agency environment before going on to refine their skills in a more relaxed in-house role, where perhaps they'd be able to exert their own control over agency suppliers. I'd speak to people working at account manager/account director-ish level at industry events who'd confide they'd been looking around for PR manager/communications director roles and the like, who, after a solid spell in-agency would quite like a different change of pace. The insinuation was always that in-house PR is somewhat easier and something an experienced PR could walk right into. The average staff turnover at PR agencies is around 20 per cent (Barker, 2014), which means one in five people will leave every year. This won't always be to in-house roles, of course, but demonstrates that agency workers are, on the whole, flighty.

I should reiterate the fact that I've never worked in-house. My entire time in PR has been at agencies in various roles, with a short spell freelancing. Based on this, anecdotes and references will show that the myth that in-house is somehow easier is, as with many of the misconceptions I'm tackling, entirely a broad-brush viewpoint.

To assume that in-house is in some way easier fails to take into consideration much beyond the fact that attention is far less divided to service multiple clients. Quite simply, agency versus in-house work is a matter of breadth versus depth. An agency will expose employees to a variety of different clients and a multitude of tactics to achieve the agreed-upon strategies. Conversely, working in a company means employees are focused solely on working to achieve the aims of that business and its products and/or services. Tactics will be chosen based on how applicable they are to the business and how it best hopes to communicate to and with its target audience.

At my first agency, I juggled as many as a dozen clients at any one time. The number sometimes increased or decreased, but more often than not, the relatively flat management structure meant if something was happening with or for one of those businesses, everybody on the account knew about it. At my second agency, it was more like half a dozen, which is commonplace, as I understand it. I also hear of people at the very biggest agencies looking after three or thereabouts, where I imagine they're very much ingrained into the fabric of the clients' business. Whether three or a dozen, you can feel stretched in many different directions a number of times a day, which when viewed from a glass half-full standpoint means no two days are the same – something most PRs would attest to.

The typical day of an agency worker has been well chronicled, and anybody with a cursory interest in PR will likely perceive a role in a consultancy to be a case of split intentions and, perhaps, long hours to achieve them. Conversely, in-house workers are more likely to have a much tighter remit: 'Here's what we're trying to achieve as a company – using PR and wider marketing tactics, what can you do to help?' When your only 'client' is the company in which you work, there's a much greater chance of you being able to see stories in all aspects of the company. Working with agency clients, I'll occasionally highlight that, as a result of being very close to the business, owners and other senior figures tend not to see the PR-able (I know how much that non-word's going to bother language purists) stories around them. A talented in-house person, though, will spot and pull stories from every department, and not just work with the subjects the marketing team assume are the best to push. Equally, and on the flipside, a good in-house professional will work to balance – and, in some cases, hopefully mute – the expectations of a managing director that wants to send a press release out about a website redesign.

Brian Adams (no, not that one) is a consultant for non-profits now working in Hong Kong. After moving away from agency-side PR in 2006, Adams worked in senior communications roles at youth support organization United Way of Massachusetts Bay and Merrimack Valley and animal welfare organization MSPCA-Angell. Adams wrote about the differences he experienced in a Medium post (Adams, 2013) also picked up by PR Daily. One of his points was that 'when you're on-site you realize that your clients are the departments that need your help sharing their stories. The workload is the same, just different; the bonus being that you can poke around.' He added that, for the most part, 'you're there to chronicle daily life'. I think this perfectly explains the more in-depth role one is able to play when embedded in a company. To think of each department as a client is a brilliant analogy, and presumably a great way to avoid tunnel vision attributable to pressure from sales or your marketing boss.

One thing's for sure, and that's that if you're keen to get closer to the machinations of a brand, to fully realize what makes a company tick, you have to work internally. 'In-house executives become brand experts and can dive deep into industry issues and the company's products and services,' Emma Dale, managing director at Prospect Asia said (Cornish, 2011). Carolan Davidge, director of brand and PR at Cancer Research UK in 2011, agrees, saying that 'one needs to completely understand the organisation, what it stands for and its people too' as an in-house professional, adding that 'teams can be quite small, so people are often expected to turn their hands to a wide variety of things', which might also include wider marketing and event management. There's also internal communications that might get thrown the way of the in-house PR – something I'm conscious is almost entirely absent from this book, but on which topic the brilliant Rachel Miller and her website All Things IC are the leading resources.

It might sound exciting to be asked to get involved in all aspects of a business, but if these areas are outside of an individual's core skill set and they're not given the time to learn, the expectation of that person will likely never align with the reality of the situation for the employer and can result in an uncomfortable time for the employee or team. The modern PR professional is expected to be versed in ever-more areas of marketing and it takes an educated and/or determined person to keep him or herself up to date.

Why do people think in-house is easier?

This misconception really is a case where I think we can invoke *Friends*' 'it was different' defence in the case of Rachel versus Ross (and his assertion that they were, in fact, on a break). It's impossible to give a final answer as to which is easier, one way or the other, but each role asks something different of the people that fill it. The insinuation that internal roles are less demanding stems almost entirely, in my view, from the fact that there are fewer disparate yet demanding voices to appease. There's also the odd habit in-agency where the earlier one clocks in and the later one clocks out somehow indicates the effort one has put into a work day, whereas in an in-house role and as one of few (if not the only) people dealing with the communications side of things, it's unlikely there'll be the pressure for the promotion-hungry to please the big bosses. I've worked in enough other roles at companies before PR came along to know it's uncommon to play this weird clock-watching game in other walks of professional life. These things, though, in and of themselves, are not enough to prove that agency-side professionals have it 'harder'.

Again, I have limited exposure beyond my relationships with and research of in-house communications types, but Chris McCafferty, whose impressive CV lists roles at Myspace and MSN and agency Shine Communications (recently merged with The Academy to form Shine at The Academy) – all before founding his own agency, Kaper – is a more than reliable source of experience. McCafferty said the idea that in-house life is easier is 'nonsense', first highlighting the number of stakeholders one needs to keep happy, highlighting that 'in an agency, you have got the camaraderie, but in-house you can be a lone voice' battling to be heard. This is a great point worth picking up, and something that I can only imagine makes in-house work all the more taxing. With fewer colleagues performing a similar role, there will be fewer people with whom to share the highs and learn from the lows. Mistakes are harder to hide from and success is, in the case of brands that use external agencies, shared at best.

Prospect's Emma Dale believes that recruiting for PR agencies is tougher, as a lot of candidates want in-house roles, and her experience close to but not within the agency and in-house worlds has also shown her that McCafferty's estimation of internal PR being easier is nonsense (Staff Writer, 2014). Many 'feel the grass is greener on the other side, and that an in-house role offers better work/life balance. There is also a belief that there will be less pressure – but I can tell you plenty of in-house practitioners would say this is a myth.'

In the instances where a business might only use internal practitioners, however, there are two other issues – and they relate to budget and the business owner's (or decision-maker's) sensibilities.

Budget is no doubt the toughest to overcome. If there is little in the coffers, you can all but guarantee the marketing arm will see the least of it because, as discussed previously, we're often seen as little more than amplification. I've seen this lead to in-house workers becoming incredibly stressed, as they talk to more or less the same journalists about their company or organization and its products and/or services that don't change all that much. Creativity can be the saviour here, but forced creativity on a tight no-to-low budget can sometimes lead to desperation. Where there isn't the money to afford external support, I've seen in-house professionals issue briefs with no intention of taking a third party on, but as a palette cleansing and refocusing exercise. As an agency owner these are getting easier to spot as I gain experience, with muted responses around the topic of budget and deliverables, and long periods of silence where the 'potential client' is 'discussing' options with a boss you'll never meet or speak to.

With one eye on the money in the bank, services that can help make the job easier will also be scrutinized by those holding the purse strings internally in a way they're often not in-agency, given we can offset the cost by charging back to clients. Fortunately, there are some brilliant free tools out there that I've already touched on in other chapters, and some useful and supportive communities like the TechJPR Facebook group for UK technology journalists and PRs. It's common to see people asking questions in groups like TechJPR about the best free or low-cost services, occasionally highlighting individual stories (without ever seeming too pitch-y) or asking for media contacts in specific areas. If you can't find a group or industry chat/hashtag that works for you by searching on Facebook, LinkedIn and Twitter, there's always the option of creating one and starting to build a community around certain industries or topics. It's a no-lose situation in which you could end up building influence simply by spending as much or as little of your time as you can spare developing something useful for others. In a way, that's exactly what PRexamples.com has been to me in terms of building my stunt/campaign credentials.

The issue of persuading risk-averse company decision-makers to pursue certain newsworthy or community-engaging stories crops up in both agency and in-house life, but I'd argue that agency workers get off easier here. If we send ideas that aren't quite right, we can always say that there are 'plenty more where that came from', and be excused as a result of being new to an organization and its framework, learning and attempting to fit to the sensibilities of the client. In-house, there will likely be a short grace period but, after that and when embedded, one might lose their early enthusiasm and every idea will be expected to be a good one on account of their access and close proximity to the business.

In an agency, even small ones, there are likely a number of people with which to throw proactive PR ideas and features angles around. In-house, though, unless the structure is in place to allow for time here, one might not be afforded the same luxury of being able to shout out a terrible idea and not be judged for it. I've rubbed some hideous ideas from various whiteboards throughout my career, but within seconds I've forgotten about them, or used them to springboard us to another. I've also led or been involved in meetings like this where non-PR people, such as might only be available in-house, get involved and might not have the same understanding of newsworthiness, or thick enough skin to be OK with not having their every idea written down. Internal politics can be an issue, here. A finance or managing director, pulled into a 'creative' meeting with one or a small group of PR/marketing employees, might not be the best addition unless you can gently divert them from ideas like 'can we send a press release out about the fact we are the best?' to something more likely to not invite ridicule.

Gerald Heneghan is content manager at Push Doctor, a medical advice app, and formerly head of content at Roland Dransfield PR, based in Manchester. He touched on this point of internal politics (Heneghan, 2015), saying that while the majority of companies of a certain size will have an in-house PR team, 'most under a certain size won't be utilizing them properly', stating that 'even teams in larger organizations can become hopelessly bogged down in bureaucracy, with in-house PR people facing an uphill struggle when it comes to gaining approval for communications'. This doesn't sound particularly easy to work around to me, though there's little doubt the only answer is to soldier on and try to effect change as well as one can, as an individual or departmentally.

Even internal PRs in bigger companies with the budget to bring in external support have pressure we don't often consider as that supplier. 'Never underestimate the work involved in ramping up your agency allies, keeping them looped in and on point with your evolving program strategy and goals', Holly Teichholtz, the vice president of marketing and communications at The Michael J Fox Foundation for Parkinson's Research said (Teichholtz, 2014). 'It requires at least the same investment of time and effort – and sometimes more – as doing the legwork yourself.' While agencies are safe in the knowledge they have a minimum notice period in which to prove themselves, all that time could also be spent explaining the need for external support and fighting the corner of an agency that might not be quite right for the business, all considered. If agency account handlers can understand and ease the pressures their client is under, not just departmentally but company-wide, they'll be their best friend.

Salaries compared

I believe I've made a good case for in-house being as stressful an area as agency life. But what of the remuneration – is it at least worth it?

According to the PRCA 2016 Census, PR agencies are most likely to be made up of between 11 and 50 people. In-house teams are 'overwhelmingly made up of 2–5 people, regardless of organisational size'.

The average PR agency salary is £44,805, down from £54,311 in 2013. According to the Census, pay at the senior levels has fallen, but professionals at account director level or below have seen a small increase. When it comes to in-house salaries, the average salary is actually less, standing at £43,591 (down from £50,438 in 2013).

It's harder to find parallels beyond averages because job titles often differ, and made even more difficult by different pay levels across sectors – for instance, financial PRs typically earn more than consumer PRs – but recruitment agency The Works' Annual Salary Survey for PR and Communications Professionals (The Works Search, 2016) sheds some light. The most recent survey, released in 2016, was completed entirely by in-house and agency professionals based in and around London, so expect these figures to be higher than elsewhere.

The Works' survey has done the job of equating a small number of roles for us in order to provide a barometer. Here are the average base salaries per year for the following roles:

- Corporate communications – in-house managers earn £60,000 per annum. Agency account directors in corporate communications earn £50,000.
- Financial PR – in-house managers earn £58,000 per annum. Agency account directors also earn £58,000.
- Consumer PR – in-house managers earn £45,000 per annum. Agency account directors also earn £45,000.

On account of there being no similar role in agencies but as a point of interest, the survey found that internal communications managers earn £53,000 per annum, in terms of average base salary.

Reuben Sinclair is a recruitment agency based in London, specializing in sales, marketing, PR and digital roles. They too released a salary survey in 2016, on which note, one must remember that the intention for these surveys is as content marketing in itself, to help promote the companies behind them. The aim is for candidates and employers to happen upon them by searching, or see them in trade media and social media circles. This very likely won't affect the data highlighted itself, but I'd be very surprised to see attention drawn to negatives, such as salary decreases, given the aim is to encourage business for the surveying company. Anyway, I digress.

Reuben Sinclair's survey found similarly to that of The Works, but didn't break down by sector. The following passage from the report stood out to me:

> Typically, it is thought that client side PR roles are slightly better paid than the agency side equivalent. Our salary survey suggests that this might be true at the more senior end of each level, for example whilst agency side Account Managers are getting paid a maximum of £41,000 (this is likely to be at Senior Account Manager level), In House PR Managers are being paid up to £51,000. The comparison is, however, difficult to make based on title alone as often In

House PR teams are a lot smaller and therefore their 'PR manager' may actually be running the PR function and have 10 years' experience, showing titles don't necessarily correlate between the two.

Another thing to consider, is that due to client side PR teams being smaller, individuals often have to wait for someone above them to leave before they can be promoted, meaning progression is generally slower. So, although salaries might appear to be comparatively higher than a like for like agency role, [the employee] may have to wait longer to progress to the next level, and during this time your agency side counterparts may have had a salary increase to match or exceed [them]. (Reuben Sinclair, 2016).

In terms of bonuses, The Works' report is almost unreadable as a comparable set of data. When considering the convolution of like-for-like roles, different sectors and no doubt location, it would be far easier for individuals to assess them personally rather than me just regurgitating figures. What Gorkana took from the bonus findings in its reporting of the survey (Bylykbashi, 2016) was as follows:

The senior roles in corporate communications fared best, with global heads of communications receiving an average bonus of £60,000 – a 3% increase on the previous year. This is slightly lower within agencies where CEOs and directors earned an average of £30,000, but senior account directors received an average bonus of £13,000 – a 27% jump from the previous year.

Financial PR agencies saw the biggest rise bonuses, with managing directors and board directors seeing a 30% jump from 2014. Here the average bonus was £50,000.

To wrap this up

Comparing the ease of in-house PR versus agency PR is an entirely subjective topic. As highlighted, there are in-house people that have experienced both sides that baulk at the notion, while agency PRs believe the grass is greener with no evidence other than whisperings of the ones that got 'out'. It makes sense that the fast-paced agency world is the place to both learn and develop as a professional, taking advantage of agency commitments to employee development and better access to tools and resources to aid in our work. With top-end in-house roles further and fewer between than near equivalents in agencies, there's a prestige attached to them, but I can see nothing in researching this and talking to people on both sides to suggest that either is 'easier' than the other. Even the idea that in-house is better paid appears not to be the case, on average.

It all comes down to personality and what individuals hope to get out of a career in PR. If favouring in-house roles for the big bucks while living on easy street is the aim, I'd suggest those people think again. Limited budgets, fewer colleagues and more immediate ROI-centric pressure from above can make in-house easily as stressful as agency types consider time sheets, client pressure and longer hours.

Further reading

Adams, B, 2013. Going in-house: shifting from the agency world – the publicity machine. *Medium*, 11 January. Available at: <https://medium.com/the-publicity-machine/going-in-house-shifting-from-the-agency-world-881d890ce71f> [Accessed 4 September 2016]

Barker, L, 2014. The real reasons why people leave PR agency jobs. *PRWeek Jobs*, 7 May. Available at: <http://www.prweekjobs.co.uk/article/the-real-reasons-why-people-leave-pr-agency-jobs/> [Accessed 4 September 2016]

Bylykbashi, K, 2016. PR saw salary rises in 2015 reports The Works Search. *Gorkana*, 13 May. Available at: <http://www.gorkana.com/2016/05/pr-pros-see-a-rise-in-salary-and-bonuses-says-survey/> [Accessed 4 September 2016]

Cornish, J, 2011. In-house or agency: which role suits you? *PRWeek*, 10 March. Available at: <http://www.prweek.com/article/1059106/in-house-agency-role-suits-you#PJP0hKFUBAEHVTRW.99> [Accessed 4 September 2016]

Heneghan, G, 2015. In-house PR people suck and other common myths busted. HubSpot, 9 February. Available at: <http://blog.hubspot.com/agency/pr-myths-busted#sm.00002rie6h8flco0sj01z1ds541ke> [Accessed 4 September 2016]

Reuben Sinclair, 2016. *2016 PR Salary Survey*. [pdf] Available at: <https://www.reuben-sinclair.com/media/34697/PR-SALARY-SURVEY-2016.pdf> [Accessed 4 September 2016]

Staff Writer, 2014. Busting common myths around PR jobs. *Marketing*, 6 February. Available at: <http://www.marketing-interactive.com/events/busting-common-myths-around-pr-jobs> [Accessed 4 September 2016]

Teichholtz, H, 2014. 4 myths of in-house PR. *PR Daily*, 11 April. Available at: <http://www.prdaily.com/mediarelations/Articles/4_myths_of_inhouse_PR_16443.aspx> [Accessed 4 September 2016]

The Works Search, 2016. *Annual Salary Survey 2015/2016*. [pdf] Available at: <http://www.the-works.co.uk/assets/uploads/downloads/Salary_Survey_2016.pdf> [Accessed 4 September 2016]

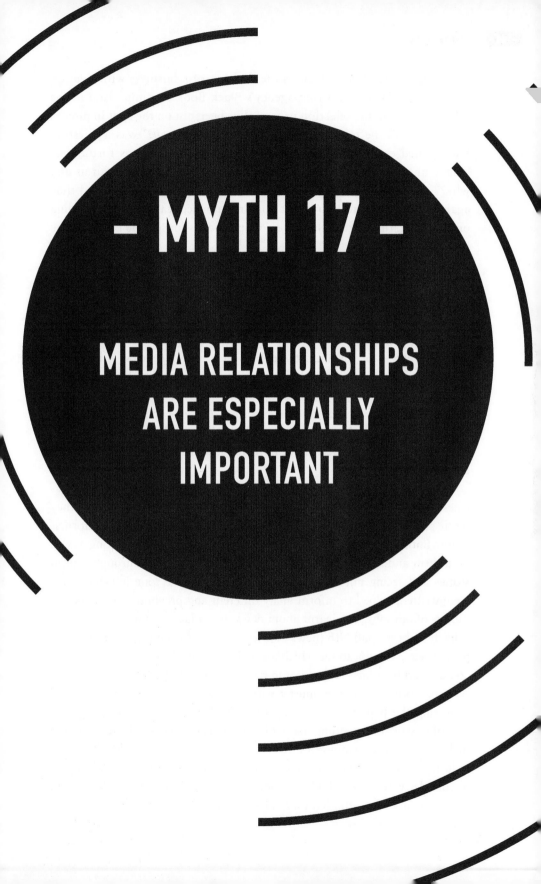

- MYTH 17 -

MEDIA RELATIONSHIPS ARE ESPECIALLY IMPORTANT

One aspect that often influences the decision of a business with relation to the agency it selects is that agency's Black Book in comparison to the other agencies in the selection process. I've been put on the spot in pitches before. 'Who's the technology editor at *The Telegraph*?' was a question I was asked early on in my career when pitching, and was fortunately able to answer. 'Which journalists do you think would care about us and why?' and variations thereof is a question that's come up time and time again. Clients need to know that you are knowledgeable, and depending on the client, the more niche or sector-specific responses you can give, the better.

Potential clients want and need you to be the expert. After all, that's what many believe they're paying for: an agency's access to certain people and the no-doubt highly cultivated relationship that agency's employees have built up with those writers and producers over time.

Specialist agencies are made up of people that profess to be experts in specific areas – for instance, there'll be leisure PR agencies, video game agencies, sports specialists and many others. Of course, there'll be specialist freelancers, too, and people looking for roles in-house in areas that align with their area of passion and/or expertise. These people might disagree, but I think, a handful of sectors notwithstanding, media relations is media relations, and the approach can be mirrored successfully without much difficulty. More on that later.

PRs of a certain age will remember poring over newspapers and magazines, cutting out or writing down journalist names in relation to what they wrote about. It's not that online media directories don't supply this information in both general and daily headline terms – they have for as long as I've used them and will continue to, I'm sure. It's that running through topical stories and seeing not only who wrote them, but the tone in which they were written, helped to inform many different and previously fundamental aspects of our jobs. You learnt about news story placement in terms of what is likely to be a small NIB (news in brief) piece and what made for a double page spread. You got to see which journalists dominated the lead pages and could ascertain a hierarchy if not in terms of writers at least in terms of the types of stories that passed muster with editors.

Buying the papers and running through them with a highlighter or a pair of scissors is something many PRs still swear by, especially for younger or less experienced employees. It's a great way to teach those new to the industry about the unique character of each news outlet while asking them to consider ways in which clients they are likely to be new to could fit in. It helps in many ways still, but there's been a shift.

When print and broadcast journalism were the only games in town, journalists were in a unique position. They held the keys to the gates, and, like the famous two-door riddle in the movie *Labyrinth*, PR people had to jump through hoops and communicate in especially particular ways to get through. Journalists held all the power, by virtue of being able to grant access to their audience should they so choose and see fit. This was a fortunate position to be in, depending on your viewpoint, and everybody keen to influence an audience has worked at ways to build a professional rapport with journalists.

Journalists, and in particular senior journalists, have always enjoyed and long expected a level of familiarity with senior public figures. Prominent politicians, entertainers and business owners keen to ensure favourable or at least informed public opinion would first have to ensure that the journalists with the ability to grant that were treated and informed well.

Newspapers have traditionally shown a political leaning. In the UK, especially with relation to the tabloid media, the allegiance shown to political parties isn't an absolute given. *The Sun* has flip-flopped in terms of support for both major parties and even issues in the last few decades, going between being pro-New Labour to backing Brexit. At its height, reaching and influencing the decisions of millions as the best-read daily newspaper in Britain, what journalists at *The Sun* thought of individuals mattered enough to senior politicians to want to cultivate good relationships with them with regular meetings and a bid to keep them informed.

'It's *The Sun* Wot Won It' is a headline that appeared on the front-page of *The Sun* on Saturday 11 April 1992, in reference to the supposedly unexpected Conservative party victory that election. It is a headline regularly cited in debates on the influence of the press over politicians and election results, and was preceded by a campaign against the Labour Party leader, Neil Kinnock, which culminated in the equally famous election day headline, 'If Kinnock wins today will the last person to leave Britain please turn out the lights'. The 'Wot Won It' was referred to again by political commentators five years later, after *The Sun* had backed New Labour's Tony Blair to office.

When even ascension to the most powerful role in UK politics is seen to have been influenced by the media, it's understandable that business owners would feel that the better a PR agency's relationship with journalists, the more likely it is they will be written about favourably and, in turn, the more likely an audience is to think favourably of them. Logic and human experience also dictate that the friendlier with and more useful to somebody you are, the more likely that person is to do you a favour. Boozy lunches are synonymous with 90s PR – the idea that you can wine and dine your way to preferential treatment. Perhaps that once worked, and perhaps journalists were once happy to take whatever was on offer, but the media, as described above, is now almost unrecognizable when compared to today's landscape.

The shift – today's reality

I hate to be the bearer of bad news for any business owners reading, or PR industry entrants desperate to be best friends with the *Mirror*'s 3 am celebrity gossip writers, but these apparently excellent relationships are few and far between today, replaced with clipped conversations where one is had at all. The insistence on them harks back to headier and happier days for the media in general that just don't exist anymore.

The jobs of the journalists whose headlines we used to spend our mornings highlighting are under threat, or have changed so as not to be entirely recognizable. They spend more time at their desk than ever before and, with dwindling resources, often have more in the way of responsibility too.

The issue of time spent writing was thrust into the spotlight in January 2016. In a move that was described by the National Union of Journalists (NUJ) as 'Big Brother–style surveillance in the newsroom', *The Daily Telegraph* had to announce that it was withdrawing devices installed to monitor the time employees spent at their desks. The decision to install the under-desk 'OccupEye' boxes, which reportedly tracked whether someone was at their desk using heat and motion sensors, was roundly pilloried both sincerely and jokingly at the time. A *Telegraph* journalist I spoke to around the time sighed and poked fun at the reason given for installing them when I broached the subject, suggesting that the official explanation that the monitors would be in place for four weeks to 'help plan measures to improve energy efficiency' was less than plausible.

The reach and influence of the media, fragmented as it now is, means any claim by any one paper or even publisher that they won or greatly influenced an election for a party would be met with ridicule. The lines in the sand of political fealty are still drawn – *The Guardian* will always be left of centre and *The Daily Telegraph* always right of centre, for instance – but the scale of influence has been hampered by a public that are less likely to define themselves by the paper they read. We're simply much more fickle in the links we click today, with less interest in who's produced what we consume.

The death of media relations has been greatly exaggerated, as I've explained throughout the book. It's still a fundamental part of what we do, but the reality is there are fewer journalists than ever before to pitch to. They move out of roles, into freelance work, to other titles, or out of journalism altogether at a rate I've not seen before, and this means you can't get too attached to the individual.

The hard facts – why journalists' jobs are at risk

The shift is unsurprising when you look at the figures.

According to the World Press Trends Database's most recent report from 2015, global newspaper circulation revenues have now actually surpassed newspaper advertising revenues, meaning that audiences have become the biggest source of revenue for publishers, taking into account both print and paying digital readers. The balance tipped in 2013, when circulation was responsible for $91 billion as compared to $90 billion in advertising revenue. The downward trend continued in 2014, when newspapers generated an estimated $179 billion in circulation and advertising revenue – $92 billion came from print and digital circulation, while $87 billion came from advertising.

These numbers are still huge, obviously, but the downward trend in global advertising spend is stark – in 2010, the figure stood at $100 billion. That's a 13 per cent drop in just five years.

Don't get too excited, though – just because readers are paying more than advertisers doesn't mean things are in great shape. The report highlights that print circulations are declining in the West, but that global print circulation is growing steadily thanks to circulation growth in India and elsewhere in Asia. In fact, of the 10 best-selling newspapers globally, just one – *USA*

Table 17.1 Global percentage increase/decrease in circulation over time

Region	One-year change	Five-year change
Africa and Middle East/North Africa	1.2 %	3.7 %
Asia	9.8 %	32.7 %
Australasia and Oceania	−5.3 %	−22.3 %
Europe	−4.5 %	−21.3 %
Latin America	0.6 %	2.9 %
North America	−1.3 %	−8.7 %

SOURCE World Press Trends Database

Today – is published outside of Asia. Global print circulation increased over 6 per cent globally in 2014 from a year earlier and more than 16 per cent over five years, but, as you can see in Table 17.1, this is heavily influenced by that Asian boom. The increase in Asia is huge and masks what is otherwise a global nosedive.

In terms of the UK specifically, Audit Bureau of Circulation figures, as reported by The Media Briefing (Taylor, 2014) showed that since January 2001, the total circulation of the UK's 10 major national newspapers declined from just over 12 million copies sold on average each day to a daily average of under 7 million copies in May 2014. That was a decline of more than 42 per cent. The same article extrapolated circulation trends for the same 10 national newspapers and looked five years ahead – finding that *The Sun* could well, the trend continuing, be selling around a million copies a day on average. This is a far cry from the paper's highest ever one-day sale at full price on 30 March 1996 when nearly 4.8 million people bought it.

Ad blockers and publisher revenue

Of course, it's easy to point at a loss in paid print circulation. Digital has shifted everything and we'd be hard pressed to find an industry untouched by it in some way. That said, the downward slide in advertising spend and the increased shift to digital, where readers are reluctant to pay, means despite impressive increases in traffic to national newspaper websites, publishers aren't in a particularly positive position.

Oh, and on top of fewer advertisers and fewer, far more fickle readers, there's been something of a consumer backlash against digital media advertising, too.

It's a quickly developing trend, but ad blockers represent a significant threat to one of the few remaining routes to monetization publishers have online, as consumers increasingly get news from social media sources and make their distaste for digital advertising known. According to an eMarketer report, more than a quarter of US-based internet users will block ads in 2016.

'At least 419 million people are blocking ads on smartphones, up 90 per cent between January 2015 and January 2016', according to a report by analytics company Priori Data and Pagefair, a company that helps publishers battle ad blockers (Kharpal, 2016), stating that there are also now twice as many mobile ad blockers than desktop ad blockers. Asian mobile users, especially those in China and India, are leading the charge, installing 159 million and 122 million ad blockers respectively.

The data isn't set yet, and a lot of projections you see reported are unconfirmed given the explosion of usage, but it's fair to say ad blockers are bad news for news organizations. Research group Ovum estimates that if ad blocking rates maintain at their current levels – and publishers do little more to combat ad blocking than they already are – they will lose $35 billion by 2020 (Davies, 2016).

Add this to the fact that publishers are continuously having to adapt to play the game in other grounds that don't bring anything definite in the way of revenue – Snapchat's Stories and Facebook's Trending news functions two ways in which people can skim news quickly and conveniently – and the future looks uncertain. Being increasingly reliant on third-party platforms to reach audiences is not a great place for established media brands to be.

What does all of this have to do with clients and agency choices?

As the above might have made abundantly clear, it's an uncertain time in which to be a journalist, and that doesn't look like changing.

It's not just newspapers and the consolidation of previously specialist journalistic roles with those of news-orientated writers, either. Magazines and niche online titles are suffering from the Grim Reaper's looming shadow, too. This is when it starts to affect the specialists I mentioned at the beginning of the chapter, as the potential pool of media outlets they can lean on for client results gets shallower.

Choosing an agency based on its insistence on 'amazing relationships' with the media shouldn't sway decisions as much as it once might. I'm not saying a passion for the media and a solid knowledge isn't important. I'm speaking from a general, consumer perspective and background, and saying, as I mentioned up top, that media relations is media relations. It's a much more democratic time to work in PR, where ideas and execution matter far more than the relationships you once had to have with people through which you want to reach an audience.

If you can come up with ways to ensure a company (or individual) both reaches and influences its audience, selfishly, it's then simply about understanding the channels you choose to use. I was never and will never be a motoring PR expert – but that didn't stop me from learning just enough about the area to launch a client in the space in a way that achieved what we set out to achieve: sales and links. The same with video games. As much as I love them – any time I've ever worked on video game clients, it's been a case of getting to know the news sites, blogs and magazines all over again, which can be done quickly. It takes a day or two, tops, to pull together an accurate media list and introduce yourself – which, in a climate where journalists are jumping ship left, right and centre, would need doing regularly even among specialists.

The main difference as I've always found it with specialists is that they might have more passion for an area and, as such, might come up with news and features ideas or ways to connect with the right people that generalists wouldn't. Picking a business area out of thin air – let's say a company that manufactured an awesome product for… horse riders got in touch – I'd be so distant from the topic that I might struggle to understand quite why it's necessary as much as somebody who spent years as a horse rider and on seeing the product exclaims, 'Yes, why didn't this exist before!?'

I'm aware that I sound like a Grinch, but the notion of a Black Book of media contacts in times of such uncertainty for the names we'd otherwise be writing in it seems entirely antiquated. I'm fortunate to have come into PR at a time just before this shift away from personal relationships happened and, as such, count a very small number of journalists still climbing the career ladder as friends, despite working over the years with countless people. I've always been conscious of being *that* PR guy, the namedropper that might impress a potential client initially but soon starts to grate if and when said relationships amount to little in the way of results. I was told early on that journalists don't want to be your friend, and, to be frank, I was never much interested in being theirs either, unless we genuinely got on and would go for lunch or a drink. It's easier when it's transactional on both sides, when it's just two people doing a job.

If not relationships, what sets agencies apart?

The best PR people and agencies are future proofing themselves, having seen this coming long enough ago that the person being pitched shouldn't matter quite so much as what's being pitched, or indeed if other channels and routes to client audiences are better pursued. For some, like my agency, this means an increased focus on areas like SEO and creative campaigns; for others, it might be building out a department in which images, videos, podcasts, microsites and other direct-to-audience content is created.

For some agencies, especially the bigger ones, they'll have people that specialize in all of the above and more, pulling the necessary components into place, dependent upon the brief.

For me, ideas, evidence of previous results and execution where available, and/or an understanding of the market and the ways in which to reach and influence them should always trump the promise of relationships.

Despite having been on one side of the pitching process more times than I can remember, I can't profess to be an expert in terms of what individuals and companies look for, or should look for. Marc Cowlin, though, who works in corporate communications for recruitment company Glassdoor, is certainly more experienced in this matter than I am. Cowlin (2014) wrote a great piece while working at Meltwater in which he described the 10 tips he'd give to anybody considering multiple agencies. These tips should be of use to businesses, students and professionals reading, and are based on Marc's experience as somebody who, in his words, has 'hired six or seven (and fired a few)'.

CASE STUDY

What to look for when hiring a PR agency   Contributed by Marc Cowlin

Tip #1 – When you hire a PR firm, decide on PR/firm goals before you do anything else!
As with all PR and marketing programs, I always advise defining goals before getting too far into making decisions about retaining an agency. We must recognize that strategy is the first step to success and leads to tactical execution. I am a firm believer that good strategy starts with goals. As you look to hire a PR firm, decide what you are trying to achieve. A few great examples are: brand awareness, thought leadership, attention for a specific product or program, etc.

Tip #2 – When you hire a PR firm, make sure you have considered all options
How does a company tackle PR effectively? Hire a PR firm? Hire in-house? The answer will be different for every company, but I venture to say it is generally a combination of the two for a very good reason: a PR firm that isn't managed by someone who understands PR will never fully realize the firm's full potential.

A PR firm needs brand and product knowledge and most importantly, access to the right internal people for both strategy and execution, and an internal

PR person makes this possible. This combination of in-house and PR firm is not always possible, so you'll need to decide what your budget warrants. If you don't plan to have an internal PR person, your PR agency is likely best managed by the CMO.

Tip #3 – When you hire a PR firm, decide on RFP or no RFP process

You can always just hire a firm that you already know or have heard good things about. However, if you have never hired a PR firm I strongly advise going through the formal request for proposal (RFP) process. And, more importantly, I advise that you hire a PR pro with specific RFP experience to help lead the process if it's your first time. If you have never been through an RFP to hire a PR agency, the process will seem daunting.

Generally the first steps are to define what you are trying to achieve, your goals, what you actually want the firm to do, and then come up with a list of 10-ish prospective firms. This list can be tricky, because you want to carefully weigh PR firm capabilities to your goal expectations. From there you contact each firm to gauge their interest and issue a request for qualifications (RFQ), a document that will help you to whittle down the prospect list. Those that choose to participate will send qualifications to be reviewed against the others and you'll select a few (I recommend three) agencies that will formally pitch/compete for your business. Each will bring a team to pitch you, and you select one from the three. While this may not seem so bad, it is time-consuming, and if you do not have experience or a network of potential agencies, the process will feel overwhelming.

Tip #4 – When you hire a PR firm, determine your PR Agency budget

Seems like a simple tip, right? In some ways it is, but it is important to make a firm decision on your top-line budget. Agencies are expensive and you'll need to make sure you clearly articulate your top-line budget, including base retainer, overages, expenses and incidentals. Believe me, it can add up. Make sure you have a clear path that requires written approval for any month expense that exceeds your budget.

Tip #5 – When you hire a PR firm, decide what size PR firm is right for you

PR firms come in all different shapes and sizes, and the firm that's right for you might not be the firm you'd predict. There are many reasons to go with large PR firms (global reach, massive relationship networks, fantastic experience), and just as many reasons to choose a boutique PR firm (smaller, more closely knit teams, local expertise, niche industries, etc). One thing to keep in mind is how much your budget dollars will mean to the firm you hire. For instance, often a $15,000/month retainer could be one of the largest accounts if you hire a small

PR firm, but a very small account if you hire a large PR firm. Keep in mind the bigger clients usually get the A-team. If your budget is modest, you may want to consider a smaller boutique firm.

Tip #6 – When you hire a PR firm, make specific requests regarding their pitch presentation

When you hire a firm, especially when you implement a formal RFP process, there will be a formal presentation when your prospective agencies pitch you in an effort to win your business. Before that meeting I recommend making three very specific asks:

1 Ask that they only send people who will be on your account from day one to the meeting. This way you will not get caught up in a situation where you're pitched by the A-team, but assigned to the D-team. Bait-and-switch situations can be painful and should be avoided at all costs.

2 Ask that everyone who will be on your team be involved in the presentation, not just the team lead. In the end, you will work with everyone – you'll want to know how each one thinks.

3 Ask agencies to keep their 'about us' description and back-patting slides to a minimum. After all, if you weren't interested in the PR firm they would not be in the room – you've already done your homework!

Tip #7 – When you hire a PR firm, don't ignore the importance of chemistry

Make sure you like the team you are hiring. Of course, it is important that they are qualified and will do a great job, but it's equally important that you like them and want to work with them. It's really no different from hiring people to your own internal team – you want to be excited to work with them every day!

Tip #8 – When you hire a PR firm, look to hire an extension of your team, not just an agency

Tip #7 really leads me to tip #8. I firmly believe that you should think of your PR firm as part of your team, not as a third party. While your PR firm team will work with more than just your account, you should never feel like they are working with anyone but you. My advice is to tell prospective PR firms, from the first time you meet, that you work with agencies differently from most clients; you want to hire an extension to your team; you're not looking for an average client/agency relationship.

Tip #9 – When you hire a PR firm, make sure they have at least one idea you're excited about!

In the pitch meetings, if the PR firms have done their homework and prepared properly, they will present a few different PR campaign ideas based on your RFP requirements. I generally take these ideas with a grain of salt – after all, these PR firms are not fully on-boarded and have limited knowledge of your brand. That said, at least one of the ideas should be out-of-the-box and cool enough to get you excited!

Tip #10 – When you hire a PR firm, understand your contract

Once you decide on which PR firm you want to hire, you will move to contract and/or statement of work (SOW). Make sure you review it carefully, with a lawyer if possible, and understand all key terms (cost/budget, duration, team, hours you receive based on budget, how they will report out results, etc). I have yet to see a PR firm contract that I have not red-lined substantially, which they fully expect. If something seems off, red-line it and negotiate. Most of the time PR firms are agreeable, assuming your asks are reasonable.

I don't intend to claim that these 10 tips will make the process easy. But, I do promise that these tips will make the process of hiring a PR firm less painful, and they will help you to make an informed and wise choice.

Further reading

Cowlin, M, 2014. How to Hire a PR Firm: 10 Tips to Finding the Right Match. *Meltwater*, 27 June. Available at: <https://www.meltwater.com/blog/hire-pr-firm/> [Accessed 5 September 2016]

Davies, J, 2016. Uh-oh: ad blocking forecast to cost $35 billion by 2020. *Digiday*, 7 June. Available at: <http://digiday.com/publishers/uh-oh-ad-blocking-forecast-cost-35-billion-2020/> [Accessed 4 September 2016]

eMarketer, 2016. *US ad blocking to jump by double digits this year*. Available at: <http://www.emarketer.com/Article/US-Ad-Blocking-Jump-by-Double-Digits-This-Year/1014111> [Accessed 4 September 2016]

Kharpal, A, 2016. Ad-blockers posing 'serious threat' as 1 in 5 smartphone users using tech: study. *CNBC*, 31 May. Available at: <http://www.cnbc.com/2016/05/31/ad-blockers-posing-serious-threat-as-1-in-5-smartphone-users-using-tech-study.html> [Accessed 4 September 2016]

Taylor, H, 2014. Newspaper circulation: how far it's fallen and how far it's got to fall. *The Media Briefing*, 1 July. Available at: <https://www.themediabriefing.com/article/newspaper-circulation-decline-2001-2014-prediction-5-years> [Accessed 4 September 2016]

World Press Trends Database. *World Press Trends 2015: facts and figures*. Available at: <http://www.wptdatabase.org/world-press-trends-2015-facts-and-figures> [Accessed 4 September 2016]

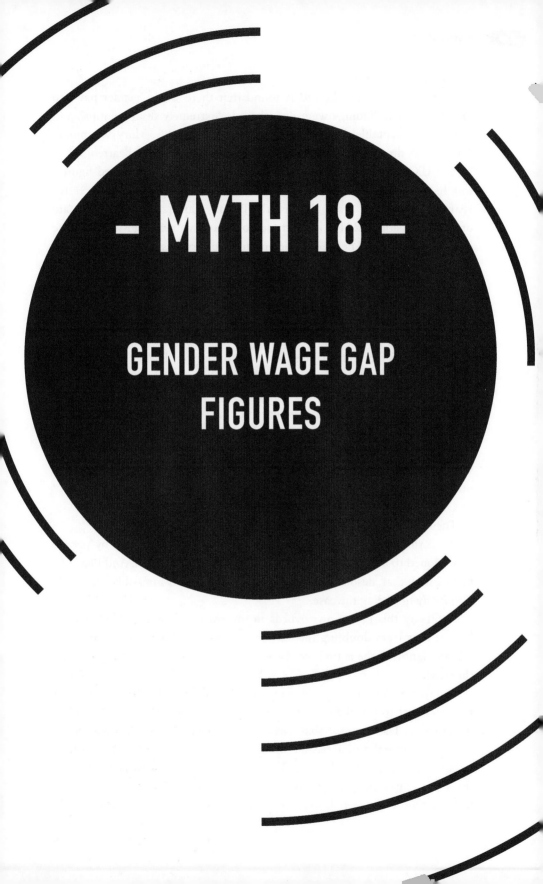

Takes a deep breath

In its 2016 Census, the PRCA found that there was a 'gender pay gap of £9,111'. The findings were described as 'extremely disappointing' and 'simply unacceptable' by the president of Women in PR, Mary Whenman. The PRCA's director general, Francis Ingham, called them 'disheartening'.

The UK's other prominent PR organization, the CIPR, released figures, too. Its 2016 State of the Profession survey showed, for a fourth successive year since the CIPR first published the PR pay gap figure as part of State of the Profession in 2012–13, that men out-earn women in PR. An average disparity of £15,040 between male and female earnings was found to exist, up 19 per cent on 2015's figures (attributed to the inclusion of freelancers in the overall results). An employee-only figure, however, shows a gap of £11,698, a 7 per cent year-on-year decrease.

Two separate 2016 surveys, two different results, each of which highlight a significant gap in earnings attributable, according to the surveys, to gender. It's a similar picture in the United States according to PRWeek's 2016 Salary Survey, which found that, overall, senior male PR executives earn $125,000 a year compared to $80,000 for women.

These are the industry figures that stick in your mind. Students will be taught them and industry entrants will begin their careers believing they are being held back. Two-thirds of PR industry employees in the UK are women, with similarly disproportionate representation elsewhere, so that's a huge number of the industry affected.

Only... (and this is the deep breath bit)

These figures aren't quite telling the whole story.

'Rich thinks the wage gap is a myth' will be the takeaway by people conditioned to accept often complex issues in 140 characters. And I have to be OK with that, despite – and I'll say this as clearly as I possibly can – that *absolutely* not being the case.

I will say this in my own words in my own way: if people choose to believe that I am doubting the existence of the wage gap, they are intentionally ignoring the actual words used. It's easy to see why that could be the case.

Today, we consume news in ever smaller bite-sized chunks, pared down to the easiest to understand and lowest common factor in order to make it shareable. The news we share, as a kind of social media currency, determines how moral and agreeable other people think you are and, as social beasts, we're concerned by this. The more likes, comments, positive reactions and shares our social posts receive, the more 'together' with others we feel – the more connected. Journalists have been informing and (sometimes intentionally, sometimes unintentionally) misleading with snappy and enticing headlines since the 17th century, when the first newspaper was established. Now, millions of people, untrained in the art, do the same.

Headlines and Twitter-friendly takeaways like 'women in PR earn £15,040 less than men' help nobody, because they're inaccurate and liable to spread like wildfire.

In fact, as a case in point, an earlier version of this chapter failed to highlight the effort the CIPR has gone to in its State of the Profession annual reports to ensure a regression analysis was done, aiming to, in the surveying company's words, 'determine the affect one variable is having on another, whilst holding for the impact that other factors might be having'. What this basically means is, all factors accounted for, the regression analysis should find the actual figure in a bid to nullify arguments such as, say, 'the reason men received higher salaries was because more men were in senior positions'.

The CIPR's 2016 report found a post-regression analysis annual gap of £6,004 in favour of men. The report showed gender has the third largest overall impact on a PR professional's earnings, after level of seniority and years in the industry.

Thanks to former CIPR president Sarah Pinch for highlighting this to me.

I say that this is a case in point, citing 'headlines and Twitter-friendly takeaways' because, in my research for this chapter, I read three industry sites and blogs reporting on the State of the Profession's findings: PRWeek, PR Moment and The Drum. Not one of them mentioned the post-regression finding. I should have read the report itself better, but if I, as somebody that makes an effort to read as much as I can about the industry, can miss this, I don't think I'll be the only one.

Again, I am not questioning the existence of a gender pay gap. I am questioning the validity of the industry figures we are routinely exposed to, which could quite easily affect the likelihood of, say, my daughter when it comes to choosing her career down the line.

'What's the difference?' one might ask. 'Why split hairs?' My answer is, again, simple: we should care about every single percentage point. If we're truly bothered by a gender pay gap, both societally and in PR, every penny should matter. We can't shun intellectual honesty in favour of simply looking like a good person.

The figures we're presented with are not inaccurate because of the sample sizes of the surveys – it would be foolish to hope for every single person in PR to respond to either report I led with. They are inaccurate because it is a simplification of a complex issue, compounded by the fact that the necessary questions to determine the pay gap have not been asked.

A helping hand

Again, for the third time – if you're reading this and rolling your eyes, I am not dismissing the existence of a gap in earnings between men and women. There is one – and we'll get onto it.

I am no economic whizz. But I know somebody who is, and she's given a lot of her time to help me and, by extension I hope, everybody who otherwise parrots the same wage gap figures to understand this issue.

Susan HayesCulleton is a Chartered Financial Analyst charterholder. As an experienced trainer and public speaker, she regularly presents at conferences and delivers keynote speeches on the subjects of economics, the financial markets, entrepreneurship and finance. Before passing the notoriously difficult CFA exams, Susan graduated from NUI Galway, ranked in the top 2 per cent of universities in the world by *Times Higher Education*, with a degree in Financial Maths and Economics.

Susan is the author of three books, one of which – *Positive Economics* (written with Trudie Murray and Brian O'Connor) – is used as the Irish 'Leaving Certificate' textbook. In the Irish education system, the Leaving Certificate Examinations are the equivalent of A-Levels in the UK – the final examination stage in the Irish secondary school system, before students go off to university.

Her other two books are *The Savvy Woman's Guide to Financial Freedom* and *The Savvy Guide to Making More Money*, published by Penguin Ireland.

Understanding the complexities

Another figure readers might well have seen is the statistic that female full-time workers earn 79 cents for every dollar a man makes. This is an accurate figure, when comparing everything women earn, and everything men earn. But it doesn't tell the full picture.

CASE STUDY

Explaining the gender pay gap   Contributed by Susan HayesCulleton

The 'average wage for a man versus average wage for a woman, unadjusted for everything', gender pay gap is approximately 20 per cent. Women earn 20 per cent less than men.

However, that's a very raw figure. It's easy to quote, but ignores a lot of things. Let's call that the *unadjusted* pay gap.

The actual pay gap – and one does exist – adjusted to take into consideration the factors we need to take into consideration to make an accurate statement of fact (such as hours worked and level of education), reduces to around 5 per cent. Not 20 per cent – the *adjusted* pay gap is somewhere between 4.8 and 7 per cent.

This is the finding of a 2009 study by the US Department of Labor (Daily Caller, 2016), which examined more than 50 peer-reviewed papers and concluded that the wage gap 'may be almost entirely the result of individual choices being made by both male and female workers'.

First, the way to fix the imbalance (assuming that is what we want to do) is to accept that 20 per cent is not the correct figure to be quoting, while still expressing distaste for the remaining 5 per cent gap. I will get onto what I mean by this after I talk about the ways in which the imbalance can be fixed. Let's see if the appetite is really there to fix it.

It is illegal to pay somebody less money for the same job, doing the same hours, on the basis of their gender. If you are able to show this to be the case, you have a legal basis to sue your employer and stand to win, and I would encourage you to. If women really were cheaper to hire than men for the same role, business owners would surely be employing more women to enjoy higher profitability, no? Given that businesses will happily outsource to other countries to save money, it's not a huge stretch to assume they'd do the same by employing women if they could simply pay less. Those highlighting the easily quotable 20 per cent figure have no answer to that. It would make simple economic sense, but is not the case.

So why do the figures say the gap is around 20 per cent, then?

A number of factors have to be considered when talking about the differences in pay between the genders. As Harvard University economist Claudia Goldin stated in 2014, the highest-paying jobs 'disproportionately reward those who can work the longest, least flexible hours'.

The key word here is 'disproportionately'.

Jobs that reward those who can work long, inflexible hours at short notice, such as being a lawyer, pay a disproportionately high salary. Not to men, not to women – to everybody.

However, these types of jobs penalize workers who have caregiving responsibilities outside the workplace. Women have disproportionate responsibility for children and caring for the elderly. Therefore, women are less likely to work in roles that do not allow them to fulfil these caregiving responsibilities.

Taking law again, let's look at what happens to the number of women in the profession at varying levels of seniority. The results of the 2014 Gender in the Law Survey by Chambers Student Guide can be found in Table 18.1 . More than 100 legal firms were asked to account for the number of female solicitors by level of seniority.

Table 18.1   Average percentage of female solicitors by level and type of firm

	Trainees	Associates	Partners
Magic circle firms	48.6 %	47.0 %	18.8 %
US firms	51.3 %	53.2 %	17.5 %
Other London firms	52.6 %	57.4 %	25.1 %
Regional/national firms	64.5 %	60.7 %	26.0 %
Overall average	57.1 %	57.2 %	24.0 %

SOURCE Chambers Student (2014)

As the results show, and as in public relations, there are more women than men in the industry, until the most senior positions.

If you were to take an average of what men earn versus what women earn in the legal profession, you would expect, with the figures above, a discrepancy – because men take up those roles in senior positions that undoubtedly pay better.

It's sometimes difficult to picture, but imagine that same imbalance in terms of female presence at a more senior level in *all* of the other industries that disproportionately reward the most value-adding positions. These will be some of the best paid jobs in the world, on account of the fact that fewer people will want to do them – again, supply and demand economics. If you were to take an average of what men earn versus what women earn across all professions, you would expect a discrepancy because, again, men will be better represented in senior positions that pay better.

And why are men better represented in senior positions?

Because, again, these types of jobs penalize workers who have caregiving responsibilities outside the workplace. And at what age do people tend to graduate to those senior positions? Of course, it's around the age where people become parents, and elderly relatives might need looking after.

A study was highlighted in *The New York Times* in 2014, based on data from the National Longitudinal Survey of Youth from 1979 to 2006 in the United States. The research, which tracked people's labour market activities over time, found that childless, unmarried women earn 96 cents for every dollar a man earns. This is much more in line with the adjusted wage gap and still something we need to work at.

Workers in many industries often face steep penalties for any interruption to their career. One 2003 study (Noonan, Corcoran and Courant, 2003) estimated that among lawyers, a year out of the labour force costs an 8 per cent salary reduction, while colleagues continue to work and earn. It is easy to see how a woman who takes her full maternity allocation with more than one child can quickly fall behind in earnings. Is this fair? Well, put another reason for a year's absence in the place of maternity – say, travelling the world – and ask yourself if you'd be happy with a colleague who did that returning to work with a pay rise despite having not been there to gain experience and add value to the company.

We are, as a society, blinded by the eminently quotable 20 per cent statistic and we're looking for a smoking gun in employment that probably doesn't exist. If women really were cheaper, it doesn't make economic sense for an employer to favour men. It doesn't make legal sense either – once more, it's illegal to pay different salaries to people doing the same job during the course of the same number of hours.

If there's a smoking gun, it lies firmly at the feet of society and the role women have been given or adopted as caregivers. Women have disproportionate responsibility for children and caring for the elderly. Therefore, women are finding they are unable to or, in many cases, do not want to progress to senior positions that expect longer and inflexible hours of commitment.

The fact that the gender pay gap is mostly due to individual choices poses the question of how these choices are constrained by gender stereotypes in society: for one camp, these stereotypes and societal norms need to be proactively addressed. For the other camp, free individual choices are what matters and shouldn't be interfered with.

These choices aren't just child-related. They relate to career choices, too – and this is an area we can and are working to fix. Women are statistically more inclined to choose careers, even from incredibly young ages, that have a lower pay packet than men. Why does this happen? For example, why would a woman choose to be a teacher and a man an engineer?

Do women positively choose to be teachers, or is it a 'second best' choice because they lack the confidence to be an engineer? Perhaps women are pressured into being teachers. Perhaps there's societal pressure to work in certain areas of employment. Perhaps women don't believe they have the ability.

There is one solution to fix the adjusted gender pay gap. But I'm not sure it is one that would be much appreciated.

As I mentioned, women have disproportionate responsibility for children and caring for the elderly and, I would say, are well rewarded holistically for doing so. There is a trade-off between staying an extra hour at work and spending more time with your family and it's a conscious decision often to do the latter. There are obvious intrinsic rewards which differ in range and scope for everybody, but there are extrinsic rewards too. As a result of time I've spent caring for my family, I have gained vital life experience. This makes me a better speaker. It makes me more conscientious and it makes me more aware of the responsibilities and emotions of people around me. These things all translate into employable, financially beneficial skills.

We have to question whether this disproportionate responsibility is given or taken. Are people expected to take this care of children or elderly relatives, or do they take on the responsibility?

One also needs to question: would women give this responsibility away, especially the time spent with children?

We often assume that men are happy with their family lifestyle. That dads are happy to work all the hours God sends. I ask men 'What's it been like to manage your work–life balance? Have you felt your career has hampered your time at home?' The answer is that men, especially men with older children, often do feel that their career has hampered time with their families. We assume they're OK with that.

In 2015, shared parental leave rules came in in the UK, allowing mothers and fathers to divide time spent at home with new babies. The rules were much-maligned – it still didn't and doesn't make financial sense for many, on account of various circumstances. According to research by Working Families, a UK charity dealing with family life and work, between 0.5 and 2 per cent of eligible dads had made use of shared leave six months after the rules changed. The government had predicted a take-up of 2 to 8 per cent in the first year.

According to the Trade Union Centre (TUC) general secretary, Frances O'Grady, 'take up has been very low and TUC research shows as many as two in five new fathers are ineligible for shared parental leave, as their partners are not in paid work, or they fail to meet the qualifying conditions'. She added, 'If the government is serious about men playing a more active role after their child is born, they must increase statutory pay and give all new dads a right to some independent parental leave that is not shared with their partners'.

Shared leave rights have existed for parents in other countries for decades. Sweden became the first country to introduce shared leave in 1974, and today each parent is entitled to 240 of the 480 days of paid parental leave. Each parent has two months reserved exclusively for him or her. Should a father – or a mother – decide not to take them, they cannot be transferred to the partner. In 2014, dads took 25 per cent of the total parental leave. Child care in Sweden is cheaper than in the UK, but still, women make up the majority of primary child carers.

A 'men-at-home' quota

If there is a genuine choice to stay at home with the kids, who takes that choice? Of course, it can come down to who earns more, but I think that many women wouldn't give the responsibility up. Surely, if they choose to stay at home, it's a positive if they can live out this ambition.

One way to fix the gender pay gap immediately would be to firmly impose a quota on how many men are in the household full-time. Rather than getting more women out of the house, the quota would be to get more men into the household.

Quotas are being put in place at board level in business worldwide. The UK has opted for a 25 per cent *target* as opposed to a quota, where women currently account for 23 per cent of FTSE 100 board seats. Imagine if, similarly, there was a quota in place for men in the home!

I don't see any appetite for it, despite the fact that this would have an obvious and immediate impact on the number of women in senior positions. I don't want this imaginary men-at-home quota by any means. That said, it would undoubtedly work, and would absolutely shine a light on the biggest issue causing the adjusted gender pay gap. Fewer men in the workplace would ensure that the jobs that disproportionately reward those who fulfil the most value-adding positions would be given to women, forced by this reverse quota to occupy them. It would affect the very fabric of society.

Now, I'm not a fan of quotas, and wanted to highlight this one to demonstrate the confusing nature of them. I'm often invited to speak at conferences, and am often the token woman. I would say that I've been given a lot more opportunities and experienced a huge amount of positive discrimination. I used to get insulted by it. Now I take those opportunities because I can work with them with a view to being asked back as myself in my own right and, secondly, to make women more visible in the world of finance, media and public speaking.

I'm of the view that female empowerment is allowing women to do what they want. Female empowerment isn't pushing a woman out the door. Women can make up their minds for themselves and shouldn't feel forced into a black-and-white choice of either looking after children or going back to work. I believe that you can have it all, but you need to be very clear about what 'it all' is and be willing to sacrifice lower priorities to get it. The pay gap can be fixed if women take only their prescribed two weeks' maternity leave, if partners take on or are given more at-home responsibility and if new parents make full use of expensive child care. I can't speak to the happiness of people that do this, but the options are there.

It all comes back to whether or not an individual – not specifically a man, not specifically a woman – can put themselves in the frame for jobs that disproportionately reward those who can work in the most value-adding positions.

I think women should make choices based on what they want to do, and there are two ways to do this.

First of all, part of the solution is both men and women supporting young girls to pursue what they want to do. There's already been a lot of work around science, technology, engineering and mathematics (STEM) subjects and jobs, but I think it starts earlier than this, in dealing with confidence. In fact, positive discrimination has been found to exist in these areas, as a 2015 study from Cornell University actually found that women were preferred by a ratio of two to one over identically qualified male candidates for assistant professor positions.

It's often said that women lack confidence in terms of asking for promotions. Women can and are helping each other here in many different ways and in many different sectors, including PR. Support networks exist, and are often at our fingertips, and free. These groups, though, are often highlighting figures like unadjusted pay gap statistics – which could be doing the opposite of encouraging women into an industry.

Secondly, I believe we need a greater conversation around pay transparency. This isn't about forcing companies to divulge exact expenditures per employee, but having pay grading per job role as standard practice in all businesses, in all industries. That way, there simply isn't the opportunity to unduly pay one employee much more or much less than another. We're not all equal in terms of ability and the effort we put in, and I'm a believer in being rewarded for effort and excellence – something banded systems still allow for.

It's up to us

If anything, I've benefited by being a woman in a society more aware of the need for equal opportunities than ever before. We can all start businesses. We can all ask for pay rises where we think they're deserved. We can all choose the subjects we want to choose, and the career we want, and whether or not we as women are primary caregivers, and, of course, if we want children at all. These choices are how we reduce the adjusted pay gap, if indeed we want to make these choices.

Let's continue to support each other to realize our value in the workplace, but let's do it with the actual facts to hand, not unadjusted and frankly useless blanket statistics that don't look at the whole issue.

I personally believe that it's this current generation we need to worry about, not the next. The teenagers of today are positive about their financial future, based on my regular interactions with them. Let's not allow them to be indoctrinated with supposed facts about the world of work that simply don't stand up to basic scrutiny. As I say, this could well end up turning women away from careers by virtue of making the problem look both bigger than it is and unfixable. Creating a culture of victimhood before they've even had the chance to make their own decisions will do little to fix the existing 5 per cent gap. On the other hand, explaining why the adjusted gap exists and showing them how to fix it for themselves can and would fix it.

How this applies to PR

Susan's experience, knowledge and no-nonsense approach is exactly what I think the PR industry needs to be paying attention to.

In an industry dominated by women until we get to the senior ranks, the pay gap is a constant conversation. It will continue to be among the key figures in every annual industry report, as it well should be – but, these conversations should be had using statistics that have been through the economic wringer. I do not think PR people, the heads of trade organizations and survey companies should be conducting surveys that will spit out figures that will get a huge amount of attention using methods that have not been checked by people with the experience and knowledge to say whether or not those methods will produce an accurate end result.

The reason I thought this chapter so important is following a recent online conversation I had with the person that handles the Global Women in PR Twitter account.

They had been promoting a survey looking into the gender pay gap on a global scale. I took the survey, and encouraged other PRs to do the same. However, even with a cursory knowledge of the unadjusted and adjusted pay gaps, it was easy to spot where questions had been missed that would undoubtedly affect the results. As such, the resulting figure – that will no doubt show a huge imbalance in terms of equal pay in favour of men – will be incorrect, and I can't imagine it will be all too different from the figures we've seen in other surveys.

This is an issue because, as I pointed out to them in a conversation I put into a Storify thread (Leigh, 2016), the exact results of the grandly titled 'Global Gender Pay Gap Survey' will be taught to students, and parroted by the media and people in the industry. I believe but am yet to see, with the results out later in 2016, that they will be well reported on and well shared by an industry paid to communicate.

As I have said in this chapter, on Twitter at the time and as Susan pointed out, we should care about every single penny – otherwise, what is the point in putting a figure to an issue?

The main concern I had with the way that the survey was collecting responses was the absolute absence of anything asking respondents about career leave.

The survey asked respondents to state their country of residence, gender, age, level of education, job title, salary, whether they received a bonus (and if so, how much), years of experience in the PR industry, and many other questions – some related to confidence around asking for promotions and even the share of domestic chores.

It looks relatively comprehensive – but the 'years of experience' question was banded. You could select nought to two years, three to six, six to ten and so on.

Without a question referencing career leave – which could include sabbatical periods as well as parental leave – the years of experience aspect is wholly unfit for purpose. Let's say a 33-year-old woman who started working in PR 11 years ago has had two children, and took the maximum amount of time off allowed by UK law – 52 weeks – with each. That's two years where she wasn't in the industry. That same person might look at the banded responses and select '11 to 15' years of experience – because she started working in PR 11 years ago – when, in reality, she actually has nine. Her role and salary will reflect the time she hasn't been in the industry when compared to male colleagues (and indeed female colleagues) who had been in a job throughout, but as per the survey, she will be seen as a female PR person who, for 11 years in the industry, is earning less than a male also with 11 years in the industry.

Without so much as asking about career leave, the results are flawed.

Another aspect is that certain key job roles were missing from the list of 22 that respondents could select. This sounds like I'm nit-picking. I am and we should. For instance, the mostly comprehensive list did not have selections for junior account directors or senior account directors – only account directors. Anybody with a knowledge of the industry will be aware that a junior account director can earn significantly less than a senior account director. The percentage difference will be marked. This isn't even a matter of gender pay here, but simply that if we are to espouse the results of a global PR study that will undoubtedly be treated with a huge degree of importance in the industry and in education, it should not be quite so easy to point out areas that won't provide accurate results. The person handling the Global Women in PR Twitter account replied exasperatedly when I highlighted the missing roles, saying 'we already have 22 choices of job role/level in the questionnaire. Not enough?!' – frankly, no it isn't. It's enough when it allows people to respond with the correct answer, not a 'close-enough' selection. I don't understand how a survey's question set that is otherwise detailed in the way it was put together could miss questions and selections that will impact on its results.

The person handling the account said they disagreed that the results would be inaccurate, as I said they would, suggesting we left the 'debate'.

We should not be worried about challenging the results, or so much as enquiring about the methodology of surveys. It might have been a personal concern and one that I'm placing more emphasis on than actually exists, but I was in fact worried about challenging these questions, and also in asking the CIPR to see the questions it used to come to its State of the Profession 2016 findings.

I was concerned that, even in daring to ask, I would be considered misogynistic at worst for my enquiry, and petty at best. I quickly got over that, though, knowing that without the facts, we can't begin to understand an issue. The nature of the issue of gender pay, being one that provokes an emotional response, should not exempt it from scrutiny.

The questions I was sent that related to pay from the CIPR were:

1 Gender.

2 Role – there were seven options here (Intern/Trainee, Assistant/ Executive, Officer, Manager, Head of Communications/Associate Director, Director/Partner/MD and Owner).

3 Current gross basic salary.

4 Were you paid a bonus in addition to your gross basic salary over the course of the last 12 months?

5 The amount of that bonus.

6 Level of education.

7 Whether the respondent worked in a private or public company.

8 Number of years in PR.

It does not appear that the regression analysis took into consideration career leave as that question was apparently not asked, and the number of years in PR again only gave options for a banded response.

Using the CIPR's data, as illustrated in a PR Moment article entitled 'The State of Salaries' (2016), women actually out-earn men between the ages of 18 to 34. The gap, as found using the above questions, is £2,651.15 in favour of women aged 18 to 24 and £285.25 in favour of men aged 25 to 34, giving a net positive for women.

It's in the age range above – 35 to 44 – that the gap is much more apparent in favour of men, standing at £13,025.80. The age range above that – 45 to 60 – shows a gap of £13,760.53, and the gap jumps hugely above the age of 60, to more than £50,000.

The CIPR's effort at a regression analysis is the closest thing we've been presented with in terms of finding the adjusted pay gap, and this should be commended. By making strides in methodology, the unadjusted pay gap in PR was found to be more than £9,000 off.

Using what's been described throughout the chapter, and especially in Susan's evaluation, there is both a potential correlation and causation for this – women give birth and adopt the role of primary caregivers.

As Susan said, the way to effectively combat the gap is to confront the issue of caregiving, especially as PR is an industry that does disproportionately reward employees who can work longer, more inflexible hours.

When at my last agency, without being too crass, I earned much more annually than I have since starting my own agency, both on account of having to build a business from scratch and also wanting to keep money in it. I saw the inequality in my wife spending much more time looking after our two children than I did while working in London four days a week, and coupled with the altogether-stronger emotion of missing my family, I made the decision to leave. I don't regret it one bit, but to say there wasn't an impact on my earnings immediately after as a result of being a parent and being conscious of my responsibilities to my kids would be untrue. I could have made the decision not to have children, or to continue with the time working away, and been rewarded for my presence.

I have a great deal of respect for the organizations, magazines and blogs that serve the industry, but we have some way to go until the figures we see are both accurately found and reported. The CIPR's report is as close as we have come and despite there being potential issues in the regression analysis on account of career leave not being asked about, combined with respondents being given bands within which they should mark their experience, we are on the right track.

This is why, despite the inevitable backlash I will receive, the unadjusted wage gap figures belong in a book about PR myths and misconceptions. The word 'misconceive' means to fail to understand something correctly, and by taking social media-friendly statistics at their word, without comprehending the issue itself, that's exactly what we're doing – and it only hurts the industry.

Further reading

Bentley, G, 2016. Global study finds gender wage gap close to zero. *The Daily Caller News Foundation*, 15 May. Available at: <http://dailycaller.com/2016/05/15/global-study-finds-gender-wage-gap-close-to-zero/> [Accessed 4 September 2016]

Boscia, T, 2015. Women preferred 2:1 over men for STEM faculty positions. *Cornell Chronicle*, 13 April. Available at: <http://www.news.cornell.edu/ stories/2015/04/women-preferred-21-over-men-stem-faculty-positions> [Accessed 4 September 2016]

Chambers Student, 2014. *2014 Gender in the Law Survey*. Available at: <http:// www.chambersstudent.co.uk/where-to-start/newsletter/2014-gender-in-the-law- survey> [Accessed 4 September 2016]

Daniels, C, 2016. The PRWeek 2016 salary survey. *PRWeek*, 29 February. Available at: <http://www.prweek.com/article/1384984/prweek-2016-salary-survey> [Accessed 4 September 2016]

Goldin, C, 2014. *A grand gender convergence: its last chapter*. [pdf] Available at: <https://scholar.harvard.edu/files/goldin/files/goldin_aeapress_2014_1.pdf> [Accessed 4 September 2016]

Leigh, R, 2016. *Discussing flaws in survey: gender pay gap survey*. Available at: <https://storify.com/RichLeighPR/discussing-flaws-in-survey> [Accessed 4 September 2016]

Miller, C C, 2014. The Motherhood Penalty vs. the Fatherhood Bonus: a child helps your career, if you're a man. *The New York Times*, 6 September. Available at: <http://www.nytimes.com/2014/09/07/upshot/a-child-helps-your-career-if- youre-a-man.html?_r=1> [Accessed 4 September 2016]

Noonan, M C, Corcoran, M E, and Courant, P N, 2003. Pay differences among the highly trained: Cohort differences in the male-female earnings gap in lawyers' salaries, *National Poverty Center Working Paper Series*. [pdf] Available at: <http://www.npc.umich.edu/publications/working_papers/paper1/03-1.pdf> [Accessed 4 September 2016]

PR Moment, 2016. The state of salaries in PR. *PRmoment.com*, 1 April. Available at: <http://www.prmoment.com/3394/the-state-of-salaries-in-pr.aspx> [Accessed 4 September 2016]

PRCA, 2016. *PR census 2016 reveals that the PR industry is worth £12.9bn*. Available at: <http://news.prca.org.uk/pr-census-2016-reveals-that-the-pr- industry-is-worth-129bn> [Accessed 4 September 2016]

CIPR, 2016. *State of PR 2016*. [pdf] Available at: <https://www.cipr.co.uk/sites/ default/files/CIPR_StateofPR_16.pdf> [Accessed 4 September 2016]

CONCLUSION

As any working in it will attest to, and as many of the statistics and anecdotes I've highlighted should demonstrate, public relations is a rapidly changing profession. Marketing disciplines that were once easily discernible from one another still exist, but digital progress has got us to a point where there's more convergence and crossover than ever before. The core goal of marketing, of reaching and influencing the decisions of a relevant audience, stands above the protestations of the marketers reluctant to adopt practices previously alien to them.

In this book, I've tried to analyse the myths and misconceptions that exist both in the public understanding of PR, and within the industry itself. Many public myths – that PR is all spin, or that all publicity is good publicity – exist often because we enjoy and prosper from our anonymity, or have allowed certain individuals to direct an image of PR that isn't true and/or ignores much of what we do. Industry myths, from the death of the press release to the apparent lack of measurement means, exist as a result of the way the internet has opened a hole in the traditional media that will now never close.

Some PRs will stick steadfastly to media relations, ignoring the ominous signs. There are two ways for those individuals, company employees and agencies to go. They will either die off, or they will stay around long enough to see similarly traditionally minded freelancers and firms go bust. By outliving the others, they will become the more obvious choice for clients and employers that will continue to exist and value these traditional tactics more highly. Media relations and the skills needed to do it well will always be important, but the PRs that will 'never be geeky enough to care', as I mentioned back in the chapter about measurement, will simply struggle.

I am, though, incredibly optimistic about the future of PR. I believe that by highlighting areas of misunderstanding, and acknowledging that we need to learn and continuously adapt to stay relevant, we can do exactly that. Ad agencies circle our clients, keen to bring both paid and earned under one roof, one eye on campaigns that gain media and public attention by virtue of newsworthiness. SEO agencies continue in their attempt to earn authoritative links for companies, having always been conscious of the very real financial benefits that high-ranking clients enjoy, which inevitably means they will find ways to place stories that lead to these links using PR methods. Social media agencies began to crop up before the turn of the new decade, and have capitalized on a base of clients we can also cater to. PR isn't all of a sudden going to hoover everybody's work up by any stretch, but the remit of public relations has and will continue to widen as future routes to audiences open up. Those that care enough to remain educated will succeed, and opportunities to increase our reach into other areas will present themselves – we just need to be open to them.

In April 2016, the Holmes Report estimated the size of the global PR agency industry in 2015 at $14.2 billion, from $13.5 billion in 2014. Growth slowed to 5 per cent, down from the previous year's 7 per cent, but is still positive. Global Communications Report research found that the industry is expected to reach $20 billion by 2020. Advertising's total global revenue according to Statista, for comparison, is more like $661 billion.

To put PR's worth in more relatable terms, global revenue for the music industry in 2015 was $15 billion (King, 2016). In fact, with the music industry on course to continue its reversed fortune, as digital subscriptions and downloads buck the still-spiralling physical sales downturn, there is another comparison in that it, too, looks set to achieve global revenue of $20 billion in 2020.

Paul Holmes, CEO of the Holmes Group that also includes the SABRE Awards, took a dim view of the decrease in year-on-year growth, but highlights many of the opportunities I see, too: 'At a time when engagement, authenticity, transparency, credibility – the things that PR is good at – are increasingly critical to successful brand-building, it is disturbing to see industry growth slowing, and indeed underperforming growth in the ad industry.' Holmes believes there are two potential reasons for this – either that PR agencies are adapting slowly to multiple digital channels, or that they're not convincing clients on ability or knowledge just yet.

A small drop in growth is important to assess and note, but the net result is still a positive. As global ad revenue shows, there's a huge amount of money out there and we are more than deserving of it in many areas. We will continue to adapt to the 'multichannel communications landscape', as Holmes puts it. Convincing clients is a matter of proving that PR is more than column inches – something readers of this book either already knew or will hopefully come away understanding.

The writing of this book, set against the often stressful early-stage development of my agency, has been tough on a personal level, but I think that in addressing misconceptions at this time we will continue to ensure enquiry and professional progress. For topics like the gender pay gap in particular, which receives an awful lot of airplay in the press, the time is right to investigate and discuss them intelligently, and not just emotionally.

I realize that I am, at present and without the clout of the heads of the big holding companies, agencies, publishers and trade organizations, little more than a tiny cog in the machine. However, a small number of individuals have been able to impact the entire reputation of PR negatively before now – so here's to hoping this book goes some small way to righting that. PR should be more than a barely understood and seemingly fringe profession, especially when you consider it's making the same revenue as global music. If we don't stand up for our own industry, and if we don't do away with misconceptions that no doubt affect the make-up of the PR workforce, we're not doing it justice.

As I touched upon in my introductory chapter, the aim was never to write a textbook. I hope I've given a reasoned viewpoint of many prevalent and some lesser myths, leaning on my time in the industry. As with any personal meditation on issues such as those I've chosen, there will undoubtedly be a level of subjection. My goal was to interpret prevailing beliefs and, in the light of day and based on my near decade working my way up the ladder, paired with available statistics and peer analyses, assess just how they stood up.

I hope, in my honest efforts to give a modern depiction of the PR world as I have seen and see it, I've given readers a thought-provoking and entertaining read.

There's a great deal to be excited about in public relations, for those hoping to enter into it, for people benefiting from the work done by the industry, and for those already in it. Let's remain positive and keep moving it forward.

Further reading

King, C, 2016. Global revenue for music industry in 2015 reaches $15 billion. Available at: <http://www.noiseprn.com/2016/04/19/global-revenue-music-industry-2015-reaches-15-billion/> [Accessed 4 September 2016]

Statista, 2016. *Global advertising revenue from 2007 to 2016 (in billion U.S. dollars)*. Available at: <http://www.statista.com/statistics/23779/total-global-advertising-revenue/> [Accessed 4 September 2016]

Sudhaman, A, 2016. *Global PR industry hits $14bn in 2016 as growth slows to 5%*. Available at: <http://www.holmesreport.com/research/article/global-pr-industry-hits-$14bn-in-2016-as-growth-slows-to-5> [Accessed 4 September 2016]

INDEX

Note: page numbers in *italics* indicate tables.